Degrees of Excellence:
The Academic Achievement Game

Degrees of Excellence:
The Academic Achievement Game

Noel J. Entwistle and John D. Wilson

assisted by Jennifer Thompson,
Jennifer Welsh and T. Brennan

HODDER AND STOUGHTON
LONDON SYDNEY AUCKLAND TORONTO

ISBN 0 340 20901 1

Printed and bound in Great Britain for
Hodder and Stoughton Educational,
a division of Hodder and Stoughton Ltd,
Mill Road, Dunton Green, Sevenoaks, Kent,
by Hazell Watson & Viney Ltd, Aylesbury, Bucks.
Phototypesetting by Print Origination, Merseyside L20 6NS

Contents

45015

Preface

This book reports results from two major research studies concerned with the problem of explaining differences in academic performance. Students are a highly selected group, and yet, in British universities, some 14 per cent of each intake fail to graduate (Heywood, 1971). A University Grants Committee enquiry (1968, p.42) showed that 3,837 students who would normally have graduated in 1965-66 left university for academic reasons during their course, half by the end of the first year. Malleson (1967) estimated that there might be 20,000 such cases annually by 1981. Yet most of these students had high academic qualifications on entry. What other factors help to explain poor academic performance and what are the characteristics of successful students in different areas of study?

Both authors developed an interest in research into higher education when they were in the Department of Education at Aberdeen University. Discussions at that time influenced the development of John Wilson's study in Aberdeen before he moved to Moray House College of Education, Edinburgh, and the planning of Noel Entwistle's project which was subsequently carried out at Lancaster. As a result of this common origin, the studies have used similar research designs and the differences in approach have become, to some extent, complementary.

In the Aberdeen enquiry, reported in Part Two of the book, students in the science and arts faculties were tested in their first year (1967) and retested in their third year. Groups of successful and unsuccessful students were formed on the basis of first-year and final examination performance. Indicators of success and symptoms of failure were identified from both head teachers' ratings and psychological test scores. Combining these variables it was possible to predict the outcome of the course for individual students with an encouraging degree of accuracy.

The study at Lancaster, described in Part Three, drew its samples from seven universities in the North of England and the Midlands as part of a larger follow-up study which also involved colleges of education and polytechnics. Again psychological test scores in the first year (1968) were used to predict academic performance later in the course. Students completed most of the tests again in their third year and hence it was possible to examine changes in personality, attitudes and values during higher education, as well as to detect the factors which were related to degree results in six contrasting areas of study. Cluster analyses were used to describe differing 'types' of successful and unsuccessful students; thus they provided an interesting alternative to conventional statistical models of academic performance.

Part Four brings together findings from the two studies to produce models which should help to explain differences in academic performance of students in all sectors of higher education. (Some checks on similarities and differences between the sectors have been possible, although they are not reported here—see Entwistle and Percy, 1971.)

The background to the studies is described in the first part of the book. As an increasing number of research workers and lecturers are becoming interested in correlates of academic performance in the different disciplines, we have provided a brief, but thorough, summary of the methodological problems involved (Chapter 2). Research into higher education is by no means a straightforward activity, and yet little has been written about the many pitfalls which face the unwary. Not least of the problems is the complexity of the literature. Chapter 3 charts the progress made in identifying factors associated with academic success and failure, providing a background to our studies and, hopefully, a coherent framework within which to examine this research area.

In sponsoring the research at Lancaster the Joseph Rowntree Memorial Trust indicated the importance of obtaining factual evidence about students in higher education before major changes in the system were planned. In an ideal world possible changes might well await research evidence. In practice, expediency and political pressures shape our educational system faster than research can be conducted. But higher education is still evolving and factual evidence relating to students' academic performance is valuable in assessing the direction which future changes might take.

Evidence on the prediction of academic success in the past has been used mainly as an aid to selecting students more efficiently. This process of selection is carried out by the institution, mainly for its own benefit. A knowledge of factors related to success in different areas of study could, however, be used to assist students' choice either of the type of institution or of a particular course. In addition such research evidence is useful to those who have to advise students who encounter difficulties and it also stimulates ideas for improving the organisation of teaching and learning in higher education.

Inevitably, in large-scale studies of this kind, many people have helped in one way or another. Both authors owe a special debt of gratitude to Professor John Nisbet in whose department at Aberdeen the early work for both studies took place. Advice and encouragement at the formative stage of any study are enormously valuable. In Aberdeen the burden of interviewing and data processing was shared with Jennifer Welsh, while the review of the literature in Chapter 3 owes much to the efforts of Jennifer Thompson.* Many of the analyses reported in Chapter 10 were carried out by Dr Tim Brennan and his knowledge of the techniques of cluster analysis proved to be crucial to

*Née Nisbet.

the Rowntree project. Sheilah Hargreaves and Jon Tudge undertook the major task of coding the Lancaster data and Barbara Cockburn provided valuable assistance both in condensing computer print-outs into simple tables and in checking the final draft of this report. The Academic Achievement Game board was designed by the Media Services Unit of the University of Lancaster; the Printing Department at Moray House College produced the packs of hazard, bonus and chance cards. Secretaries in both Edinburgh and Lancaster coped with a succession of drafts over several years, but a special word of thanks must go to Mrs Pamela Gordon, who typed much of the final version of the manuscript. Our greatest debt, however, is to the staff and students who provided the data which made the studies possible. Those who delight in castigating students for idleness should reflect on the amount of effort spent in completing psychological tests by the 2,500 students in these two studies. Their only reward was a feeling that the results of these investigations might benefit subsequent generations of students.

A final acknowledgement must be paid to the Working Party of the Committee of Vice-Chancellors and Principals (ISPIUA) who made available to the Rowntree Project part of their experimental Test of Academic Aptitude.

Both studies depended, to some extent, on outside financial support. The Social Science Research Council gave a small grant to facilitate the processing of the Aberdeen data, while the whole expense of the Lancaster project was borne by the Joseph Rowntree Memorial Trust.

PART ONE
Preliminary Work

Chapter One

Selection, Guidance and Choice

Our starting point is to place our research against a wider background of current issues in higher education. The problems we raise here are wider than those tackled in either of the two studies, but our more restricted research objectives should be seen in relation to this broader perspective.

In 1966 there were 339,000 students taking full-time courses in higher education throughout Britain. In 1972 the planning projections envisaged some 750,000 students by 1981, although this figure has since been reduced. The increased demand for higher education in the mid-sixties was attributable, in part, to the 'bulge' in the birth-rate. By the late sixties this peak had passed but the expansion in demand for higher education continued, fed by the increasing proportion of the age group who were staying on at school beyond the age of sixteen.

The increased demand for higher education is a product of changing social and economic conditions, and of changes introduced into secondary education. Qualifications for many employments have been upgraded to degree level, and the vocational relevance of higher education has been appreciated by many parents whose relative affluence has enabled them to allow and encourage their sons and daughters to continue with their education. At school level the ending of selection and the introduction of comprehensive education (now almost universally adopted in Scotland) means that most pupils attend a school in which progression to national certificate examinations is accepted as a reasonable goal for at least a substantial minority of children, and pupils are now able to choose from a wider and more attractive range of courses in the sixth form. A continued expansion of voluntary staying-on and an increasing demand for higher education seem inevitable in the long run, although the last few years has shown a levelling-off in applications (Williams, 1974).

A demand for increased provision of higher education in a period of continuing financial stringency may lead to a demand for more rigorous selection, particularly by the universities. Our studies into the prediction of academic success provide explanations of the differing levels of performance and may thus help to improve the accuracy of selection. They may also lead to more effective instruments or selection procedures for admissions tutors to use. But additional or alternative criteria for selection may need to be devised. It has already been suggested by one ex-minister that pupils should be forced to break their studies for at least a year between school and higher education. Such a year would certainly act as a practical test of motivation, weeding out by a process of 'natural selection' those who might otherwise drift into higher education for no good reason, but it might also differentially deter pupils from poorer homes. Sixth-formers should certainly be made to consider carefully the type of institution and course they will take in higher education. The choice is crucial to their subsequent success and enjoyment, and yet faced with the many universities, polytechnics and colleges of education offering courses at different levels, with varying structures and with contrasting content, a fully rational decision is difficult to reach.

In *Diversity and Choice in Higher Education*, Watts (1972) presented a clear structure by which the wide range of institutions may be classified. He also developed a theoretical model of the process of pupil choice which emphasised the 'image' of the institution in terms of social stereotypes. There is no doubt that institutions are perceived in this way, and a pupil is certainly unlikely to apply to an institution whose image he dislikes. But his main concern is surely to find an interesting and relevant course and a department which is likely to accept him. In making his selection the pupil is likely to adopt a strategy which balances ideal choice with probability of acceptance, but without accurate information about the parameters in operation he may well be making a blind guess. There is an urgent need to help pupils make informed choices so that their interests and ambitions match the demands of the available courses. Most schools advise pupils about university and college entrance requirements on the basis of myth and hearsay as much as knowledge. Some teachers have developed effective strategies to help pupils, but the flow of information to schools on entrance qualifications and on how courses are organised and taught needs improvement. An equally important need is to collect evidence on the types of student likely to be successful in the various courses. At this point the Rowntree study may have a contribution to make.

The situation for sixth-formers is confused enough, but acceptance of a place at university or college does not guarantee an untroubled future for the student. Even if the availability of fuller information and useful research evidence improved his choice, there would still be unexpected difficulties ahead. Statistics collected by the Universities Central Council on Admissions (UCCA, 1967, 1969) indicate that some 9 per cent of students fail outright at some stage of their course (besides those who withdraw for other reasons), and for each failure there must be many other students whose academic performance has been disappointingly low. It is difficult to resist the implication that there should be more effective methods of advice and guidance within, as well as in advance of, higher education.

The provision of effective counselling depends, initially, on its importance being recognised by schools, colleges and universities. A recent symposium at Lancaster (Warwick, 1973) demonstrates a growing awareness of the need to provide effective counselling in colleges of education, and universities and polytechnics have begun to appoint professional counsellors. But in Britain most counselling is still carried out by untrained amateurs. Lecturers are often expected to act as 'personal tutor' to a group of students, and they have to rely almost entirely on their own experience in giving advice. The successful academic may find it particularly difficult to provide appropriate help for a struggling first-year student; he may not even begin to understand how such a student perceives the academic and social demands being made of him. It is difficult enough for the experienced professional counsellor to appreciate how these problems arise. While research evidence which pin-points factors commonly associated with study difficulties cannot be of *direct* help in solving the unique problems of the individual, such research can provide a coherent framework of ideas and possible explanations which enable perceptive tutors or counsellors to understand how different types of student react to the pressures they meet at university or college. It is here that our studies may have their greatest impact.

The organisation of teaching and learning is central to a student's experience of higher education, and his academic performance is an index not only of his own ability, but also of the effectiveness of the teaching he has received. Thus research into academic performance may well raise questions about teaching methods. For example, if we were to show that extraverts consistently obtained worse examination marks on average than introverts, what is the implication? Do we decide to select fewer extraverts? Do we accept that having an outgoing personality is an inevitable handicap to concentrating on academic work? Or should we recognise that the effect may be a function of the way in which we currently teach our courses and discuss ways of altering the courses?

Higher education provides students with opportunities and challenges, as well as difficulties and disappointments. It is important not to paint too gloomy a picture. However, educational research is often directed towards improving the efficiency of the educational process and may necessarily involve a detailed examination of possible weaknesses in the existing system. Even so, research evidence cannot be expected to provide ready-made solutions to the problems it raises. Too many value judgements are involved in assessing the efficacy of education. Even if we accept the institutional definitions of academic success and failure, research is unlikely to explain these in any simple way.

When we started our studies of higher education it was already clear that we would not find any single variable which could explain more than a small proportion of the variations in academic performance. Many factors are involved and it is only from an examination of how these interact that progress can be expected. But the lack of progress in previous research was still disconcerting and puzzling. Our first task was thus to try to explain these disappointing results and to extract from the literature whatever consistent and significant findings there were.

Chapter Two

Methodological Problems

There have been few large-scale prediction studies carried out in Britain. Until recently only the UCCA analysis (1969) of the relationship between 'A' level grades and degree performance had used a large representative, cross-institutional sample. The correlations reported in this survey were not high, averaging no more than 0.3. This value is lower than equivalent relationships found in the American studies summarised by Fishman (1962) and Lavin (1965). They reported some studies which had used combinations of intellectual tests and attainment measures, but even then correlations of 0.6 were rarely exceeded. Similar prediction studies of secondary school attainment on the basis of batteries of tests given in primary school have led to multiple correlations as high as 0.8 (Nisbet and Entwistle, 1969).

However, the prediction of undergraduate success might reasonably be expected to be more difficult. Correlation coefficients underestimate the relationships present in higher education studies because the ranges of scores on some variables have been restricted in the process of selecting students. For example, the full range of 'A' level grades will not be represented among university students, since only those with high grades are selected. British students are a relatively homogeneous group in terms of intelligence and, besides having an effect on correlational analyses, this makes measurement of differences in their abilities more difficult, again reducing the likelihood of close relationships with academic attainment. Moreover the courses taken in higher education are more varied, and freedom of action allowed to students is greater, than in secondary education. All these factors would lead us to expect some drop in predictability from school to higher education, but not its disappearance. However, some psychologists (e.g. Drever, 1963; Parkyn, 1967) have suggested that the academic behaviour of students is necessarily unpredictable, resulting mainly from chance experiences. Many of the factors affecting success and failure are 'not merely indeterminate, but indeterminable. An inspiring teacher, a pretty face, a subject encountered for the first time, may decisively affect the outcome.' Drever's comment emphasises the existence of important individual causes of differing levels of academic performance, but it by no means rules out the possibility of general trends which would be amenable to statistical analysis. Most empirical social scientists would expect a substantial proportion of unexplained variance in predicting degree results, but it still comes as a shock to find that academic performance shows low correlations with almost every predictive measure.

In any research area where many of the findings are insignificant or contradictory there must be a suspicion that methodological weaknesses are affecting the results. Before accepting the complete unpredictability of academic performance, we must be satisfied that appropriate techniques of research have been applied.

Research strategies

The following description of research strategies commonly adopted in prediction studies fills in the background to our own work and may also provide a necessary introduction to methodology for those unfamiliar with this field. While we naturally hoped to avoid the methodological weaknesses detected in earlier studies, practical problems made this impossible. Perhaps, at present, the only perfect study in higher education is the next one—at least while it remains on the 'drawing-board'. And perhaps the most outspoken critics of research into higher education are those who have themselves yet to conduct such a study.

The problems we have encountered are presented within a framework which indicates the stages followed in most prediction studies. The first seven of these stages provide appropriate categories for the discussion which follows:

1. Deciding on the general research design.
2. Setting out hypotheses or precise questions.
3. Selecting a representative sample from the target population.
4. Obtaining a satisfactory criterion of academic performance.
5. Choosing effective measures with which to predict later success.
6. Collecting data under appropriate and standardised conditions, followed by the various stages of data processing.
7. Applying statistical analyses to condense the data into interpretable form.
8. Comparing the results with the original hypotheses and with previous research findings, thus allowing conclusions to be reached and educational implications to be suggested.

1. Research design

A majority of prediction studies on academic performance are surveys of three basic types—case studies, comparisons of contrasting groups and surveys of the complete ability range. These categories are in no way mutually exclusive; more than one approach can be used with advantage in any study. But they do indicate a different focus of interest and may imply differing methods of measurement or analysis.

A *case study* represents an intensive investigation of a small number of people. The technique most commonly used to collect information is the interview, although other methods may also be used. Much of the early work on the causes of student failure was undertaken by psychiatrists using depth interviews. Inevitably the portraits of unsuccessful students tended to over-emphasise psychiatric disturbances and the retrospective opinions of students contained rationalisations as well as more objective reasons for failure.

One common approach in prediction studies is to identify *contrasting groups* of unsuccessful students and either 'average' students or those who have done outstandingly well. Again, rationalisations of the causes of differing levels of performance may be expected, if the groups are not identified until patterns of success or failure have already been established. Studies of extreme groups also produce the problem of the 'missing middle'. Among average students, some will have entered with what appeared to be an outstanding potential for academic success, whereas others may have had only borderline entrance qualifications. Changing patterns of performance among this group of average students may provide additional insights into differences in degree results.

Clearly the most satisfactory research design is one which allows a maximum of information to be analysed without unnecessary limitations. Thus a follow-up study of a sample of the *complete intake* of students is by far the most satisfactory procedure. The particular strategy adopted will then depend on circumstances but it is often helpful to start, or to end, the investigation with detailed case studies. As a way into a study, interviews throw up a variety of ideas to be investigated further and, at the end of a questionnaire survey, they help to ensure that the interpretations of the statistical analyses fit in with the experiences of those more directly involved. The interviewer may be able to obtain the 'feel' of the situation as perceived by the student, but this 'feel' is most difficult to report in any convincing way. A combination of questionnaire, to obtain quantitative information and to investigate relationships between variables in a representative sample, and interview or participant observation, to counteract the simplifications or distortions created by mass testing, together provide a more convincing basis for theory-building than either approach used separately.

2. Hypotheses

The influence of empirical social scientists is particularly strong in research on prediction. Thus the paradigm most frequently encountered, at least at the idealistic level, is that of the hypothetico-deductive method. For this strategy to be effective there must be an established body of theory from which to deduce operational hypotheses. In education itself there are, as yet, no theories of this type and many studies are essentially atheoretical. This approach is commonly criticised as leading to weak *ex post facto* explanations of findings, but there are other ways of deriving hypotheses.

Economy of effort and ease of communication are the main advantages in starting from a formal theoretical framework. The theory brings together a range of human behaviour into a simplifying explanatory system from which verifiable hypotheses emerge. The ensuing measurements are related to accepted concepts and will thus be readily intelligible to other research workers. But, as we have said, there are no theories in education which lead directly to hypotheses. Must we then be content with *ex post facto* reasoning? Certainly not. There are a number of alternative strategies.

The first possibility is to make use of a theory developed in another context, perhaps in psychology or sociology. However, transplanting a theory into a different setting cannot be wholly satisfactory. The framework systemises but also constrains, and inappropriate limitations may be counter-productive. The next method of obtaining hypotheses is from the results of previous studies, using what Feldman (1972) has called the actuarial method. Previous studies using comparable techniques indicate the direction of relationships and would certainly allow hypotheses to be formulated. But in higher education, all too often, the research worker obtains little guidance from previous studies. Previous studies may for example, have produced contradictory findings. In this case all that can be done is to mount a pilot study and make use of its findings to generate hypotheses for the main study.

These three strategies for avoiding *ex post facto* reasoning are again by no means mutually exclusive. Studies should, where possible, draw ideas from theoretical perspectives, previous research, and pilot studies before formulating definite hypotheses. But that is still the pattern recommended within one particular research paradigm. Recently some research workers have been commenting on the artificial and restricting nature of the pursuit of the hypothetico-deductive ideal (see, for example, Parlett and Hamilton, 1972). Hypotheses clarify thinking, but also narrow the perspective and, where complex inter-relationships are anticipated, any artificial restriction of view may be damaging. Furthermore there is a real worry that human behaviour may not, after all, be susceptible to mechanistic explanations. Nevertheless a majority of attempts to explain differences in academic performance continue to adopt traditional approaches.

3. Sampling

Choosing an appropriate sample may seem straightforward, but representative groups in higher education can be elusive or ephemeral. In a follow-up study not only have you to obtain a sample, you have to keep it for perhaps three years. It is easy enough to define the target population as, say, first-year students under the age of twenty-one who were born in Britain. What is much more difficult is to persuade a large representative sample of such students to participate. In studies on schoolchildren it is often possible to obtain the co-operation of virtually every school in a particular area and to ensure that almost all pupils take part. In higher education the population is far from captive and, in the past, it has been difficult to carry out prediction studies 'away from home'. Part of the problem has been the reluctance of academic staff to provide details of first-year performance to outsiders. But even if the research worker is able to convince institutions that the confidentiality of academic records will be maintained, he may still have severe problems in persuading the students themselves to co-operate in the project. The unwillingness of students to submit to enquiries of this kind is not at all unreasonable when it is recognised that they may have to give up a considerable amount of their time to provide the required information. In return the students may receive nothing but valedictions; frequently they will hear nothing more of the project or of its findings. Repeated experiences of this kind build up resistance to co-operation in subsequent projects and hostility may be passed on to future generations of students.

In planning a research project there can be no initial expectation that students will be eager volunteers. They must first be persuaded that the project is worthwhile and that it may be of value—to students in the future, if not to themselves. Even where a fair number of students do come forward it is exceedingly difficult to arrive at a truly represent-ative sample. Having chosen the sample and used all acceptable methods of persuasion, the final sample will almost certainly be partly self-selected, as it is impossible to apply compulsion. The resulting volunteer samples inevitably over-represent the more highly motivated, enthusiastic and idealistic students, and generalisation from such samples is difficult unless some check is made on relevant characteristics of students who did not volunteer. Furthermore, where students from only one department are included in the sample, the study can be little more than exploratory. Such studies have their value, but confirmation of the results by replication in other institu-tions is essential before much weight can be placed on the findings.

4. Criterion of academic performance

In any prediction study the most important single measure is the criterion, and here it is whatever index of success or failure in higher education which has been chosen. The terms 'success' and 'failure', if taken in a general sense, are themselves not easy to define. First, who decides whether the course has led to a successful outcome? Is it the institution, or is it the student? An analysis of the meaning of 'success' in the work situation has been carried out by Stott (1950) and contains useful parallels with the student's position. Stott suggests that there are five factors in success—progress, competence, satisfaction, fitness and adjustment—and for an individual to be described as 'successful' all must be related harmoniously. He must be 'progressing' satisfactor-ily, whether up the career ladder or towards graduation; he must be 'competent', satisfactorily performing his duties in a qualitative as well as a quantitive sense (attaining a high standard as well as sufficient output); and he must experience an adequate level of 'satis-faction' or sense of well-being in the work in which he is involved.

A student's success is generally judged on examination performance, which includes only the first two elements in Stott's definition of success. The feelings of the student are not taken into account. A student who passes all his examinations may still be wasting his time on an unsuitable course. Only if he fails is action likely to be taken, and then the action is rarely designed to help the student towards better adjustment. He is more likely to find himself prematurely ejected from higher education. Again, a good second-class honours graduate may feel himself to be a failure because he missed a 'first', or a student who fails at the end of his first year may have found the university or college environment so uncongenial that he leaves with a feeling of relief.

Although it is important not to forget that 'success' may finally have to be evaluated in relation to feelings of personal satisfaction, follow-up studies must, of necessity, put considerable emphasis on objective measures, such as examination results. Such a limited definition makes sense, as a successful examination performance is crucial evidence that a student has benefited from a course of study (Wiseman, 1961). Certainly nearly all British studies, and over 90 per cent of all American studies (Fishman, 1962), have relied on first-year assessments or final examinations as criteria of performance. Of course, the reliability and validity of these criteria is a vexed question (Cox, 1967). Briefly, examinations are likely to be unreliable (that is, to lead to different assessments of the same student's work on separate occasions) where essay-type questions are marked without appropriate safeguards. Examinations of this type may fluctuate in standard from year to year, markers may adopt varying criteria in deciding what is a 'good' answer and the small number of questions asked may lead to an inadequate sampling of the student's field of knowledge. Indeed Pieron (1963) has gone so far as to say that 'in the determination of . . . marks, the part played by the examiner can be greater than that of the performance of the examinee'. If the marks used as the criterion of success are, at best, not wholly reliable and, at worst, almost randomly allocated, it would come as no surprise to find low correlations with such a criterion.

Although critics have vehemently attacked the accuracy of examination marks on theoretical grounds, there is still a feeling among a majority of lecturers that these results do represent an accurate indication of a student's academic standard. After watching a student working under a variety of conditions for a period of three or more years, even a consensus of opinion from the staff might be a worthwhile criterion of success. The assessments used in higher education certainly represent a quantification of such a consensus of opinion, if nothing more. As to the validity of the criterion of success, evidence is difficult to come by. Degree classification may well represent a reasonable estimate of certain academic qualities in the student. It may, or may not, be a good indication of success later in life. Little is known about this question but in terms of justifying selection we can return to Wiseman's comments and accept examination results as providing an appropriate criterion, at least in the short term.

The acceptance of examination results as our criterion does not conclude this section. There are still two important considerations which may affect the validity of this measure. First there is the problem of combining marks from different subjects. It is still not widely realised that percentage marks do not immediately have the properties of numbers. It can be grossly misleading to add together marks from different subjects such as mathematics and philosophy or even to combine unscaled marks from differing forms of assessment. Marks may have quite different meanings. In mathematics a good student may be given 90 per cent and a poor student may get little more than 20 per cent, while in philosophy the range may only be between 65 per cent and 35 per cent. In objective tests there is usually a wide range of marks; in course-work essays there may well be a small range. A mark of 60 per cent thus will indicate a different level of performance in each subject or mode of assessment.

In the first year at university the best criterion of performance is likely to be the sum of the student's academic performance in all subjects taken, but only if the marks have first been re-scaled in some way to compensate for difference in range and level of marks in the various subjects. In carrying out the scaling procedure some assumptions have to be made. The simplest way of re-scaling the marks is to assume that the mean and the spread of marks (standard deviation) should be equal between the various subjects and to re-calculate the scaled marks on this basis.

Even after such careful readjustment of first-year marks there remains the second possibility of error in the use of this criterion. Although the numerical scales involved are now equivalent, we still cannot assume that examiners in different departments are looking for the same intellectual qualities. If differing mental skills are taken into account in arriving at examination marks, any analysis which groups together students studying widely different subjects may still find only weak relationships. Separate analyses by faculty, or even by honours subject, may be necessary before any confidence can be placed in the findings.

5. Predictive measures

What are likely to be the characteristics of the successful or the unsuccessful student? While the probable importance of hard work, effective study methods, intellectual ability and motivation is almost self-evident, there remains the problem of finding suitable measures of these dimensions. The tests chosen have, for a start, to be appropriate for the students in the sample. For example, American tests are rarely ideal for use in Britain. Systems of higher education, and also language usage, differ and cause confusions in the wording of items. Also norms (expected patterns of scores) are unlikely to be equally appropriate in both countries. Although it is comparatively easy to find well-validated British tests at school level, the situation in higher education is difficult. The research worker may be faced with the problem of either 'translating' an American test or designing his own. Both these procedures are technically intricate and time-consuming, but they are necessary if we are to obtain useful predictive measures. If inappropriate or inaccurate predictive measures are used, the relationships with the criterion will necessarily be disappointing. An indication of the types of tests which have been used in Britain will be found in the review of the literature, and descriptions of tests used in the present studies will be found in Chapters 4, 5 and 8.

6. Data collection

As there can be considerable differences in the way students react to the tests they are asked to complete, some control of the conditions is important. It is essential if timed tests are being used. Variations even in the introductory motivating remarks may affect the students' subsequent performance or answers. If questionnaire items are not taken seriously, the data will be useless. With attainment or ability tests it is, of course, necessary to try to obtain well-spaced tables, but it is impossible to ensure that students put their maximum effort into answering the questions. All that can be said is that any additional uncontrolled variance due to differences in instructions or in physical conditions must be avoided.

Some of the practical difficulties which are involved in the apparently simple matter of collecting data have already been described elsewhere (Entwistle and Nisbet, 1972). In a study which involves over, say, 500 students, the logistics of collecting and systematising the data have to be carefully considered—lay-out and pre-coding of questionnaires, provision of envelopes to keep tests together, careful pre-timing of tests, consideration of the order in which they are to be presented, and many other details, are all vital to the successful collection of complete data sets.

The next stage is to mark and code the information obtained, if direct computer-marking is not possible. Marking and coding have to be checked at each stage before the data are stored on punched cards for ultimate computer analysis. Statistical programs reduce the burden of computation to a minimum, but only if the data pack is 'clean'. The problem of eliminating every single error from the data may well cause substantial delays and frustrations. Computers do not allow for human fallibility.

7. Analysing results

The existence of valid and reliable measures is a necessary pre-requisite to the discovery of substantial correlations with academic performance. But it has already been indicated that the value of the correlation may still be lowered by statistical artefacts, such as the homogeneity of the sample. The use of correlational technique implies, moreover, that each variable has scores distributed along the normal curve and that the relationship between the variables is rectilinear (increases in one variable create proportional increases in the other). There is little violation of either of these assumptions when intellectual tests are used with school children from the full ability range, but if relationships between personality and attainment among students are being investigated, correlational techniques may not summarise the relationships accurately. Non-linear relationships or non-normal distributions may well be found (e.g. Lynn and Gordon, 1961).

While linearity of relationship between individual measures is an essential pre-requisite to correlational analysis, in complex social situations we are forced to examine the inter-relationships between several, perhaps many, variables. Multiple regression techniques or factor analyses, which are derived from correlations, are based on even more stringent assumptions than simple correlations. In particular, non-linearity in any of the predictor variables would invalidate the outcome. Fishman (1962) reported that when non-intellectual measures were added to tests of aptitude and attainment the multiple correlation rose by only 0.05 on average. But if there were different relationships at different levels of the non-intellectual variables (as in Lynn and Gordon's study on neuroticism) such a finding is to be expected. A regression analysis cannot allow for interactions of this type, as correlations average out relationships over the whole range of scores. Eventually it may be possible to increase substantially the levels of prediction currently found in higher education by matching sophisticated statistical models of analysis with the complex patterns of interactions, all within a fully adequate research design. Progress towards such an ideal is likely to be slow, but alternative methods of analysis have been reported, some of which affected the approaches adopted in our own studies. For example, Forehand and McQuitty (1959) compared a configural approach to measuring patterns of response on aptitude, achievement and interest questionnaire items with the standard multiple regression model. Their multiple regression analysis proved stable on a split-half sample (r varied from 0.499 to 0.383) while the configural prediction shrank from 0.735 to 0.237. Another study (Walton, Drewery and Philip, 1964) used factor analysis in a performance study of 102 medical students grouped into six constituencies on the basis of their academic performance. The factor analysis grouped together dichotomised variables to create a 'delegate' to represent each constituency. The delegates were then treated as persons, accorded scores on each of the test variables, and correlated with one another. A second factor analysis was then undertaken to obtain final delegates to represent and typify the whole population.

Macnaughton-Smith (1965) suggested a method of prediction based on a hierarchical classification of dichotomised variables—predictive attribute analysis (PAA). This involved classifying students on the basis of similarities and differences on the variables studied either divisively, by splitting a sample into two sub-sets on one variable and then further dividing sub-sets as each attribute in turn is examined, or agglomeratively by combining pairs of individuals or sub-sets to form larger sets. Final sets are defined arbitrarily as containing a minimum number of individuals, or as having a minimum value of chi-square defined in relation to the attribute for which a prediction is desired. This method, like Forehand and McQuitty's, involves the random splitting of the initial sample into two half-samples. The analysis to define the final sets is carried out on one of these samples and the results are then cross validated on the other.

No study has been reported using PAA in student performance, but Simon (1971) employed the technique to predict the likelihood of reconviction of young men on probation. She was trying to devise an instrument, based on pre-probation data, which would distinguish likely successes from failures (i.e. men reconvicted). Her study compared PAA with multiple regression analysis. She separated her sample into control and validation sets, but reported similar results from both analyses. After reviewing forty prediction studies in delinquency, Simon concluded that valid predictive data need not be objective, but might include data collected 'clinically or at least with the use of some subjective judgment, if it can be made reliable'. With regard to techniques of analysis she commented (p.154 ff.) 'Choice of a method may be determined as much by convenience as anything else ... it seems unlikely that the degree of power so far generally obtained can be greatly improved by further sophisticated statistical techniques for combining variables ... in practice they all seem to work about equally well.' In short, more reliable and valid data are needed rather than more sophisticated treatment.

A much simpler method—and that closest to the method adopted in the Aberdeen study—was devised by Small (1966) who attempted to predict the first year performance of 99 students at the University of Canterbury, New Zealand. The students participated in lengthy interviews and completed tests of intellectual and non-intellectual variables. Small then standardised his three indices of academic aptitude—intelligence test score, school certificate mark and reading test score—and reduced the scores on each to a five-point scale. The sum of the scaled scores of each student was obtained, and after inspection of the distributions and several screenings, an accurate prediction was made for 75 per cent of the students. In a second prediction, ratings on fifteen personal characteristics were categorised as 'favourable' or 'unfavourable'. Successful students (N = 33) were highly likely to have fewer unfavourable personal attributes than unsuccessful students (N = 19). On a further analysis with the eight most objectively assessed personal characteristics the relationship was only slightly less significant than before.

Small gives few details about the precise composition of his sample, the content of the interviews or the means by which students' responses were classified, and it is surprising that he made no attempt to combine the 'hard' data of test scores with the 'softer' data on personal characteristics in a further analysis. Nevertheless the simplicity of his method recommends it, and his results, which became known only after the Aberdeen study has been planned, are encouraging.

Finally, Wankowski (1973) combined scores on four variables which were negatively related to academic achievement—extraversion, neuroticism, GCE 'A' level result and motivation—to obtain an index of success and failure, which provided a more effective predictor than any of these variables used separately. Dividing the resulting distribution of scores into three zones—high, moderate and low—he found that a low score (implying introversion, stability, clear goal orientation and high GCE 'A' levels) isolated 31 per cent of his interview random sample (N = 64) as entirely free from failure. The moderate score group had a failure rate well below the university average (1 : 13) and the high scores (i.e. extraverted, neurotic, poor goal orientation and low GCE 'A' level grades) had a failure rate (1 : 6) very much higher than the university average. On a simple dichotomy of the distribution he identified a low score group with a low fail risk (1 : 70) and a high score group with a high fail risk (1 : 8).

Summary

This discussion of methodology was undertaken for three main purposes. First, it was intended to draw attention to possible weaknesses in previous research, which might to some extent account for the many disappointing results reported. The second aim was to indicate to those not familiar with this particular research area the various pitfalls which should be avoided. Finally it was intended to introduce, at least implicitly, the rationale underlying the subsequent descriptions of the Aberdeen and Lancaster studies.

Some of the problems described still appear to be insoluble in practice, but it is often possible to mitigate their effects by careful research designs. Prediction studies might well be expected, for example, to make use of more than one research approach. They will also have to include a variety of reliable and appropriate measures and may have to adopt complex statistical procedures to extract recurring patterns of behaviour from apparent confusion.

Some recent multivariate analyses were mentioned in the preceding section, but most of these approaches were reported after our investigations had begun. Nevertheless each of our studies has been able to explore methods of analysis which appear more appropriate than correlational techniques. In the Aberdeen study prediction was based on a combination of 'symptoms' of failure or indicators of success. In the Lancaster study, besides the usual correlational procedures, techniques of cluster analysis were applied to the data. Details of these methods are given in Chapters 5 and 10.

The combination of demands to improve research designs, methods of measurement and techniques of analysis is formidable, but necessary, if progress is to be made. As the next chapter will show, the existing research literature provides no straightforward explanation of variations in academic performance, but it does allow us to isolate some of the factors associated with success and failure in higher education.

Chapter Three

Factors Associated with Success and Failure*

The task of providing a coherent summary of the amorphous literature on the prediction of academic performance is daunting. This review includes mainly British studies, although comparisons are drawn with a number of important investigations in the United States, Australia, Canada and New Zealand. Most of the large-scale British studies are mentioned here, although it has not been possible to describe each of them in detail. Throughout, the intention has been to identify whatever consistent trends emerged in these investigations without indulging in repetitive methodological criticisms. Many of the studies were small-scale and in only a few were analyses reported separately by area of study. However, the cumulative effect of small studies, even with methodological weaknesses, is to highlight those variables which relate consistently with academic performance. This chapter seeks to identify these predictive variables and to discover where the directions of the relationships have been clearly established.

Coherence demands structure and, in this research area, there is no obvious framework to apply. The predictive variables have been described under two main headings in terms of when the information becomes available—before or after entry. The sub-headings represent variables, or groups of variables which appeared to be relevant to our particular approach.

Information available at entry
1. Entry qualifications
2. Tests of intellectual aptitude
3. Headteachers' reports
4. Age at entry and sex differences
5. Social variables

Information collected after entry
6. Mental health
7. Neuroticism and anxiety
8. Extraversion and sociability
9. Academic motivation
10. Study methods
11. Intellectual climate

It cannot be pretended that these lists are exhaustive nor that there would be wide agreement about our choice. There is a psychological bias and that will be found throughout our study. But within this orientation our choice of variables can be defended, as the studies described have not been selected to support any preconceived theory of student behaviour. The choice is intended to be a fair cross-section of

*This chapter was written in collaboration with Jennifer Thompson.

the literature, being representative of others which might have been mentioned. The attempt to condense the findings into one chapter has led to some oversimplification of complex issues and perhaps less critical analysis than might have been wished. However a much longer review would have caused a serious imbalance in the report and several detailed reviews are already available (Wilson, 1969; Miller, 1970; Watts, 1972; Thompson, 1976).

1. Entry qualifications

Most studies have found that secondary school examination results provide the best single predictor of university performance. Presumably the same qualities of ability and application are tested by both. Eysenck (1947) has suggested that a prospective student's standing at school gives an indirect measure of his studiousness. But the relationships are not all that close; some well-qualified students do badly, while poorly qualified students excel. Studies based on the General Certificate of Education examinations at 'Ordinary' level (taken about age 16) and at 'Advanced' level (two years later) have been reported by Williams (1950), Forster (1959), Austwick (1960), Furneaux (1961), Petch (1961 and 1963), Richards and Wilson (1961), Himmelweit (1963), UCCA (1967; 1969), Pilkington and Harrison (1967), Bagg (1968 and 1970), Elton (1969), Wankowski (1973), and Choppin *et al.* (1973). Correlations of numbers of passes, aggregate scores and grades of passes with overall performance in first and final year at university have been calculated, and values ranging from 0.14 to 0.73, depending on subject and faculty, have been reported.

The studies by Petch and by the Universities Central Council on Admissions both used large samples. Petch (1961) found considerable agreement between GCE 'A' level performance and class of degree. Students who passed in three 'A' level subjects did better than students who passed in two. The 1963 report showed an overall correlation between 'A' level and degree of 0.40, with the agreement closer for history and geography than for French, chemistry and physics. Ninety-two per cent of the students in the top three 'A' level categories graduated. In a subsequent analysis of these data Barnett and Lewis (1963) (quoted by Butcher, 1968) found that 'prediction was impaired by ignoring differences between universities, and that if these were taken into account, different predictive formulas would be required for success at particular universities, or at least types of university' (p. 338).

The Universities Central Council on Admissions has reported the relationship between entry qualifications and subsequent performance in final examinations for a sample of eleven thousand students. The overall correlations varied between 0.17 in social science and 0.33 in technology. Bringing together information presented in two statistical supplements, Table 3.1 shows the degree performance of students entering university with different levels of 'A' level grades. From this table it can be seen that students with three 'A' level passes did better than students with two. Forty-one per cent of students with

Table 3.1 Percentage of students at each level of entry qualifications obtaining different classes of degree (adapted from UCCA Statistical Supplements, 1965-66, 1967-68)

'A' Level grades	First Class	Upper or Undiff. Second	Lower Second	Third	Pass or Ordinary	Failed‡	With-drew	(N)
				Degree awarded				
Three C's or better*	9.33	32.11	27.45	9.52	12.66	5.89	3.03	(6,200)
Two C's or better	4.17	24.06	33.20	10.14	15.31	9.34	3.78	(503)
Worse than Three C's	3.38	19.57	26.95	11.52	22.75	11.94	3.89	(3,525)
Worse than Two C's	1.74	12.57	23.79	11.99	24.95	18.76	6.19	(517)
No information	4.75	21.36	20.00	12.20	21.01	12.20	8.47	(295)
Overall	6.72	26.54	27.18	10.37	16.80	8.75	3.63	11,040**

* 'A' level grades divided into students with three subjects or two subjects above or below an average of a 'C' grade.
‡ Including those who withdrew through academic failure.
** Students with an unclassified honours degree, or whose results are unknown, have been omitted from this analysis.

three 'C' grades or better obtained a first-class or upper-second-class degree, compared with 23 per cent of those with three poorer grades and 14 per cent of those having weak passes in just two subjects.

Similar findings have also been reported in Scotland, based on the Higher Grade examinations which are normally taken at age seventeen. Gould and McComisky (1958) showed that students among the top ten per cent in entrance qualifications had a better academic record at university. At the same time a quarter of their sample had minimum entrance qualifications and yet 77 per cent of these students still graduated. Nisbet and Welsh (1966) at Aberdeen, and Nisbet and Napier (1970) at Glasgow, have also confirmed the validity of the number and grades of passes in the Scottish Certificate of Education in predicting first-year and final degree performance. Pilliner (1960) reported correlation coefficients of 0.3 and 0.4 between entry qualifications and degree results for two year groups in various disciplines. However, he found 'a disconcerting lack of consistency between subjects in the two years' and this comment has been echoed by Nisbet and Welsh (1966), who found that 'the predictive value of different aspects of entrance qualifications fluctuates from year to year and between faculties'. The difference in relationships between faculties has again been reported by Jones, Mackintosh and McPherson (1973a), who also found rather higher values of correlation at Edinburgh University than had Pilliner. The correlations varied from 0.31 in vocational social science subjects such as commerce, to 0.69 in pure science. A recent report by the Scottish Council for Research in Education (Powell, 1973) shows a similar pattern of correlations.

As mentioned earlier, studies from other countries have reported higher correlations than those usually found in Britain. But even so Lavin (1965) could only report a median value of 0.5 from a large number of American studies, and similar values have been obtained in New Zealand (Parkyn, 1959) and Australia (Schonell, Roe and Meddleton, 1962). These levels of correlations are still low and leave a considerable amount of the variation in academic performance unexplained. This lack of precision has led investigators to use high-grade intelligence tests to provide additional information about academic potential at entry.

2. Tests of intellectual aptitude

From a review of thirty-four studies which satisfied his conditions for design, administration and statistical analysis, Eysenck (1947) suggested that the highest correlation likely to be obtained between intelligence test scores and degree performance was 0.58. But as these tests were expected to cover intellectual dimensions not adequately measured in school attainment, their use in selection might improve the overall accuracy of prediction. Himmelweit (1950) predicted the degree results of 232 students from the London School of Economics using eleven tests of intellectual aptitude and personality. The effect of combining these tests was to produce a multiple correlation of 0.55, which is identical to the value reported by Fishman (1962) in reviewing American prediction studies. In a later study Himmelweit (1963) added the Nufferno tests of speed and level of intelligence and a test of research ability to her test battery and found specific relationships between these variables and academic performance in three different disciplines. Other intelligence tests specifically designed for university students have also given what appeared at first to be promising results (Heim and Watts, 1960; Kelvin, Lucas and Ojha, 1965). But when such tests are combined with 'A' level performance (Pilkington and Harrison, 1967) the multiple correlations show little improvement on the use of the entry qualifications alone.

The successful use of scholastic aptitude tests in college selection in the United States led to the development and validation of a British test of academic aptitude which was designed to be taken by sixth-form pupils well in advance of the 'A' level examinations. Thus 'supplementary predictive information' could be made available to admissions tutors in higher education, thereby improving the accuracy of selection procedures.

Early development work on this test was reported by Sainsbury (1970) on behalf of a working party of the Committee of Vice-Chancellors and Principals, and validity studies were undertaken by the National Foundation for Educational Research (NFER). A similar study, but using an American test, was undertaken by the Scottish Council for Research in Education (SCRE) and the results of both studies have recently been published. They provide what should be definitive evidence about the value of this type of test in the British setting.

The SCRE (Powell, 1973) followed up 2,781 students who sat SCE Higher Grade examinations in 1962 and subsequently entered Scottish universities. These students had been tested with the American 'Scholastic Aptitude Test' while still at school. Using a dichotomised criterion of academic performance the highest correlations obtained were 0.27 (with mathematical ability in faculties of medicine) and 0.24 (with verbal ability in faculties of law). More typical values were around 0.10. It was also found that this test gives a poorer prediction of degree performance than did school attainment, a finding supported by Nisbet and Napier (1970).

In the NFER study (Choppin *et al.*, 1973) the validation was based on 4,175 students who had taken the test while still at school. Correlations with degree results ranged from 0.33 with mathematical ability among linguists (sic) to =0.12 with verbal ability among medical students. In the total sample correlations of –0.02 with mathematical ability and 0.13 with verbal ability were reported. The effect of adding aptitude test scores to information already available to universities at the time of application (number of 'O' level passes and headteachers' recommendations) was not encouraging. It raised the multiple correlation, but only from 0.28 to 0.30. Adding 'A' level results increased the final multiple correlation to 0.42, but this value did not represent any great improvement on prediction based on 'A' levels alone. The authors concluded that this test of academic aptitude appeared 'to add little predictive information to that already provided by GCE results and school assessment in general', although they did suggest that the test might still be useful in particular areas of study. A more detailed criticism of these two important studies has recently been published elsewhere (Entwistle, 1974a).

Studies in Australia and New Zealand have also given disappointing results with high grade intelligence tests. Sanders (1961) reported a correlation of 0.35 with first-year performance at university; leaving-certificate results correlated 0.61 with this criterion. Again combination of the two variables in a multiple correlation boosted this latter value only slightly. Parkyn (1959), Schonell *et al.* (1962) and Small (1966) have reported even lower correlations. Schonell did however find that the combination of attainment and aptitude scores improved the prediction for students with low scores on both intelligence and school record.

Although the multiple correlations reported by Fishman (1962) from American studies are also rather low, higher values have been reported elsewhere. Using large representative samples Scannell (1960) found an average multiple correlation of 0.65 between intelligence score at school and college marks. The prediction was slightly better for women

(0.69) than for men (0.61), and these values were increased (to 0.75 and 0.69) when high school rank was included. Bloom and Peters (1962), using both intellectual and non-intellectual tests, obtained a multiple correlation of 0.75 after scaling school results to counteract for variations in grading.

Some of the American evidence does suggest a high predictive value for aptitude tests, but the large-scale studies in England and Scotland indicate that such tests may be useful only in certain academic disciplines. Perhaps the abilities so far identified are not sufficiently close to the specific academic skills required within the British 'honours degree' system of higher education.

3. Headteachers' reports

The validity of teachers' estimates of the academic potential of their pupils has been demonstrated at school level by Vernon (1959) and Astington (1960). Part of the literature at university level has been reviewed by Kelsall (1963). One of the most detailed studies was carried out by Furneaux (1961), who used both global estimates, and ratings based on specific handicaps, for a sample of 2,000 sixth-formers. Following up 503 of these pupils into university he found that the correlation between the school rating on 'lack of ability' and subsequent performance was –0.50, while that with non-intellectual disabilities reached an average value of –0.23. Letters of recommendation from the headteachers were scored for favourable intellectual and non-intellectual qualities and correlations with criterion of 0.32 and 0.17 respectively were obtained. Himmelweit (1963) found that overall assessments were less useful than specific indications of intellectual calibre.

The recent NFER study (Choppin *et al*, 1973) also investigated the predictive value of headteachers' ratings of pupils. A simple five-point scale proved to be second only to mean 'A' level grade in predicting the degree results. An overall correlation of 0.26 was obtained with the criterion, while higher values were found in certain subject areas (0.54 in mechanical engineering and 0.39 in mathematics).

While the general relevance of teachers' comments has thus been demonstrated, Nisbet and Welsh (1966) found that teachers' ratings of ability and persistence failed to discriminate among students who had minimum entrance qualifications. Unfortunately it is for precisely this group of applicants that the ratings could be of most value to admission tutors.

4. Age at entry and sex differences

McCracken (1969) investigated the relationship between age at entry and subsequent academic performance. He followed up three cohorts of students entering Leeds University. There was a significant tendency for age at entry to increase over the period 1965-67 and in two of the intakes nineteen-year-olds did significantly worse in final examinations than did younger students. Other studies have confirmed this general tendency for older students to do less well (SCRE, 1936; Forster, 1959; Malleson, 1959; Sanders, 1961; Small, 1966), but the populations are not strictly equivalent. Older students are unlikely to have obtained university entrance requirements at the first attempt and they are thus less able, on average, than younger students. However there may well be differences between arts and science students. Forster (1959) found that eighteen-year-old school leavers were superior to younger students in science but not in arts, while an Australian study (Sanders, 1961) showed that older students taking English, philosophy, law, psychology, history and economics had a superior performance. Sanders commented that the greater maturity associated with being older and more experienced could be an understandable benefit in studying the humanities. The American studies summarised by Lavin (1965) did not provide evidence on this point, but in studies in which ability was controlled, age was unrelated to academic performance.

It has recently been suggested that there might be an advantage in delaying entry to university for a year or more, during which period students might work in industry or take part in community service at home or abroad. There is no direct evidence as to the effect of having this type of experience prior to entry into higher education. Gammie (1963) showed that for students matched on age and entrance qualifications there was no difference in academic performance between those who entered Aberdeen University from the fifth year at secondary school and those who had stayed on for a sixth year. Other studies (Brown and McComisky, 1955; Lewis, 1958) have looked at the effect of the experience of national service on subsequent success at university. These investigations cannot be used as evidence for or against the type of intervening experience which is currently being discussed, for example voluntary service overseas, but Orr (1974) has suggested that this type of experience may be advantageous.

In several studies sex differences in relationships with academic performance have emerged, and in most cases the differences are in line with those reported by Scannell (1960), who found academic performance of girls to be more predictable. Abelson (1952), in another large-scale American study, found a significant sex difference in relationship between high-school grades and college attainment, but concluded that 'the factor chiefly responsible, for the greater predictability of girls' college grades was not the higher validity of predictors for girls than for boys, but was instead the greater homogeneity of girls' college grades' (p. 644).

Whatever the reasons for such differences, their significance cannot be overlooked. Wankowski (1973) found that 'male and female attributes, attitudes and temperaments are strikingly dissimilar in relation to educational progress. Any results of analyses which, for the sake of larger numbers, are confined to mixed populations should, of course, be regarded as begging an obvious question: "what happens to this trend when males and females are analysed separately?"' (p. 92).

5. Social variables

At school level, social variables such as father's occupation, parental education, family size and position in family have shown consistent, and well publicised, relationships with academic attainment. Even in terms of father's occupation, the situation is less clear in higher education (Hopkins, Malleson and Sarnoff, 1958; Malleson, 1959; Dale, 1963; Robbins Report, 1963; Nisbet and Napier, 1969; among others). In the first two of these studies, professional workers' children who had been educated at public schools were found to fail more regularly than did students from other backgrounds. The Robbins Committee found a slight tendency for Scottish students from the families of 'manual' workers to have a higher wastage rate than did those from 'non-manual' homes and Jones, Mackintosh and McPherson (1973a) stated that the 'working class underachieved in all faculty groups . . . except pure science'. But for some reason this result has only been reported in Scotland; most other studies have reported insignificant relationships. It may be that social class disadvantages have already had their effect and created 'wastage' in the early stages of the various selection procedures. As a result Marris (1964) has suggested that working-class students who actually reach higher education may be more intelligent than students from other backgrounds. Klingender (1955) certainly found that such students were atypical of their class of origin; the 1951 Census indicated that their home conditions were well above the average for this social group. Dale (1963) put forward a more complex hypothesis in arguing that there may be different degrees of bias against working-class pupils in selection for different subject areas. Where it is hard for a student from a working-class background to obtain a place, low social class would then be associated with high academic performance. Recent results from studies in Bradford (Smithers and Batcock, 1970; Cohen and Child, 1969) appear to support this hypothesis. An inverse relationship was detected among the highly selected social scientists, while for applied scientists drop-out rates were higher for students from 'manual workers' families.

Other social variables have been included in studies of academic performance but with few significant findings. Investigating the effect of parental education, Hopkins, Malleson and Sarnoff (1958) found that, compared with a control group, a significantly higher percentage of students who failed had parents who had been to a university. McCracken (1969) found a similar effect for students with graduate parents but found the more usual negative relationship between family size and academic attainment. He also reported that first- and third-born children were more successful than those who were second in their family.

On the whole it appears that the effects of social variables in higher education have been reduced by repeated 'elimination bouts' in which potential students with adverse home backgrounds have failed to reach the necessary academic standards. As a result there may be no continuing disadvantage for those working-class students who are selected for higher education. On the contrary it appears that the students most at risk will be those who have come from professional families and from high-status schools which are geared to examination success. For such students 'A' level grades may provide an unrealistically high estimate of their ability.

The first five sections of this review have dealt with characteristics which exist prior to entry into higher education. The remaining six sections relate to characteristics which may themselves be influenced by the experience of higher education and which are best measured during the course.

6. Mental health

The starting points of many British studies derive from the work of psychiatrists who have examined the causes of mental breakdown among students. Early interest in student mental health was aroused by claims by Dale (1954) and Rook (1959) that suicide rates among students were higher than among the whole age-group. Dale also reported that 13 per cent of students at the University of Wales had major psychological disorders and a further 20 per cent were suffering from minor ones. This evidence has sometimes been used to suggest that students are, psychologically, a particularly vulnerable group. However, other studies (Still, 1954; Davy, 1960; Malleson, 1963) have found that the number of students with severe disorders is no more than 3 per cent.

Ryle (1969) maintains that students have more minor and moderate disorders, but fewer severe disorders, than other young people. Better diagnostic services at universities may account for the higher proportion of minor ailments recorded, while selection procedures may eliminate some applicants with serious mental weaknesses. On the other hand Malleson (1963) appears to accept that there really are a large number of minor problems: 'It is because student life demands such a continuously high standard of intellectual efficiency, not because students are psychiatric weaklings, that the incidence of those attending for psychological help is high.'

While the impact of serious mental breakdown on academic performance cannot be denied, the effect of minor disorders may not always be deleterious. Kelvin and his co-workers (1965) found that half the failures in their sample reported mild psychiatric problems, but so did two-thirds of those who obtained first-class degrees. Many of these psychiatric disorders are anxiety states, and anxiety, or neuroticism, forms one of the two major dimensions of personality consistently identified in factor analyses of personality inventories.

7. Neuroticism and anxiety

The previous sections have reported research studies which have only loose connections with any particular body of theory.

The work of Eysenck (1957, 1967, 1970 and 1972) on personality theory and measurement has provided an opportunity for research hypotheses on student achievement to grow out of theoretical ideas. Both his theory and the associated measurement instrument (Eysenck Personality Inventory) have provoked considerable interest in the dimensions of extraversion/introversion and neuroticism/stability.

The items used by Eysenck to measure his dimension of neuroticism or emotional instability/stability suggest that it is characterised by unnecessary worrying, by feelings of restlessness, by moodiness and by general nervousness. The stable person shows behaviour which is generally controlled; he tends to be reliable, even-tempered and calm. In terms of theory, Eysenck sees neuroticism as a drive which is likely to elicit behaviour designed to reduce this state of stress. Neuroticism might thus be expected to correlate positively with academic performance, but Eysenck draws attention to complications. First there is evidence, from animal studies, of a non-linear relationship between drive and performance (the Yerkes-Dodson law). Translated into human terms, too much anxiety, or too little, may lead to poor performance; optimum performance may stem from the right amount of tension. This suggestion is intuitively satisfying, but the empirical support is not strong. Only in studies by Lynn and Gordon (1961) and by Savage (1962) has such non-linearity been demonstrated among student samples.

Secondly, he has criticised research workers who have concentrated on simple predictions derived from the Hullian equation *Performance = Habit × Drive*. The implications are, in fact, not straightforward. Anxiety will certainly increase activity levels so as to reduce the level of anxiety, but different types of behaviour will occur:

'Thus to reduce (these feelings of stress) one student may go out on a drinking spree . . . get home late, and be in no fit state in the morning to cope successfully with his examination. Another student, perhaps more introverted, may try to reduce . . . (the tension) by going over his notes again and again; this might prove beneficial and improve his chances of passing the examination . . . Theoretically at least, introverted habit systems would seem likely to predispose students to engage in good study habits so that high anxiety drive in introverts would lead to even more strenuous study' (Eysenck, 1972, pp. 43-4).

Eysenck also draws attention to a measurement problem. Tests of neuroticism ask questions about general levels of anxiety, while examination performance is likely to be related to the specific anxiety aroused at a particular time. The failure to make this distinction between trait and state anxiety may explain some of the weak relationships in the literature. Both Furneaux (1962) and Kelvin and his co-workers (1965) found a small positive association between neuroticism and performance over the complete sample but in both studies it was the neurotic introverts who were the most successful and the neurotic extraverts who did least well. The poor performance of neurotic extraverts was also noted in preparatory work for the present studies (Wilson, 1968; Entwistle and Wilson 1970; Entwistle and Entwistle, 1970), but neurotic introverts did not do particularly well. Stability was related both to good study methods and to above average attainment.

The detailed follow-up of a random sample of students at Birmingham University by Wankowski (1973) yielded much the highest correlations reported in Britain between neuroticism and attainment (− 0.37) and within a zonal analysis by personality type a correlation of − 0.66 was obtained, but this was in a very small sub-group.

The American literature reveals similarly contradictory findings, but in terms of rather different measures. Lavin (1965) found it useful to distinguish between tests of general anxiety and measures of specific test anxiety. The American studies measuring general anxiety produced equivocal and inconsistent findings; those measuring test anxiety indicated a small, but consistently negative correlation between test anxiety and examination performance. This consistency may have been produced by measuring a dimension more relevant to the criterion measure.

Other complications in the American literature emerge from discussions about the extent to which drive, in the form of general anxiety, facilitates performance. Spielberger (1962) investigated the relationship between general anxiety and academic performance at different levels of ability. His findings suggest that anxiety had apparently facilitated attainment in the highest ability group. For all the remaining students, and particularly for students of average ability, high anxiety was associated with poor performance and was strongly related to actual failure.

Another distinction was introduced by Alpert and Haber (1960) who were unhappy about the way in which previous studies had assumed that *all* anxiety necessarily led to poor performance. They suggested that there might be two types of anxiety, the one facilitating and the other debilitating academic performance. Their results supported this contention, but the precise nature of the dimensions they were measuring is still far from clear.

The contradictory nature of both American and British evidence makes it particularly difficult to make adequate hypotheses about the ways in which anxiety or neuroticism will be related to academic performance. This personality dimension may well be an important determinant of academic performance, but the precise nature of the relationship is still unclear. It is likely that complex interactions will rule out the observation of simple relationships even within specific academic disciplines. Fortunately the relationships with Eysenck's other main personality factor appear to be much more straightforward.

8. Extraversion and sociability

Eysenck (1965) has drawn popular pen-portraits of typical extraverts and introverts, which have apparent implications for academic performance:

'The typical extravert is sociable, likes parties, has many friends, needs to have people to talk to, and does not like studying by himself. He craves excitement, takes chances, often sticks his neck out, acts on the spur of the moment, and is generally an impulsive individual. He is fond of practical jokes, always has a ready answer and generally likes change; he is carefree, optimistic, and likes to "laugh and be merry". He prefers to keep moving and doing things, tends to be aggressive, and loses his temper quickly. Altogether, his feelings are not kept under tight control, and he is not always a reliable person.'

'The typical introvert, on the other hand, is a quiet retiring sort of person, introspective, fond of books rather than people; he is reserved and distant, except with intimate friends. He tends to plan ahead, "looks before he leaps", and distrusts the impulse of the moment. He does not like excitement, takes matters of everyday life with proper seriousness, and likes a well-ordered mode of life. He keeps his feelings under close control, seldom behaves in an aggressive manner, and does not lose his temper easily. He is reliable, somewhat pessimistic, and places great value on ethical standards' (Eysenck, 1965, pp. 59-60)

These descriptions suggest that the extravert will be easily distracted from studying either by a need to take part in social activities or by an inability to concentrate on studying for long periods. Eysenck's theory suggests more fundamental reasons for the behaviour of extraverts. Drawing on the idea of Pavlov and Hull, he postulates the existence of 'reactive inhibition'—'kind of neural fatigue, produced whenever a response occurs, and as such (acting) as a barrier to repetition . . .' (Eysenck, 1957). Evidence derived from laboratory experiments on the learning of manual skills and on simple conditioning indicates that extraverts build up reactive inhibition more quickly than introverts and condition less readily. Lynn and Gordon (1961) developed hypotheses about students' behaviour from these ideas. They predicted that extraverts would be handicapped in academic studies through their slower rates of conditioning. Also the quicker build-up of reactive inhibition would reduce their ability to withstand the strain of prolonged revision and to work continuously well under pressure. Finally Eysenck (1970) has drawn attention to empirical evidence derived from simple verbal learning which suggests that, while extraverts are superior at immediate recall, introverts are more efficient after a delay of over, say, twenty minutes. This finding could imply that the introverts are able to code material more effectively into the long-term memory. In all these ways Eysenck's ideas would suggest an academic advantage for introverts.

The educational results, both in Britain and elsewhere, support these predictions with unusual consistency. Lavin's (1965) summary of American studies indicated that high academic performance was associated with low levels of both extraversion and impulsivity. Bendig (1960), using the Maudsley Personality Inventory, reported a correlation of -0.17 with achievement on a course of introductory psychology. Investigations by Savage (1962) in Australia, and by Small (1966) in New Zealand, confirmed the poor performance of extraverts while studies in Britain by Furneaux (1962) and Kelvin, Lucas and Ojha (1965) identified a majority of introverts among the most successful students. In the latter study, however, the authors commented that a normal degree of extraversion was quite compatible with academic success and Kline and Gale (1971) found the relationship between extraversion and academic performance to be near zero among psychology students. Nevertheless a majority of studies has confirmed the academic superiority of introverts. In one of the pilot studies for the present work (Entwistle and Wilson, 1970) it was suggested that introversion may be an important characteristic associated with the highest levels of achievement, while poor study methods are more closely related to poor performance. In the other pilot study (Entwistle and Entwistle, 1970) introversion was again linked with above average marks, with a correlation coefficient of -0.25 for university students at Lancaster. Introversion was also associated with good study methods, but the relationship between introversion and academic success remained significant even after the effect of these good study methods had been removed.

Extraversion contains two components—impulsivity and sociability. While consistent findings have been found from the composite dimension, studies on sociability have produced less clear-cut conclusions. Some writers (Burgess, 1956; Sanford, 1959) report that the socially passive and introverted students do better in academic competition than do their more socially active colleagues. On the other hand enquiries by Hopkins, Malleson and Sarnoff (1958) and by Lucas, Kelvin and Ojha (1965) both found a tendency for unsuccessful students to be characterised by social isolation and by a restriction of their personal interests.

Nevertheless there is convincing evidence for the overall superiority of introverts, at least under the present system of teaching and examining. An interesting study by Beach (1960) draws attention to the fact that these relationships *are* dependent on the methods of instruction adopted. Using four different learning situations he was able to show that lack of sociability was related to achievement only with the lecture method and for a small leaderless discussion group. The relationship did not occur for an interactive discussion group or for an independent group. This is an isolated finding, but one of potential significance. Personality clearly interacts both with teaching methods and with a student's attitudes to his courses, or his determination to be successful.

9. Academic motivation

One of the most popular explanations of failure by students is that they lack motivation. This comment usually implies that the students are lazy or, at least, that they are not interested in the syllabus provided. In the psychological literature 'motivation' is sometimes treated as synonymous with 'drive' and is thus linked with anxiety. The conceptual confusion surrounding the use of 'motivation' in the psychological literature has been criticised by Peters (1958). He reminded psychologists that most human behaviour appears to be directed towards specific outcomes—it is goal-orientated. He concluded that theories which seek to explain wide ranges of human behaviour in terms of simple physiological drives are unlikely to prove satisfactory. Peters did, however, consider it useful to follow the distinctions between *extrinsic* and *intrinsic* motivation. Essentially extrinsic motivation is aroused by rewards external to the learning situation—a present for doing well in an examination, for example. Intrinsic motivation is aroused by the task itself. Another philosopher, Wilson (1972), is still not satisfied with this level of clarification. He wished to distinguish between intrinsic motivation, which is clearly related to the activity itself (learning for learning's sake), and intrinsic motivation which feeds on some inner need, such as the need to maintain self-esteem.

The division into 'push' theories of drive reduction and 'pull' theories of goal direction does, however, help to make the literature more intelligible, even if the separation into extrinsic and intrinsic types of motivation has yet to be explored psychometrically. The idea of intrinsic motivation as a cognitive drive (Ausubel, 1968) seems to fit in with 'learning for learning's sake', but most attempts at measuring motivation reflect the current state of uncertainty. They combine, inextricably, different types of motivation and other aspects of students' attitudes and study methods. This mixture is frequently the result of harnessing factor analysis to the search for predictive validity, as distinct from explanation. The empirical connection between responses to items, or between item and criterion of success, does not guarantee conceptual clarity. Scales need to be conceptually consistent and psychologically meaningful, not simply statistically homogenous, if they are to allow satisfactory explanations of the findings.

The 'goal orientated' type of motivation is often measured by single questions about students' motives for entering higher education. In Britain, studies by Hopkins, Malleson and Sarnoff (1958), and by Wankowski (1969, 1970, 1973), have shown that unsuccessful students are likely to have entered university for 'extrinsic' reasons such as 'parental pressure', rather than out of 'intrinsic' interest in a particular discipline. Wankowski also showed that students who were progressing normally had clearer short-term and long-term goals than students who had failed their first-year examination. Jones, Mackintosh and McPherson (1973b) have criticised such studies for failing to examine inter-disciplinary distinctions. Among students at Edinburgh University they found that successful psychologists tended to endorse reasons for entering university such as 'studying subjects relevant to a future job', while successful sociologists gave negative responses to vocational reasons; their choice of higher education was 'the least unattractive of alternatives' and it also allowed 'the postponement of a career choice'. The authors point out that a rejection of conventional motives may be of positive benefit in courses which demand an imaginative consideration of alternative social structures. In other words the effectiveness of goal-orientated motivation is dependent on the confluence of student values and the educational objectives of the course they are attending.

The work on *need for achievement*, 'n-ach', derives from a view of motivation as an underlying drive. McClelland (1953) and his associates used thematic apperception tests to measure this dimension, in which drawings of ambiguous situations are used to evoke stories, which may indicate underlying needs for achievement. Elaborate scoring procedures are necessary to quantify the contents of the stories with any certainty, but the technique has been widely used. Atkinson and Feather (1966) developed from it a theory of achievement motivation which identified both 'hope for success' and 'fear of failure'. Within this theory 'hope for success' is expected to be linked with high scores in attainment, while fear of failure is associated with poor performance. However, Birney, Burdick and Teevan (1969) have challenged this view. They provide evidence that 'fear of failure' may either facilitate or debilitate performance, depending on the person's perception of the tasks involved. As fear of failure has been linked conceptually with anxiety (Atkinson and Feather, 1966) and as projective measures of fear of failure appear to be related to neuroticism (Easting, 1973), a parallel may perhaps be drawn between this research on motivation and the studies on facilitating and debilitating anxiety mentioned earlier. The overlap between explanations in terms of motivation and those related to anxiety is found repeatedly in the literature, but there are other aspects of the dimensions which remain distinct.

In spite of the intuitive appeal of the ideas of Atkinson and Feather, the use of thematic apperception tests of 'n-ach' has not consistently improved the overall prediction of academic success (Lavin, 1965). One reason for low correlations may be that 'n-ach' is a fairly general drive; it is not directly linked to achievement within an educational setting. More successful approaches are those which measure achievement motivation specifically in relation to academic performance (Mitchell, 1961). In the United States Finger and Schlesser (1965) used their Personal Values Inventory to measure different aspects of 'academic motivation'. They reported that these scales were particularly effective in predicting academic performance, while remaining almost independent of scholastic aptitude.

In spite of the usefulness of scales of motivation in predicting academic success, the continued conceptual confusion still affects their explanatory value. Inter-disciplinary differences such as those indicated by McPherson and his colleagues may weaken any general conclusions and there is also the possibility of sex differences. Men and women may have different motives for entering higher education and they may also express 'motivation' in differing ways. General scales of motivation would be insensitive to such differences. A scale developed by Mehrabian (1968) has separate male and female forms, but it is too early to say whether this scale will be appropriate for British use. Some exploratory work suggests that it may well be valuable (Cohen, Reid and Boothroyd, 1973).

Motivation is by no means a straightforward dimension, although it is popularly used to explain student success and failure. At the common-sense level it should certainly appear as a close correlate of academic performance, but the research literature does not entirely endorse this view. There is a need for a clearer definition of the term itself, followed by the development of conceptually unidimensional scales. Consistent relationships between academic motivation and performance might then be anticipated, but, of course, motivation in itself cannot guarantee success. Effort must be applied effectively.

10 Study habits

The simplest measure of study habits is an indication of the number of hours of private study carried out each week. Thoday (1957) reported a 'fairly clear relation between examination results and the amount of work done', but subsequent research workers (Malleson, 1963; Cooper and Foy, 1969) did not substantiate these findings. The lack of relationship may simply indicate the difficulty students have in remembering their work patterns in retrospect, but it may also point to the importance of how these periods of studying are spent. Long hours of obsessive, but ineffective, work are unlikely to correlate with success. In fact 'obsessiveness' is one of the symptoms of study difficulties identified by psychiatrists (Malleson, 1963; Ryle, 1969). Another common pattern involves unconscious conflict created by a desperate need for autonomy in which the student rejects pressures to conform to conventional academic requirements (Blaine and McArthur, 1971).

This clinical tradition in describing study difficulties has been made the basis of a recent questionnaire (Crown, Lucas and Supramaniam, 1973). Factor analysis indicated three dimensions: anxiety/depression; obsessiveness/work satisfaction; and low motivation/disorganisation. The first of these factors describes neurotic symptoms and may be similar to 'fear of failure'. The second factor may relate to 'syllabus-boundness' (Hudson, 1968), while the third factor looks like the negative pole of Schlesser and Finger's 'academic motivation', but with an additional component of *organisation*. This aspect of study methods is present in most descriptions of effective technique. It is certainly to be found in many of the items of a well-known American study habits scale which was developed by Brown and Holtzman (1966).

In their Survey of Study Habits and Attitudes they identified four sub-scales:

(*a*) work methods (effective study procedures);
(*b*) delay avoidance (promptness in completing work);
(*c*) teacher approval (favourable opinions about teachers); and
(*d*) educational acceptance (approval of educational objectives).

In their validation studies (Brown and Holtzman, 1955), correlation coefficients of over 0.4 were found with grade-point average. In Britain correlations of 0.3 have been reported (Cowell and Entwistle, 1971), delay avoidance and educational acceptance being most closely related to academic attainment.

These results imply that it is possible to generalise about effective study methods, but this idea has been challenged by Newman (1957). The alternative position is that students must develop their own characteristic approaches, and Small (1966) agrees with this view up to a point. He accepts that individual approaches are necessary, but, in his sample of new Zealand students, the successful group did adopt *systematic* study methods. Their systems certainly differed, and in some it was difficult to understand why the methods were successful, but the element of organisation, idiosyncratic or not, was apparently important. Pond (1964) compared the comments of contrasting groups of Australian students. The 'high-achievers' reported that they organised their studying and time allocations, worked during free periods, decided on priorities and tried to improve their study techniques. The 'low-achievers' did not consider organised study to be important. Their comments suggested a transfer of blame for their poor performance. They tended to be critical of facilities, mentioning too much chatter, over-crowding or scarcity of books. Presumably better-organised students modify their study strategies to overcome any defects in the academic environment and so maintain a more positive attitude to their studies.

Perhaps the most interesting recent work on study methods has been provoked by the ideas of Hudson (1968). He suggested that students adopt different styles of studying which parallel the cognitive distinctions between convergent and divergent thinking. He described 'sylbs' who were syllabus-bound, and 'sylfs' who were syllabus-free. Parlett (1970) explored these differences further and developed a scale of syllabus-boundness which he used with American students. Essentially syllabus-bound students may be expected to have systematic and conscientious study-habits, but these will also be associated with anxiety and obsessiveness in some students (cf. Crown, Lucas and Supramaniam, 1973). Syllabus-free students demand independence and they may thus come into conflict with their tutors. It is easy to see that extreme syllabus-freedom may be associated with that pathological demand for autonomy which has been identified by the psychiatrists.

Although Parlett's scale produces a single score of syllabus-boundness it is composed of two sets of items, representing acceptance of academic requirements (scored positively for syllabus-boundness) and imaginative independence of mind (scored negatively, indicating syllabus-freedom). The summation of these different types of item seems to make little sense, although the two parts may well be statistically related. Perhaps some of the best students will see acceptance of the system as only a minor constraint on their intellectual freedom. There seems no reason why such students should not be both syllabus-bound and syllabus-free. In the Lancaster study syllabus-boundness and syllabus-freedom were scored separately to investigate this possibility.

A recent Canadian study (Biggs, 1970a) isolated six study dimensions which fit, to some extent, into the frame-work suggested by Hudson's speculations. The factors included study organisation, intrinsic motivation, tolerance of ambiguity and independence in studying. An examination of the items defining the first two factors suggests syllabus-boundness, while the others represent aspects of syllabus-freedom. Although Biggs (1970b) did not find consistently significant relationships with academic performance, there were interesting relationships with other measures. Both 'syllabus-free' dimensions were found to be negatively related to dogmatism and, except in one sub-group of his sample, they were positively correlated with divergent thinking. Intrinsic motivation was related to introversion,

while high scores on study organisation were associated with conformity (high scores on a 'lie' scale) and with convergent thinking (fewer
'uses of objects').

Biggs is firmly of the opinion that study strategies reflect more
fundamental personality dispositions and Eysenck (1972) certainly
expected, on theoretical grounds, that neurotic introverts would have
efficient study habits. Relationships between study methods and
personality have been found, but recent British studies have found that
stability and introversion are related to good study methods (Entwistle
and Entwistle, 1970; Cowell and Entwistle, 1971). This relationship
may, however, simply indicate that neurotic introverts adopt study
methods which differ from those conventionally thought to be effective; no doubt students with differing personality types will need to
study in different ways. As with 'motivation', the dimension of 'study
habits' appears to be promising but unrefined. The value of *organised*
study methods comes through clearly in many investigations, but
apparently very different systems can be used effectively. Even so
there is sufficient in common within these different approaches to
allow study methods scales to be used in predicting academic success,
and the syllabus-boundness scale may produce particularly interesting findings.

One might anticipate curvilinear relationships between academic
performance and syllabus-boundness, where conscientiousness
shades into obsessiveness and neurosis on the one hand, and where
imaginative independence leads towards paranoia and demands for
total autonomy from the system on the other. The inter-relationships
with personality emphasise the complexity of this area and the analyses by Biggs (1970b) draw attention to the probability of inter-
disciplinary variations. Indeed the importance of intellectual climate
in mediating relationships between predictor variables and academic
performance is gradually being accepted.

11. Student sub-cultures, intellectual climate and fields of study

Much of the literature on intellectual climate is American and has been
exhaustively reviewed by Feldman and Newcomb (1969). It has been
concerned with measuring college environments and studying their
impact on students. Stern (1963), Pace (1967) and Pervin (1967) have
developed instruments to measure both social and intellectual aspects
of the student and of his college environment. The Center for Research
and Development in Higher Education at Berkeley recently produced
fascinating profiles of six contrasting colleges (Clark *et al.,* 1972).
These profiles showed striking differences in student intakes and some
differential changes in personality and attitudes during the college
years.

The long-term aim of much of this research has been to achieve
'goodness-of-fit' between student attributes, such as personality, values or cognitive style and institutional characteristics in an attempt to

minimise academic failure. But Baird's (1974) recent review of the literature raises serious questions about the whole idea of 'fit'. Besides the obvious problems of securing valid measures and communicating the results in an intelligible way to potential applicants Baird concluded that when measures of student characteristics (e.g. subject matter knowledge, values, career plans) are compared at entry to college and on leaving, the impact of the college environment, where it is detected, is still a small effect. It is also *inconsistent*—with factors which lead to change in some attributes being negatively related to change in others. Even where congruence between students' values and college ethos has been demonstrated, the evidence on student satisfaction is weak and inconsistent. However, some studies showed that students who choose 'inappropriate' major courses are likely to feel less satisfaction with their educational progress and are likely to change subjects or even to withdraw from college.

Student values can also be viewed in another way. They help to define friendship patterns and even 'sub-cultures' among students. Clark and Trow (1966) proposed a model which identified four distinct student sub-cultures in terms of involvement with ideas and identification with college (see Figure 3.1). Both academic and non-conformist

Figure 3.1   Student sub-cultures (from Clark and Trow, 1966)

INVOLVED WITH IDEAS

		Much	*Little*
IDENTIFY	*Much*	Academic	Collegiate
WITH			
COLLEGE	*Little*	Non-conformist	Vocational

students are interested in ideas, but one distinction is that the former link their intellectual interests with the official curriculum while the latter pursue theirs outside it. (There are hints of 'sylbs' and 'sylfs' here too.)Thus academic students identify with the staff, work hard, get the best marks and talk about course work outside class. Non-conformists are more likely to be involved with ideas in the wider society of art, literature and politics, although Clark and Trow admit that non-conformists are a residual category including such diverse types as fashionable bohemians, hippies and apathetic/alienated students, not all of whom are involved with ideas.

Collegiate students look out for fun. They are strongly attached to their college, but resistant or indifferent to serious intellectual demands; their values and activities focus on social life and extra-curricular activities. Vocational students are neither intellectually oriented nor particularly attached to or generally involved in their college: they pursue their diplomas wholeheartedly with no time for the luxuries of scholarship, ideas and extra-curricular activities. Clark and Trow caution that they are describing types of *sub-cultures* (a point disputed by Feldman and Newcomb, 1969) and not types of students. Thus an individual student might participate in more than one sub-culture (or in none), although in most cases only one of them will embody his dominant orientation. In practice, therefore, it does seem that there will be an identifiable typology of students defined in terms of their predominant values and attitudes.

Peterson (1965a) operationalised the typology by means of vignettes to represent the different sub-cultural orientations and reported (Peterson, 1965b) results for nearly 13,000 freshmen tested at twenty-three colleges and universities. He found that the percentage of students endorsing an academic or non-conformist orientation varied from 16 per cent at a moderately selective private technical institution to 72 per cent at a highly selective women's independent liberal arts college. Other studies (e.g. McDowell, 1967) have related shifts in first-year student orientation to the climate of the institution.

Similar research in Britain is not well developed, perhaps because our universities are less heterogeneous and students spend much of their time in a single department. The equivalent unit for analysis may thus be field of study, honours subject or even individual department. We can hardly assume that excellence in, say, history demands the same combination of intellectual skills and personality attributes as, say, engineering, and yet a majority of studies in higher education has ignored these possible differences. However, Jones, Mackintosh and McPherson (1973) at Edinburgh did use different combinations of predictors in each faculty and were able to report some substantial improvements in the overall prediction of academic attainment. For example, in the faculty of law, a correlation of 0.37 between school attainment and first-year performance in the university was boosted to 0.75 by the addition of four non-cognitive variables. Much smaller increases were, however, found in other faculties.

The different reasons for attending university given by successful psychology and sociology students at Edinburgh have already been mentioned and Wankowski (1973) has commented on the large subject-area differences he encountered at Birmingham. In terms of Eysenck's scales he reported that arts students tend to be neurotic, while scientists, and especially applied scientists, are stable. Subject areas designated as 'practical' appeared to attract stable students with varying levels of extraversion, theoretical subjects such as physics or history attracted stable introverts, while subjects involving 'people orientation' (such as social sciences and literature) contained more unstable extraverts.

Such differences in student characteristics within subject areas might well vitiate attempts to identify general correlates of academic performance. Analyses by faculty or by honours subject would certainly control for possible variations in relationships, but where students spend a considerable proportion of their time in a single department, it may be the intellectual climate of that particular *department*, rather than the general characteristics of the discipline or of the institution as a whole, which affect their academic performance. An interesting study by Beard, Levy and Maddox (1962) did suggest that the intellectual ethos of the individual department may be important. Their results, based on aptitude test data, questionnaire measures and examination results, showed that university engineering departments differed in the demands they made on their ablest students and that there were parallel differences in the students' attainments and in their attitudes to the subject. Such analyses of individual departments are uncommon in the literature, but potentially of great significance in trying to understand the effects of intellectual climate on academic performance.

Summary

Although few variables show close relationships with degree results, this may reflect the lack of any coherent strategy in analysis. If both sex and area of study are significant intervening variables which alter the nature of the relationship, low overall correlations are inevitable. Thus the first lesson from the literature must be to try, wherever possible, to identify important sub-groups in advance and to keep the results from these analyses separate—or at least to report that no significant differences were found.

In spite of the disappointingly low correlations it is nevertheless possible to fulfil the main objective of this review; that is, to identify a series of variables which have been predictive of academic success. The empirical evidence suggests strongly that scholastic attainment, head-teachers' ratings, and introversion will be effective predictors. While the evidence is less strong, it is likely that academic aptitude, goal-orientated and intrinsic motivation, organised study methods and academic values will all be positively related to degree results. Other variables, such as neuroticism, social attitudes and values, may have low overall relationships, but may neverthless provide useful information about students in different areas of study.

The rationale for the choice of variables in the two studies reported here will be found in this chapter, but it must be remembered that the investigations were planned between 1966 and 1968. Since then a clearer understanding has been reached about this area of research and hindsight would have affected both the research designs and the methods of measurement.

Chapter Four

Measuring Motivation and Study Methods

The review of the literature has indicated the wide variety of variables which might be related to success and failure at university and at least some of the relationships which might be expected. The choice of variables included in the Aberdeen study and in the Rowntree study at Lancaster was not identical and different measurement instruments were used for the variables which were common to both studies. The tests chosen reflected not only differing research orientations, but also differential limitations in the time allowed for testing and in the resources available. It was thus not possible to make direct comparisons of either test scores or relationships with academic performance. As a result separate research reports are presented in the following chapters. However the same psychological 'domains' relating to study behaviour have been tapped using methods of measurement which were basically similar. The two approaches thus turn out to be complementary and Chapter 11 identifies the common threads which draw the studies together.

Each study included indices of school attainment (GCE 'A' level or Scottish Highers), a test of academic aptitude or intelligence and an Eysenck Personality Inventory. As no suitable scales of motivation or study methods were available in Britain, the collaborative early work involved creating a pool of items from which scales were subsequently developed in pilot studies. As items relating to motivation and study methods are essentially 'transparent' (the 'correct' responses will generally be obvious) a Student Attitude Questionnaire (SAQ) was developed where these items were imbedded in a matrix of 'distractor' items. In the pilot version of this inventory, personality items were included for this purpose; in the version subsequently used in the Rowntree study, questions related to social attitudes were used. Of course these distractor items served the additional purpose of measuring dimensions which were expected to be relevant to the investigation.

The starting point in developing the motivation and study methods scales was the work already carried out in the United States (Finger and Schlesser, 1965; Stern and Pace, 1958; Brown and Holtzman, 1966). The American items were not directly applicable to the British educational system, but they did indicate the types of question which should be included. Rewritten American items and additional British items

38

were discussed with colleagues and graduate students before the pilot inventory was printed. The first validation study, carried out in Aberdeen (Entwistle and Wilson, 1970), confirmed the value of the scales of motivation and study methods as correlates of degree performance. A slightly modified version of this inventory was used in the Aberdeen enquiry. A further validation study (Entwistle and Entwistle, 1970) led to another version of the scales being used at Lancaster.

The inventory used in the Rowntree study is shown in Appendix A1, but the dimensions can best be understood by examining a small number of typical items.

'Distractor' items measuring personality*

Extraversion ('correct' response shown in brackets)

1. I'm not keen on parties: I prefer to be alone or with one or two friends. (*Disagree*)
2. I'd like a job where you're always having to meet new people. (*Agree*)
3. Sport or social activities take up a lot of my time. (*Agree*)
4. I like to be in the swim of things: if anything is going on I like to be there. (*Agree*)

Neuroticism

1. I get depressed easily—too easily. (*Agree*)
2. I seem to spend a lot of time wondering what might happen in the future. (*Agree*)
3. My friends seem to think that my moods are unpredictable. (*Agree*)
4. If I have a sudden pain, I always think it may be something serious. (*Agree*)

'Distractor' items measuring social attitudes

Radicalism

1. Our treatment of criminals is too harsh; we should try to cure them, not to punish them. (*Agree*)
2. The death penalty is an effective deterrent and should be reintroduced. (*Disagree*)
3. Workers in industry should have a voice in the running of their factory. (*Agree*)
4. The threat of unemployment is the only incentive which will cause people to work hard at unpleasant jobs. (*Disagree*)
5. Unofficial strikes should be declared illegal. (*Disagree*)

*Not included in the final scale.

Tendermindedness

1. Persons with serious hereditary diseases should be compulsorily sterilised. (*Disagree*)
2. Our present difficulties are due rather to moral than to economic difficulties. (*Agree*)
3. There is no survival of any kind after death. (*Disagree*)
4. Immigrants should be encouraged to return to their country of origin. (*Disagree*)
5. Only by going back to religion can civilisation hope to survive. (*Agree*)

Scales of motivation, study methods and syllabus-boundness

Motivation

1. It's important for me to do really well in the courses here. (*Agree*)
2. I hate admitting defeat, even in trivial matters. (*Agree*)
3. I play any game to win, not just for the fun of it. (*Agree*)
4. I get disheartened and give up easily if something is too difficult for me. (*Disagree*)
5. I enjoy the challenge of a difficult new topic in lectures. (*Agree*)

Study methods

1. I'm rather slow at starting work in the evening. (*Disagree*)
2. I usually plan my work in advance, either on paper or in my head. (Agree)
3. It is unusual for me to be late handing in work. (*Agree*)
4. I need to be in the right mood before I can study effectively. (*Disagree*)
5. My habit of putting off work leaves me with far too much to do at the end of term. (*Disagree*)

Syllabus-boundness

1. I usually study only what I am required to study. (*Agree*)
2. Worrying about an exam or about work that is overdue often prevents me from sleeping. (*Agree*)
3. I consider the best possible way of learning is by completing the set work and doing the required reading. (*Agree*)
4. I like to be told precisely what to do in essays or in other assignments. (*Agree*)

Syllabus-freedom

1. I like to play around with certain ideas of my own even if they do not come to very much. (*Agree*)

2. I tend to learn more effectively by studying along my own lines than through doing set work. (*Agree*)
3. I should prefer the set work to be less structured and organised. (*Agree*)
4. Often I try to think of a better way of doing something than is described in a lecture or book. (*Agree*)

In each version of the SAQ, students were asked to either 'agree' or 'disagree' with each statement. This forced choice simplifed the scoring and followed the method adopted in the Eysenck Personality Inventory (EPI), but the comments of some students indicated that they would have preferred the greater freedom offered by a five-point scale. Scores on each scale were obtained by summing the 'correct' responses.

Evidence of the reliability and validity of personality and social attitudes scales has been presented elsewhere (Eysenck and Eysenck, 1964; Eysenck, 1951). The personality items used in the pilot version of the SAQ were not taken from the Eysenck inventories, but nevertheless the scales correlated closely (0.7) with EPI traits. The social attitude scales were almost identical to those originally described by Eysenck, with only minor modifications being made to avoid anachronisms. The reliability and validity of the final version of the motivation and study methods scales has already been reported (Entwistle *et al.*, 1971). Briefly, the test-retest reliability coefficients for motivation and study methods, after an interval of a fortnight, were 0.78 and 0.83 respectively ($N = 124$). These values are high for this type of scale and indicate a satisfactory level of consistency in the scores obtained.

Evidence of validity is less easy to obtain and more difficult to interpret. The scales must first be inspected for 'face' validity. The earlier discussion on the conceptual confusion underlying the measurements of both 'motivation' and 'study habits' makes it difficult to demonstrate even this simple form of validity. It is possible, however, to specify how these terms have been defined in our scales. The type of motivation being measured is mainly 'intrinsic' and indicates attempts to maintain or enhance self-esteem through high standards of performance. The items also hint at a physiological drive directed towards competitive success. An examination of the items on one of the pilot studies (Entwistle and Entwistle, 1970) suggested a picture of·a student who has 'a certain obsessiveness towards being correct in behaviour which, coupled with independence and self-confidence, ties in with the determination to do things well. In some people this combination might add up to ruthlessness, but this did not emerge clearly from this analysis.'

The study methods items put substantial emphasis on organisation, planning and punctuality. Quoting again from the pilot study : 'An intuitive impression can be built up of the student who plans his work carefully and thinks ahead, and who is conscientious and recognises the importance of finding conditions suitable for efficient studying.' This description corresponds well with the impression of 'good' study

habits obtained from the literature review. It must be admitted, however, that even the final scales were not conceptually as clear-cut as,
subsequently, we should have wished. Perhaps, in retrospect, too much
reliance was placed on the statistical analyses of the items and as a
result several of the statements do not fit happily into the conceptual
framework we have since used to describe these dimensions.

Concurrent, or to be more accurate retrospective, validity was
obtained by administering the scales to a group of 72 graduates
embarking on the Diploma in Education courses at Aberdeen University. These students were asked to relate the statements in the SAQ to
their activities in the previous year—the year leading up to 'finals'.
Academic performance was described in terms of three categories
based on their degree result and their overall undergraduate record.
(By chance each category contained twenty-four students.) Initial
analyses showed that both motivation and study methods scale were
significantly related to degree result ($p < 0.01$). Combining the scores

Table 4.1 Motivation and study methods scores in relation to degree result

Degree result	S A Q scores			(N)
	High scores on both	High scores on one	Low scores on both	
Good honours	13	9	2	24
Honours/Ordinary	8	11	5	24
Poor ordinary	2	8	14	24

produced the close relationship shown in Table 4.1 ($x^2 = 19.55$, d.f. $= 4$,
$p < 0.001$). But, of course, this evidence of validity is weakened by the
retrospective approach which was adopted. Predictive validity is likely
to provide a more acceptable indication of the value of the scales. The
preliminary report of the Rowntree study (Entwistle, Percy and Nisbet,
1971) showed the correlation of the scales (completed early in the
second term) with end of year assessments for 898 students from three
universities. Consistent, and statistically significant, correlations
were found in most areas of study with values ranging from 0.10 to 0.41.
The median value was, however, only 0.18 which, while significant, is
not impressive.

Construct validity can be inferred from correlations with independent measures of the same dimension. In the above report the inter-
correlation between the two scales was shown to be 0.40. There is thus
considerable, but by no means complete, overlap between the two
scales. Motivation was found to be related to self-ratings of ambition
(0.23) and hard-work (0.26), while study method scores were associated
only with hard-work (0.35). Evidence of relationships with other
measures of study habits is found from a small-scale investigation in

two technical colleges (Cowell, 1970). 124 students were asked to complete the SAQ and the Brown-Holtzman inventory on separate occasions. The combined SAQ score correlated 0.77 with the total score on the Brown-Holtzman scale. Correlations between sub-scale scores showed that study methods correlated 0.69 with 'delay avoidance', while motivation had close relationships with both 'delay avoidance' (0.58) and 'educational acceptance' (0.60). As we started by querying the validity, in a British setting, of the American scales of study methods, any closer relationships would have been embarrassing. But as the various American scales guided the creation of the original pool of items, a degree of similarity was anticipated. In summary it can be said that the evidence of reliability and validity of the scales is satisfactory, but their predictive value is still an open question.

No evidence of validity or reliability can be reported at present for the scales of syllabus-boundness. These scales were included only in the follow-up phase of the Rowntree study and were based on the items used by Parlett (1970). However, as mentioned earlier, the two types of item (syllabus-bound and syllabus-free) were treated as separate sub-scales.

The final, and simplest, measure of study methods was based on a question about the number of hours spent on private studying in the previous week. As this is not a question which can readily be answered by students, a grid was developed to assist students in reporting, day by day (by morning, afternoon and evening periods) how long they had spent studying. Adding up the columns of this grid provides a total number of hours which proved to give a reliable indication of this variable (Entwistle and Entwistle, 1970), which was used in both phases of the Rowntree study.

This chapter has concentrated on measures which were either used in both our studies or were developed specially for one or other of them. Some of the findings which emerged from the pilot studies have been reported here, while others have already been mentioned in the literature review. The attempt to reach definite hypotheses even from a combination of theory, previous studies and pilot studies was abortive. This research area proved to be still too confused and contradictory. While it was possible to identify important predictors and to anticipate some simple relationships with academic success, it became clear that there would also be unpredictable interactions between variables and variations between areas of study. In the absence of straightforward hypotheses the two studies must remain exploratory, but being based on large samples from, in all, eight universities, the findings should at least provide valuable guidance for future research workers.

In Part Two John Wilson describes the background to the Aberdeen study and presents results relating to the prediction, separately, of success and failure. He also describes the results of a questionnaire survey of students required to leave at the end of the first year because of academic failure.

In Part Three Noel Entwistle describes part of the Rowntree project based at Lancaster. Prediction of academic performance at university is reported in six areas of study and also in a number of separate disciplines using correlational techniques. Finally, cluster analyses are used to identify different 'types' of students in relation to their academic performance.

PART TWO
The Aberdeen Study

Chapter Five

Background and Methods

The Aberdeen study grew out of work on student performance which was being undertaken by the university's Department of Education on behalf of the science faculty. Nisbet and Welsh (1966) developed an 'early warning system' which used first-term examination results to identify students at risk of failing in the first year. In an extension of this work the present author interviewed 91 arts and science students who were doing very well or very badly at the end of their first term at university (Wilson, 1968). Five aspects of ability, personality and study methods which were associated with failure were identified, and an accurate prediction was made of the first-year degree results of 74 of the students. It was then decided to study the range of performance of a complete intake of students, the work being undertaken for a higher degree in education.

Research design

Our discussion of success and failure in Chapter 2 suggested that there are many different interpretations of an individual's performance. Monocausal theories which attribute performance levels to the presence or absence of specific attributes have not been substantiated by research. In studies of matched groups (see, for example, Small, 1966) students who are making normal progress often lack key attributes, just as much as students who fail. In the Aberdeen pilot study eighteen of the thirty students whose progress was well above average had one or more symptoms of failure. McClelland (1958) has shown that high ability is not a necessary corollary of success for creative individuals. He argued that once a person had attained a minimal (or threshold) level of intelligence his performance might be uncorrelated or poorly correlated with his measured ability. Studies of failure have shown that students of moderate or even high ability may still fail; conversely many who graduate have a measured ability which is only average. Presumably in such cases other factors such as temperament, study methods, level of interest, and so on, intervene to influence the individual's final level of performance. At secondary school, Fraser (1959) has shown how, for example, a supportive home environment can compensate for moderate ability in pupils.

On this view the basic problem in the prediction of student performance is to identify the variables which are associated with specific criteria of success (indicators) and failure (symptoms) for homogeneous groups of individuals and to study the interactions of these factors in individual cases. Ideally one would wish to explore patterns of strengths and weaknesses exhibited by individuals, to determine if a critical number of symptoms or certain combinations of symptoms would be lethal (i.e. would lead almost inevitably to failure) or if certain indicators would be fructuous (i.e. would lead almost inevitably to success).

Clearly, in view of the effect of different departmental environments on success and failure levels, as, for example, the variation in percentage fail rates, a highly accurate prediction could only be made in relation to students following similar courses of study.

The above considerations were influential in the design of the study and in the method of analysis of the data. The review of the literature and the findings of the pilot study had suggested the variables to incorporate and also the need to analyse data separately by sex and faculty. In addition, Lavin (1965) had suggested that it was desirable to control ability, socio-economic status and certain personality dimensions such as level of anxiety. However, the rapid reduction in size of the sub-groups created by repeated division of the sample imposes practical limitations on the method of analysis. Also the more one highlights different sub-groups—subject of study as well as faculty, age as well as sex—the more one is driven inescapably to the conclusion that every student is a special case for which only the case study would be appropriate. Some researchers (for example, Small, 1966; Parkyn, 1967) have indeed come to just this conclusion, but one task of research is to establish a common framework as a guide to those who must deal with each individual.

Initially the research sought to identify factors which were related to first-year performance, and to explore techniques for combining these factors to predict individual outcomes. First-year examination results provided a valid short-term criterion, and this was also the year in which most failure occurred. But the study focused on excellent performance as well as failure, partly because the topic had been virtually ignored by previous British research workers, but mainly because it was unlikely that an adequate theory of academic performance could be generated on the basis of the study of failure alone.

It was decided to collect data on the characteristics of one complete intake of students to the two largest faculties in the university. As the research was in the nature of an extended pilot study, with relatively untried methodology and test instruments, it seemed inappropriate to extend it beyond the 'home' institution. Besides, it was argued that a detailed study in one university would provide useful pointers for future research.

An additional aspect was a follow-up of failing students to find out their reactions to failure and their future plans. It was hoped that this would provide a check on the reliability of the statistical analysis, and also suggest explanations for weaknesses in the predictions. This part of the study is reported in Chapter 7.

The project was subsequently extended by obtaining details of the students' final examination performance and repeating the analysis against the criterion of type and class of degree taken. The attitude scales were readministered by means of a postal questionnaire in the third year and additional information collected on the students' attitudes to university.

Hypotheses

In view of the absence of a coherent body of theory it seemed a pointless academic exercise to formulate specific hypotheses at the outset of the investigation. Nevertheless it was anticipated that there would be sex and faculty differences in the predictive variables which were significantly associated with failure and success, and that students with a high proportion of 'symptoms' would be more likely to fail than students with a low proportion. Similarly students with a high proportion of 'indicators' were expected to have a better performance than those with a low proportion. It was also expected that the percentage of failing students correctly predicted would be higher in the first than in the final year, but that the percentage of excellent students correctly predicted would be higher in the final year than in the first year. Other expectations were that predictions for women students would be more accurate than for men, and those for excellent students more accurate than for fails.

Sampling and data collection

The complete intake to the arts ($N = 639$) and science ($N = 376$) faculties at Aberdeen University in October, 1967, was selected for study. Background data, headteachers' estimates of potential, and academic records were collected for almost all the students from their application forms or university records, while 624 (61 per cent) were tested on various measures of ability, personality and attitudes.

Application forms contained the student's age, place of home residence, school(s) attended and date of leaving, and the level of degree (honours or ordinary) anticipated. They also provided information on academic performance at school in the Scottish Certificate of Education and GCE examinations. Three aspects of SCE higher grade examination results were considered: (*a*) the number of passes obtained at the first attempt at the examination, (*b*) a score based on the level of grades obtained on those passes which counted for university entrance requirements, and (*c*) a coding to indicate whether these requirements had been obtained at the first or second attempt at the examination.

Application forms included estimates by the headteacher of a candidate's likely level of degree, his diligence and (by means of a general report) his general suitability for university. Heads were also contacted by letter in May, 1968, and asked to rate their former pupils retrospectively on a check list of nine handicaps to good performance at university (details are shown in Appendix A2). Handicaps included 'lack of adequate intelligence', 'lack of stable personality' and 'lack of perseverance'. Handicaps, where they were identified, could apply 'to some extent' (scored 1) or 'to a great extent' (scored 2). Each student's total check-list score was calculated. Ratings were returned for 94 per cent of the students.

The names of university entrance bursary winners were noted. These students have been shown (Kirk and Crockett, 1971) to have excellent academic potential. A record was also made of students gaining first- or second-class merit certificates for class work in the first year. Merit certificates are normally awarded to between one-third and one-quarter of the students in each class for good performance in essays, practicals and class examinations over the session. Finally, marks in the first- and second-term class examinations in each first-year subject were collected, and coded according to whether they fell into the top, middle or bottom third of the class distribution.

Collecting data from the students themselves proved much less straightforward. Assessments of ability, personality (neuroticism and extraversion), motivation and study methods were required, but making contact with the students was a major problem. Testing could have taken place at matriculation, but it would have proved difficult to supervise the administration of the test instruments, and besides, it was desirable to measure variables such as motivation and study methods during the course and not prior to it. It was certainly possible to invite all the students, or a selected sample of them, to volunteer for the tests, but this would have presented its own problems, as the Rowntree study will show (see Chapter 8).

An alternative strategy was to test the students in class time. This depended on finding a class or classes with sufficient first-year students to provide a reasonably sized sample, and getting the co-operation of the department and lecturer concerned. Even so, it was unlikely that time would be available to administer all the test instruments, but if contact with the students could be established they might be persuaded to co-operate at a later date.

In the event test data were collected by a variety of strategies and with instruments which differed slightly for the two faculties. In science 355 first-year students were found to be taking ordinary chemistry, and, by a coincidence, the chemistry department was participating in a survey of student attitudes to first-year chemistry in Scottish universities, which was being carried out in the summer term of session 1967-68. The present authors had helped to prepare the survey, which included a version of the Student Attitudes Questionnaire, containing short scales of neuroticism, extraversion, study methods and motivation (see Chapter 4). The survey team agreed to supply the relevant data for the present report. (An account of the main findings of the survey can be found in Hoare and Yeaman, 1971).

It was still desirable, however, to obtain some assessment of ability and to do so during the same lecture period that attitude data were being collected. The time factor seriously restricted the range of instruments that could be considered, and it was decided to give a short vocabulary test, using the seventeen most difficult words from the Wechsler Adult Intelligence Scale vocabulary sub-test.* This had discriminated between good and fail students in individual testing in the pilot study. The vocabulary test was administered by John Wilson. Each word in turn was read out, and the students wrote the meaning on a duplicated response sheet.

Testing of the chemistry students was actually spread over two consecutive lecture sessions because the lecture theatre was too small to accommodate the whole class. On completing the questionnaire, the first class left by an emergency exit so that students in the second class, who were waiting at the normal entrance, should not find out what was in store for them, and perhaps decide not to attend. Despite these precautions the men who were tested had a significantly superior academic performance ($p < 0.01$) to those who were not, and the results for science men probably underestimate the relationship of the predictive variables to fail performance. Complete test data were obtained for 281 students.

In arts, no subject was taken by such a large proportion of first-year students as chemistry. However the psychology and geography ordinary classes, which were timetabled together, were taken by almost half the first year. Both departments were highly co-operative and were prepared to allow access to students in class time. Admittedly neither was a typical arts subject, but many students would be taking these classes as part of a general degree, or as an outside subject for an honours degree in a different subject. Nevertheless it was desirable to collect data from students in other ordinary classes, but it would have been awkward to do so directly since geography and psychology students would probably have been present. Instead, therefore, a one in ten sample of thirty students (15 men and 15 women) taking other first-year subjects was selected and invited for interview. All the students who were approached agreed to co-operate.

The test instruments used with arts students were the Moray House Adult Intelligence Test 1 (MHAI), the Eysenck Personality Inventory-Form A (EPI) and the Aberdeen version of the Student Attitudes Questionnaire (SAQ), which included scales of motivation (16 items) and study methods (17 items). In addition, information was requested on father's occupation, parents' education, and (where appropriate) on the usefulness of sixth year at school for preparation for university.

The choice of test instruments, though guided by the evidence in the literature, was not entirely fortuitous, for most Psychology students had taken both the MHAI and EPI as a practical class exercise. The SAQ was included as the first of a battery of tests administered by student demonstrators at a practical class in the middle of the spring term. The geography department allowed John Wilson fifteen minutes of practical class time to introduce the project, administer the SAQ and EPI, and invite students to volunteer for the MHAI, which was offered

*The sub-test correlates 0.86 with the full verbal score of the WAIS and 0.83 with the full test.

at several times in the following weeks. Only 53 of the 115 geography students volunteered, however, despite repeated requests by letter and in person—a poor response which can perhaps be attributed to the spell of exceptionally fine spring weather which lasted all the time the test was on offer. The thirty interviewees completed all three tests, filling in the SAQ and the EPI during the interview.

As a check on the representativeness of the sample it was found that, at the end of the first year, the academic performance of arts students who had been tested ($N = 343$) did not differ significantly from that of other arts students.

Detailed as the above description may sound, it does of course considerably oversimplify the process of collecting data from students. It omits, for example, the delicate negotiations with different departments to obtain permission to approach students in class time, the briefings given to student demonstrators, the frequent visits (over most of the spring and summer term) to practical classes to contact irregular attenders, and to persuade them to take tests they had missed, and the writing of follow-up letters to reluctant interviewees.

It is clear from the description above that most confidence can be placed in the data from university records and school reports, and that great caution is necessary in interpreting test scores, very few of which were obtained under normal test conditions. The intelligence test, for example, was taken either as a class exercise, or by volunteer students whose motivation probably differed in important respects from that of non-volunteers. Collusion was possible in the vocabulary test through the inadequate spacing of the chemistry students, and the geography students had barely enough time to complete the questionnaires. The absence of common measures of ability, personality, motivation and study methods is a further weakness. In educational research expediency is sometimes necessary. It would have been foolish to ignore relatively 'good' and complete data from the MHAI and the EPI just because there was no time to use these instruments with the science students. In the circumstances it seemed desirable to collect the best data possible for each group. By introducing a control for faculty of study, the analysis took account of the different measures of common variables.

Further data were obtained by means of a postal questionnaire (see Appendix A3) which was sent out to the same students in the spring term of their third year (February, 1970). This included the short scales of personality, motivation and study methods, which had been previously administered to first-year science students. It also involved ranking four vignettes—the vocational (passport to a job), non-conformist (idealistic, self-fulfilment), academic (love of subject) and collegiate (stimulating social experience) philosophies—adaptations of Peterson's (1965a) operationalisation of the typology developed by Clark and Trow (1966). Finally, information was requested on each student's degree and career expectations, his reasons for coming to university, problems of transition from school, general feelings about courses and university facilities, and involvement in sporting and social activities on the campus. After two reminders, replies were received for 535 students (90 per cent of the sample who were still at university).

Criterion of performance and performance groupings

The principal criterion of excellence and failure was degree examination performance in the first and final years. In addition, for the prediction of excellence, first-year merit certificates for class work were used to discriminate amongst students with a good academic record. Students with different examination results were grouped into broader academic categories to create viable groups to sustain an analysis.

Each student's subject passes in degree examinations, and his class and level of degree at graduation, were collected, but not the marks actually scored. It was sufficient to know that fails had not reached an acceptable standard after two attempts at a subject, while it was argued that merit certificates would provide better evidence of high attainment over a course than unstandardised examination marks, and that they would effectively discriminate between students with a 'clear run' of subject passes.

1. First-year performance

For the prediction of failure all students were grouped into three academic categories on the basis of their degree examination results by the end of the first year (September, 1968), that is, after the opportunity to re-sit any subject(s) failed at the first degree examination:

(a) *'Good'* students had passed all three (arts) or four (science) subjects.
(b) *'Weak'* students had failed one subject.
(c) *'Fail'* students had failed two or more subjects. Students in this category are 'unsatisfactory', and are required by university regulations to discontinue attendance, but they may re-sit their failed subjects in the following June and September, and, if successful, may apply for re-admission.

The prediction of excellent performance was restricted to 'good' students, as defined above. This category was subdivided as follows:

(d) *'Merit'* students had passed all degree examinations at the first attempt (June, 1968), and gained a certificate of merit for classwork in one or more subjects.
(e) *'Non-merits'* had passed all subjects at the first attempt, but had no merit certificates, or had passed all subjects only after a re-sit.

The number of students in each category in the two analyses, by sex and faculty of study, is shown in Table 5.1. There was the expected higher rate of failure in first-year science than in arts ($p < 0.05$).

54   *Degrees of Excellence*

Table 5.1 *Number and percentage of students in predictions of outcome of first year, by sex and faculty*

	Academic category at end of first year				
	Fail N (%)	Weak N (%)	Good N (%)	Merit N (%)	Non-merit N (%)
Arts men (N = 295)	36 (12)	57 (19)	202 (69)	107 (53)	95 (47)
Arts women (N = 344)	34 (10)	64 (19)	246 (71)	119 (48)	127 (52)
Science men (N = 264)	40 (15)	64 (24)	160 (61)	73 (46)	87 (54)
Science women (N = 112)	14 (13)	26 (23)	72 (64)	32 (44)	40 (56)
Total (N = 1,015)	124* (12)	211 (21)	680 (67)	331 (49)	349 (51)

*Five of these students were allowed to proceed to second year.

Notes 1. No information was available for a further ten students: viz. arts men (6), arts women (1) and science women (3), none of whom completed first year.
2. On the 'fail', 'weak', 'good' categories, arts students have a significantly better academic performance than science students, (x^2 = 7.58, df = 2, $p < 0.05$). No significant difference was observed on male-female performance or on performance in the merit categories.

2. Degree results

Most of the students taking ordinary degrees graduated in 1970, and the majority of those studying for honours in 1971. But almost ten per cent of the sample (111 students) were 'still studying' in 1971-72, made up mainly of honours students taking modern languages and joint honours degrees, and of first-year fails who had returned to university. It was impossible to delay the analyses of failure long enough to include these students in the results.

The same three broad categories of performance were again used for the prediction of degree failure:

(a)   *'Good'* students had been awarded first- or second-class honours, or were still studying for honours, or had taken an ordinary degree in three years (the minimum time) with no failure. (The 96 students still studying had the following results: 75 first- or second-class and 10 third-class honours; 8 ordinary degrees and 2 no awards. One student died.)

(b)   *'Weak'* students had been awarded third-class honours, or had taken an ordinary degree in three or four years, with failure in one or more subjects, or were still studying. (Nine of the 15 still studying had been unsatisfactory in the first year, but had been re-admitted. Their results were: 2 low-second-class and 1 third-class honours, 9 ordinary degrees and 3 no awards).

(c)   *'Fail'* students had been unsatisfactory in the first year, and had permanently left university, or had left without graduating between

October 1968 and September 1971. The great majority of students in this category were academic failures, therefore, but a small number of students who withdrew voluntarily were also included. Most of the latter had a very weak academic record, which suggested that they were about to fail anyway.

The prediction of excellent performance was delayed until all results were available. The 'good' category was again divided into two groups:

(*d*) *'Merit'* students had first- or upper-second-class honours, or ordinary degrees in three years with no academic failure over the course, and one or more merit certificates in the first year.
(*e*) *'Non-merits'* had lower-second class honours, or ordinary degrees in three years with no academic failure, but no merit certificate.

The inclusion of the best ordinary graduates in the merit category can be justified on three grounds. First is the status of the degree, which is seen by some academics to be in some ways harder to achieve than honours. Second is its popularity, especially with women. Half of the women in the present study took ordinary degrees. A third reason was the need for a criterion of 'merit' which was common to both sexes, and which would produce reasonably sized groups to sustain an analysis.

The number of students in each category in each prediction, by sex and faculty, is shown in Table 5.2.

Table 5.2 Number and percentage of students in predictions of outcome of course, by sex and faculty

	Academic category at end of course								
	Fail N (%)		Weak N (%)		Good N (%)		Merit N (%)		Non-merit N (%)
Arts men (*N* = 295)	64	(22)	51	(17)	180	(61)	65 (38)		105 (62)
Arts women (*N* = 344)	46	(13)	128	(38)	170	(49)	70 (43)		94 (57)
Science men (*N* = 264)	63	(24)	71	(27)	130	(49)	57 (47)		64 (53)
Science women (*N* = 112)	24	(21)	37	(33)	51	(46)	23 (48)		25 (52)
Total (*N* = 1,015)	197	(19)	287	(28)	531	(53)	215 (43)		288 (57)

Notes 1. Numbers in the 'merit' and 'non-merit' categories are less than in the good category because of the exclusion of a small number of students who did not meet the criteria.
2. There are no significant differences (by sex or faculty) on the merit prediction. Since some of the students in the good, weak and fail categories in fact achieved at a different level no tests of significance were applied to these results.

3. Personality, motivation, study methods and performance

An analysis was undertaken, for men and women separately, of the predictive validity of the scales of personality, motivation and study methods included in the third-year questionnaire. Data were available for 265 men (46 per cent arts, 54 per cent science), and for 270 women (71 per cent arts, 29 per cent science). Performance categories were regrouped to take account of the small number of fails for whom information was available, as follows:

(a) *'Good honours'* students had graduated with first- or second-class honours.
(b) *'Honours/ordinary'* students had third-class honours, or an ordinary degree in three years with no academic failure.
(c) *'Poor ordinary/fail'* students had taken ordinary degrees in three or four years with some academic failure, or had left university without a degree through failure or voluntary withdrawal.

Table 5.3 *Number and percentage of students in each academic category at end of course, for analyses of personality, motivation and study methods, by sex*

Academic Category	Men N (%)	Women N (%)
Good Honours	160 (60)	78 (29)
Hons/Ordinary	33 (12)	76 (28)
Poor Ordinary/Fail	72 (28)	116 (43)
All	265 (100)	270 (100)

χ^2 = 55.45, df = 2, $p < 0.01$.

Table 5.3 shows the number and percentage of students in each academic category. There is a statistically highly significant sex difference in performance ($p < 0.01$).

The distributions of personality and attitude scores were dichoto-

Table 5.4 *Number of students in high and low groups on scales of personality motivation and study methods, by sex*

Scale	Men (N = 265) Range of score	N	Women (N = 270) Range of Score	N
Extraversion	High (5—10)	163	(5—10)	145
	Low (0—4)	102	(0—4)	125
Emotional instability	High (3—10)	159	(5—10)	116
	Low (0—2)	106	(0—4)	154
Motivation	High (6—11)	84	(4—11)	126
	Low (0—5)	181	(0—3)	144
Study methods	High (6—11)	145	(6—11)	150
	Low (0—5)	120	(0—5)	120

mised to give approximately equal numbers of 'high' and 'low' scoring students. Table 5.4 indicates the range of scores and the numbers in each group.

Method of analysis

All the data collected for the study were entered on to individual coding sheets, and then transferred to IBM punched cards for analysis by sorter counter. Systematic checks for accuracy were carried out at every stage of the scoring, recording and transcription of data.

The method of analysis was similar to that described by Small (1966) (see Chapter 2), but was developed independently following McClelland's (1958) ideas on the threshold effect. Essentially, academic performance is predicted not in terms of scores, but by reference to the number of 'symptoms' of failure or 'indicators' of success which students show. This method of analysis had already been used in the pilot study. Then five variables associated with poor performance had been identified for a small group of first-year students for whom full data had been collected. Each person's score had been calculated in terms of presence or absence of these symptoms and on the basis of the scores it had been possible to distinguish between levels of performance. 'Good' students had had relatively low scores, while 'weak' and 'fail' students had had high scores. In the main study it was necessary, first, to identify the variables associated with excellent and fail performance, and second, to decide how best to combine them when full data were not available for the whole sample. The full list of variables is shown at the end of this chapter.

Separate analyses were carried out by sex and faculty. Each variable was related to excellent and fail performance in first and final years by chi square. This was straightforward with variables which were already dichotomous (such as being awarded or not being awarded a university bursary), but other variables, such as attitude scores, had to be dichotomised at a point which best discriminated between students at the appropriate level of performance. It was seldom obvious where a dichotomy should best be made. The problem was exacerbated in the prediction of failure by the fact that there were often five or six times as many students in the 'good' category as in the 'fail' category. The aim of dichotomising was to identify the maximum number of fails and the minimum number of passing students above or below the cut-off point chosen. Inevitably several of the dichotomies were arrived at subjectively after a number of screenings. Dichotomies often differed for the different sub-groups. Variables significantly associated with excellence were termed 'indicators'; variables associated with failure were termed 'symptoms'.

The review of the literature had suggested various ways of combining significant variables, but most of these had produced unremarkable results, or required sophisticated computer treatment. PAA computer facilities were not at that time available in Aberdeen, but, in any case, the untried nature of the attitude measures made the author unwilling to attempt too complex an analysis. Besides an adaptation of the simple but successful method used in the pilot study seemed called for. Eventually two methods were employed —a simple cluster analysis technique used only exploratively in the prediction of failure in the first year among arts women, and the main method based directly on the pilot study. In the latter it was easy enough to calculate the number of symptoms or indicators applying to each student. This total was then expressed as a fraction of his potential score (omitting variables on which data were not available). Since the amount of data collected for each student varied it was necessary to express symptom or indicator scores on a common scale so that comparisons could be made between students. This was done by converting the fraction to a decimal on a scale which ran from 1:00 (all symptoms/indicators apply) to 0 (no symptoms/indicators apply). The predictive efficiency of the resulting scores (ratio scores) was then examined. Students for whom no information was available on half or more of the symptoms or indicators were dropped from the rest of the analysis.

An example will clarify what was involved. Let us suppose that 'low motivation' was a 'symptom' for arts men (i.e. a low score predicted failure). A plus was recorded against the code number of each student who had scored 'low' on the scale, to show that the symptom applied in his case. Code numbers of students who had scored 'high' were left blank, and an X was recorded for those who had not completed the questionnaire. When each symptom in turn had been examined in this way each student's symptom score was calculated. A student who had six symptoms out of a possible eight (6/8) had a ratio score of 0.75.

Naturally it was expected that fails and excellent students would have a higher proportion of symptoms and indicators respectively, and consequently higher ratio scores than other students. On the whole this was so, but the distributions of scores were rarely normal, and there was considerable overlap between groups of students with different academic performance. In these circumstances it was not possible to apply the conventional techniques for dichotomising distributions described by Rorer *et al.* (1966) or Darlington and Stauffer (1966). Dichotomies were made by trial and error to take account of the number of fails correctly predicted, and the proportion of fails to good students.

The method described above allows individuals to be compared even when full data are not available for all. It thus overcomes the problem of shrinkage in a sample when several variables are introduced. But there is the disadvantage that the technique makes the somewhat dubious assumption that all symptoms or indicators are equally predictive, irrespective of the number of students for whom data are available. In fact this weakness was less serious than it may appear, as several separate measures of such 'hard' data as entrance qualifications, which were available for nearly all the students, were used in most predictions. A further problem when such large numbers of variables are examined for *ex post facto* relationships with the criteria is that some of the symptoms and indicators probably occur by chance alone. Nevertheless the approach was novel and seemed worth exploring.

List of variables included in the Aberdeen study

Criterion measures

1. First-year examination performance in June and September coded on a five-point scale.
2. First-year merit certificates gained.
3. Outcome of course by September, 1973, coded on a nine-point scale.

Predictive measures

Attainment and academic aptitude

4. Number of higher grade passes of the Scottish Certificate of Education gained in 5th year at school.
5. Awarded a university entrance bursary.
6. Grades of SCE Highers counting for entry to university. Numerical values were assigned (A = 1, B = 2, C = 3) and the student's average calculated.
7. School year (fifth or sixth) by which university entrance qualifications were gained and in which student left school.
8. Verbal Reasoning Score—raw score from Moray House Adult Intelligence Test I (arts students only).
9. Vocabulary Score—seventeen most difficult words on the Wechsler Adult Intelligence Scale (science students only).
10. Performance in the first- and second-term class examinations in first year.

Headteachers' estimates

11. Headteacher's confidential estimates of
    (*a*) standard of degree student could gain (on a five-point scale).
    (*b*) the student's diligence.
12. Headteacher's general report on the student's suitability for university.
13. Items from check-list ratings.
14. A handicap score derived from check-list ratings.

Motivation and study methods

15. Motivation score in first year on SAQ (arts version) and in third year on science version SAQ (arts students).
16. Study methods score in first year on SAQ (arts version) and in third year on science version SAQ (arts students).
17. Motivation score in first and third years on science version of SAQ (science students).
18. Study methods score in first and third years on science version of SAQ (science students).

Personality

19. Neuroticism from the Eysenck Personality Inventory, Form A, in first year (arts students).
20. Extraversion from the Eysenck Personality Inventory, Form A, in first year (arts students).
21. Neuroticism from the SAQ in third year (arts students).
22. Extraversion from the SAQ in third year (arts students).
23. Neuroticism from the science version of the SAQ in first and third years (science students).
24. Extraversion from the science version of the SAQ in first and third years (science students).

Student ratings

25. Usefulness of sixth year at school.
26. Level of degree sought by the student (honours or ordinary).
27. Class of degree expected (third-year questionnaire).
28. Post graduate qualification expected (third-year questionnaire).
29. Career intended (third-year questionnaire).
30. Attitude to university study measured by rating of vignettes representing vocational, non-conformist, academic and collegiate standpoints (third-year questionnaire).
31. Do you wish you had changed your course of study? (third-year questionnaire).
32. Deficiencies of university (third-year questionnaire).
33. Problems in making the transition from school to university (third-year questionnaire).

Social factors

34. Continuity or length of break between school and university.
35. Father's occupation—coded 'professional, clerical, skilled, semi-skilled and unskilled'.
36. Parents' education—coded 'one or both university education, one or both further education, one or both senior secondary education, both no further education'.
37. Participation in sport at university computed by scoring 1 for each team or sporting activity the student had participated in, and by scoring 3 for each position of responsibility held (third-year questionnaire).
38. Participation in other social activities, computed as in 37 (third-year questionnaire).
39. Age of student (at 1st October, 1967).
40. Area of home residence (defined as University Region, Rest of Scotland, Rest of United Kingdom or abroad).

Chapter Six

Indicators of Success and Symptoms of Failure

In a study of this scope it is necessary to select from the large number of results that are potentially available. Such a selection will normally reflect the research design. In the present report selection was made partly on the basis of the experience of the pilot studies and partly on the evidence from previous research. Thus the pilot study had suggested a procedure for predicting individual outcomes which involved identifying the variables significantly associated with different levels of performance and then combining them. There was also the desirability of confirming further the validity of the scales of personality, motivation and study methods first developed for the investigation. In addition the literature had suggested that headmasters' estimates had considerable potential as predictors and it was desirable to check specially on the effectiveness of the data collected from headteachers for the inquiry. Fuller reports of some of the results presented in this chapter have already been published (Wilson, 1969, 1973, 1974).

Before proceeding to these results let us look at how the 1967 intake to

Table 6.1 Degree examination results at September 1973 for students entering the faculties of arts and science at Aberdeen University in October 1967, by sex and faculty

Final degree result		Arts		Science		Total
		Men (*N*=295)	Women (*N*=344)	Men (*N*=264)	Women (*N*=112)	(*N*=1,015)
		N (%)	*N* (%)	*N* (%)	*N* (%)	*N* (%)
Hons Degree	First class	7 (2)	9 (3)	12 (5)	4 (4)	32 (3)
	Upper second	54 (18)	24 (7)	40 (15)	14 (13)	132 (13)
	Lower second	94 (32)	64 (19)	61 (23)	17 (16)	236 (24)
	Third class	6 (2)	12 (4)	17 (6)	5 (4)	40 (4)
Ord degree	No failure (3 years)	18 (6)	67 (19)	12 (5)	15 (13)	112 (11)
	Some failure (3 years)	28 (10)	96 (28)	37 (14)	26 (23)	187 (18)
	Some failure (4 or more years)	21 (7)	26 (7)	19 (7)	6 (3)	72 (7)
No degree	Unsatisfactory	60 (20)	43 (13)	57 (21)	22 (20)	182 (18)
	Voluntary withdrawal, transfer, etc.	7 (2)	3 (1)	9 (4)	3 (3)	22 (2)
All		295 (100)	344 (100)	264 (100)	112 (100)	1,015 (100)

Aberdeen University fared over its course. The degree results for the students at September 1973 are presented in Table 6.1.

The Table shows that 44 per cent of the students graduated with honours, 29 per cent took ordinary degrees in minimum time, and a further 7 per cent after a year's delay, while 18 per cent were unsatisfactory. A surprisingly small percentage of students were awarded first-class honours, even in science, where examiners traditionally give high marks. The breakdown by sex and faculty shows that arts women underachieve compared to other groups: the percentage taking upper-second-class honours degrees is only half that of men, but they take twice as many ordinary degrees, including the highest proportion with no failure. Arts women are also the group with the smallest percentage of unsatisfactory students. Another point of interest is the large number of students who experienced some failure over their course. If voluntary withdrawals are excluded but third-class honours graduates are included as students encountering failure, 48 per cent of the intake failed at some stage in their course. The percentage failing was lowest for arts men (40), while the figures for the other groups were arts women (52), science men (51) and science women (54). In their study at Glasgow, Nisbet and Napier (1970) reported that 68 per cent of arts students and 61 per cent of science students experienced failure in one or more degree examinations. Their results also showed that 11 per cent of honours graduates in arts and 19 per cent in science were awarded firsts. At Aberdeen the corresponding figures are 6 per cent (16/270) and 9 per cent (16/170).

It is also interesting to see to what extent students who were classified as 'good', 'weak' and 'fail' in the first year remained in the same performance category at the end of the course. While some fluctuation might be anticipated, these categories reflect broad levels of performance which students might be expected to maintain. Appendix B1 shows that the academic performance of one student in three improved or deteriorated over his course, and that this fluctuation was quite uniform in the different sub-groups (33 per cent arts and 36 per cent science). The fail category (which includes a small number of voluntary withdrawals after the first year) increased by half from 124 to 182, but twenty-five first-year fails returned to graduate; on the other hand forty-three 'good' students in the first year failed their course. It is possible, of course, that some voluntary withdrawals and fails may by now have returned to university and graduated. The results show that failure is an experience which many students—up to half—encounter, even those who look most promising at the outset. At the same time a number who start disastrously eventually complete their course.

The predictive variables

We now turn to the prediction of performance. Tables 6.2 and 6.3 list the indicators and symptoms which were identified by chi square analysis against first-year and degree examination performance. Table 6.4 lists

Table 6.2 Indicators of success in first and final years, by sex and faculty

Indicators of success	Arts				Science			
	Men		Woman		Men		Women	
	First year (202)	Final year (170)	First year (246)	Final year (164)	First year (144)	Final year (121)	First year (72)	Final year (48)
1. Residence in univ. region						5		
2. Many SCE passes at first attempt (or GCE qual.)	1		1	1	5	1	1	
3. Good SCE grades	1		1		2	1	x	
4. Entrance quals. at first attempt	1		5				x	
5. Bursary competition place	1	5	1	1	x	5	x	
6. Student seeks hons degree	1		1			x		
7. Head's estimate: hons degree	1		1	5	5	1	2	
8. Head's report: no reservations						5		
9. Head's rating: hard-working							x	
10. Good check-list rating			1	1			2	
11. Check-list handicap: *Not* lacking:								
(a) maturity				5				
(b) independence				5				
(c) perseverance				2				
(d) articulateness				5				
12. Top third: 1st class exam (yr. 1)		5		1		1		
13. Top third: 2nd class exam (yr.1)		1		1		1		
14. Merit certificate (yr.1)		1		1		1		
15. Level of parents' educn			2	5	2			
16. High intelligence/voc. score	5		1			5		
17. High neuroticism (yr.1)	5							
18. Low introversion (yr.1)					1			
19. Low motivation (yr.1)				5				
20. Good study methods (yr.1)					2	2		
21. High motivation (yr.3)		5						
22. Career choice (yr.3)						1		
23. Deficiencies of univ. (yr.3)						5		
24. Father's occupation		2		5				
No. of indicators	8	6	10	13	7	14	7	0
Dichotomy of ratio scores	.33	.50	.30	.45	.29	.43	.50	-
Percentage 'correct' prediction	67	66	64	73	65	76	71	-

Notes: 1, 2 and 5 signify $p < 0.01$, < 0.02 and < 0.05 respectively.
x = Numbers too small for analysis, relationship clearly significant.

the stable variables, that is the variables associated with performance in both analyses.

What strikes one about these results is the large number of variables which are predictive, and the variation in the pattern of significant variables by sex and faculty. In some analyses data were available for too few students for tests of significance to be applied, but where a relationship seemed on inspection to be clearly significant, the vari-

Table 6.3 Symptoms of failure in first and final years, by sex and faculty

Symptoms of Failure	Arts				Science			
	Men		Women		Men		Women	
	First year (295)	Final year (285)	First year (344)	Final year (340)	First year (264)	Final year (244)	First year (112)	Final year (104)
1. Residence in university region			1	1				
2. Age 20 or more						1		
3. Few SCE passes at first attempt	1	1	1	1	1		x	
4. Poor SCE 'H' grades	1			1	1	5		
5. Entrance quals. at second attempt	1	5	1	2	1	2		
6. Student seeks ord. degree		1	1	1	2	1		
7. ·Head's estimate: not hons	2	1	1	1	1			5
8. Head's rating: not hard-working	1	2	1		1	1	2	1
9. Head's report: reservations	1		1	5				
10. Poor check-list rating	1	1	2	1	1	1	1	1
11. Check-list handicaps: Lacks:								
(a) intelligence			1	2				
(b) maturity	1	1			5E	2		
(c) stability					1E	2	2E	
(d) perseverance	1	1			1E	1	5E	
(e) independence	1				5E	1	1	1
(f) interest	1						1	
(g) articulateness	2						5E	
12. Low neuroticism			1	5				5
13. High extraversion	2		1					5
14. Low motivation	2	5		5	1	5		
15. Poor study methods	1	2	2	5		1E		1E
16. Parents not ed. at univ.				5				
17. Break in education						1		
18. School sixth year not useful						2		
No. of symptoms	15	10	12	13	12	14	8	7
Dichotomy of ratio scores	.34	.50	.39	.49	.38	.29	.40	.50
Percentage 'correct' prediction	61	62	62	56	63	60	70	69

Notes: 1, 2 & 5 signify $p < 0.01$, < 0.02 and < 0.05 respectively.
E = Excluded from the prediction.
x = Numbers too small for analysis, relationship clearly significant.
Failure to win a bursary was subsequently included as a symptom in the final analysis; third-year questionnaire data were excluded.

able concerned was listed. One of the most puzzling results was the absence of any indicator of degree result for science women. Even first-year class examination and merit certificate performance failed to predict for them although they were indicators for all the other groups. Admittedly the sample was rather small, but this result does suggest that it is difficult to predict high achievement amongst women in science.

Table 6.4 Variables related to success (indicators) and failure (symptoms) in both first-year and degree analyses

	Arts		Science	
	Men	Women	Men	Women
A. Indicators of success				
1. Bursary competition place	x	x	x	
2. First-year class exam perf.*	x	x	x	
3. First-year merit certificate*	x	x	x	
4. Many SCE passes/GCE qual.		x	x	
5. Good SCE grades			x	
6. Head's estimate: honours		x	x	
7. Good check-list rating		x		
8. Good study methods (yr. 1)			x	
9. Education of parents		x		
B. Symptoms of failure				
1. Few SCE passes	x	x		
2. Poor SCE grades			x	
3. Entrance quals. at second attempt	x	x	x	
4. Head's estimate: not honours	x	x		
5. Head's report: reservations		x		
6. Head's rating: not hardworking	x		x	x
7. Poor check-list rating	x	x	x	x
8. Rated on lack of intelligence		x		
9. Rated on lack of maturity	x		x	
10. Rated on lack of perseverance	x		x	
11. Rated on lack of stability			x	
12. Rated on lack of independence			x	x
13. Student seeks ord. degree		x	x	
14. Low neuroticism		x		
15. Low motivation (yr. 1)	x		x	
16. Poor study methods (yr. 1)	x	x		
17. Residence in university region		x		

Notes: x = Variable applies.
  * Included only in degree analysis.

The most consistent indicators were winning a place in the university bursary examination, obtaining many SCE passes at the first attempt at the examination (or having a GCE qualification), and the headteacher's rating of being capable of taking an honours degree. Some of the associations shown have almost certainly occurred by chance. Thus it is surprising to find that low motivation (sic) is an indicator of a good degree result for arts women. Level of parents' education also has an obscure relationship. In first-year arts, women whose parents were at university do best, but by the final year those whose parents had no post-school education are superior. Neither neuroticism nor introversion appear to be useful indicators.

In Table 6.4 (A) bursary result is the best of the stable indicators from the background and test data, while first-year performance is also important. Number of SCE passes at first sitting, or a GCE qualification, and the headteacher's estimate of capacity for honours are stable for both arts women and science men. Good SCE grades and good study methods are predictive for science men, while a good check-list rating predicts for arts women.

In Table 6.3 the symptoms most consistently related to performance are derived from headteachers' ratings and entrance qualifications. A poor rating on the check list is predictive in every analysis while the rating for 'hard work' discriminates for all groups except arts women (degree result). Three symptoms—few SCE passes at the first attempt, entrance qualifications at the second attempt, and headteacher's estimate that the student was not capable of honours—apply in six of the eight analyses. There is a suggestion that a low neuroticism score is associated with failure for women, but extraversion is not consistently related to poor performance. Motivation score is associated with failure for men, while poor study methods are predictive in arts.

Table 6.4 (B) shows the different pattern of stable symptoms for each sub-group from this analysis. Science women again emerge as the least predictable group, with only three stable symptoms applying. It is clear that different aspects of entrance qualifications and heads' estimates are predictive for different groups. Number of SCE passes discriminate in arts, grades of SCE passes discriminate for science men. Ratings on maturity and perseverance apply to men, while lack of intelligence is a stable symptom for arts women, and lack of independence is predictive in science. The student's level of aspiration (honours or ordinary degree) predicts for arts women and science men, while arts women whose homes are in the university region are more likely to fail.

To what extent are the same variables predictive for good and poor performance? Table 6.4 shows that only four variables are predictors in both analyses and three of these apply to arts women. The variables concerned are (*a*) number of SCE passes at the first attempt or GCE qualification (*b*) headteacher's estimate of level of degree and (*c*) check-list score. SCE grades are a predictor for science men.

The prediction of individual outcomes

We turn now to the combination of these variables to predict the performance of individual students. In the first-year analysis of failure several symptoms were excluded when it was seen that they did not increase the accuracy of the prediction, while in the degree fail prediction failure to win a bursary was added. There were in fact relatively few bursary winners (66 in all), and this variable contributed little to the final result and might well have been left out. At the foot of tables 6.2 and 6.3 can be seen the point at which the distributions of ratio scores were dichotomised to separate merit students from non-merits and good and weak students from fails. Ratio scores, it will be recalled, ran from 1.00 (all indicators or symptoms apply) to 0 (none apply). A score of 0.34 (Table 6.3 arts men) means a dichotomy of the distribution of ratio scores so that students with six or more of the fifteen symptoms are in the 'at risk' category, and those with five or less are in the 'not at risk' category. The 'percentage correct prediction' entry shows the overall accuracy, that is the students predicted to fail who failed, plus those predicted to pass (either good or weak) who passed, as a percentage of all those for whom a prediction was made.

(a) Prediction of success

If we exclude science women the results in Table 6.2 are reasonably consistent. The cut-off points for arts students and science men are comparable in both the first-year and degree analyses, but the point of dichotomy in the latter is higher. The accuracy of the prediction in first year is similar for all groups. In the final year, however, the prediction improves for arts women and science men, while it is unchanged for arts men. This result may reflect the different number of indicators available to each group for the degree analysis. A more accurate degree prediction might also be anticipated from the inclusion of first-year data (merit certificates and class examination performance) as indicators.

There are only three clear indicators for science women in the first year and four other variables where the relationship appears significant. When these variables are combined a relatively high point of dichotomy distinguishes quite successfully between good and average students. Indeed the most accurate first-year prediction is that for science women. At degree level, however, science women with excellent performance do not appear to differ on any of the background characteristics or test scores from students with average levels of attainment.

While differences in the number and pattern of indicators, and the cut-off point in each analysis, justified the need to control for sex and faculty of study it was also desirable to combine the results to give an overall picture. In Table 6.5 it will be seen that a correct prediction was made for 65 per cent of the students in the first year. Eighty-five per cent of those who actually had a merit performance were correctly identified, but only 47 per cent of those who were 'non-merits'. In the degree prediction, from which science women were excluded, the prediction was accurate for 71 per cent of the students. On this occasion only 73 per cent of merits were correctly identified, but 69 per cent of the non-merits.

(b) Prediction of failure

In Table 6.3 we find that science women have fewest symptoms of failure in both the first-year and degree prediction. In the first year the dichotomies range between 0.34 (arts men) and 0.40 (science women), and the percentage 'correct' prediction is between 61 and 70 per cent. In the degree prediction the dichotomy is higher for arts men and science women and there is little change in the accuracy of the prediction. Arts

Table 6.5 Prediction of success in first and final years: number and percentage of students: all groups

Academic category	'Ratio Score' indicates					
First year	Potential merit		Not potential merit		Total	
	N	(%)	*N*	(%)	*N*	(%)
Merit	275	(85)	49	(15)	324	(100)
Non-merit	181	(53)	159	(47)	340	(100)
All	456	(69)	208	(31)	664	(100)
Degree examinations						
Merit	138	(73)	52	(27)	190	(100)
Non-merit	79	(31)	181	(69)	260	(100)
All	217	(48)	233	(52)	450	(100)

Predictions
First year: Correct prediction (275 + 159) = 434/664 students (65 per cent)
(All students)
Degree result: Correct prediction (138 + 181) = 319/450 students (71 per cent)
(Arts men, arts women, science men)

Table 6.6 Prediction of failure in first and final years: number and percentage of students: all groups

Academic category	'Ratio Score' indicates					
First year	At risk		Not at risk		Total	
	N	(%)	*N*	(%)	*N*	(%)
1. Fail	97	(80)	24	(20)	121	(100)
2. Weak	128	(61)	81	(39)	209	(100)
3. Good	217	(34)	430	(66)	647	(100)
(*a*) Non-merit	142	(43)	188	(57)	330	(100)
(*b*) Merit	75	(24)	242	(76)	317	(100)
4. All students	442	(45)	535	(55)	977	(100)
Degree examinations						
1. Fail	134	(70)	57	(30)	191	(100)
2. Weak	165	(60)	109	(40)	274	(100)
3. Good	163	(32)	345	(68)	508	(100)
(*a*) Non-merit*	92	(36)	163	(64)	255	(100)
(*a*) Merit*	56	(30)	130	(70)	186	(100)
4. All students	462	(47)	511	(53)	973	(100)

*Merit/Non-merit category does not include science women
Predictions
First year: Correct prediction (97 fail + 81 weak + 430 good) = 608/977 students (62 per cent)
Degree result: Correct prediction (134 fail + 109 weak + 345 good) = 588/973 students (60 per cent)

women also have a higher dichotomy, but the accuracy of their prediction is poorer than in the first year, while both the dichotomy and the percentage prediction are lower for science men. In both analyses the percentage 'correct' prediction is best for science women. The higher dichotomy for all groups except science men indicates that at degree level fails possess a higher proportion of symptoms than in the first year. Science men, on the other hand, can be identified on a lower proportion. As in the merit prediction the control for sex and faculty was justified by the different pattern of results for each sub-group, but the combined results in Table 6.6. give an overall picture. In the table 'good' students are subdivided into the 'non-merit' and 'merit' categories.

In the first-year analysis the ratio scores of 45 per cent of the students fell into the 'at risk' category. In the degree analysis 47 per cent were at risk. It is interesting to note that at each stage the group which encountered most failure had the highest percentage of students at risk, and that the groups with the best performance had the lowest percentage. In the first year 80 per cent of fails were at risk, compared with 34 per cent of good students and 24 per cent of merits. In the degree analysis the corresponding figures were 70 per cent, 32 per cent and 30 per cent.

What proportion of those 'at risk' actually did fail? The answer depends on whether failure is defined narrowly to mean simply students who discontinued attendance, or broadly to include students with any experience of failure. On the narrow definition only one in five (97/442) of those with low ratio scores failed the first year; on the broader definition (including 'weak' students) approximately half experienced failure (225/442). In the degree analysis the figures are three in ten (134/462) and two in three (299/462).

Finally, what of the overall accuracy of the predictions? On the narrow definition a correct prediction was obtained for 62 per cent of the students in the first year and for 60 per cent in the final year. The lower level of accuracy in the final year is not unexpected, and indeed it is somewhat surprising that the fall from the first year was not greater for the sample was more homogeneous by the end of the course, and the predictive validity of the data which were collected before entry and in the first year would also have declined. A further reason (as was mentioned in Chapter 5) is that a number of 'good' students (twenty in all) had degree results which in fact put them into the weak and fail categories.

Several further analyses were undertaken to check on the validity of fail ratio scores. For example, the ratio scores of thirty two students who graduated with first-class honours were examined in the expectation that none would be at risk of failing. Data were available for thirty one students. In both first-year and degree analyses five students had ratio scores which put them into the at risk category. A check was also made on the scores of the incomplete students who were classed as 'good' but who experienced failure: six of the twenty had high scores. Next, eight first-year fails and voluntary withdrawals who resumed classes and took degrees with honours were examined: six had high scores in the first-year, four in the degree analysis. Finally fifty-eight first-year 'good' students who subsequently failed or voluntarily withdrew were checked: twenty-three (40 per cent) had a high score in the first-year, twenty-seven (47 per cent) in the degree analysis. All these results did no more than confirm those reported in Table 6.6 and showed the difficulty of obtaining an accurate prediction.

(c) Discussion

Many of the predictive variables are consistent with those described in the review of the literature. It is no surprise to find that the best indicators of degree success are first-year performance criteria and that different aspects of entrance qualifications and headteachers' reports are the surest symptoms of failure. Local indicators (bursary place) and symptoms (home residence in the university region for arts women) are also important. Personality, however, is not clearly related to either success or failure. Perhaps this reflects the composition of the sample. The Rowntree study also reported no significant associations with performance at degree level for social science and pure science students although extraversion was so related in languages and humanities (see Chapter 9). The scales of motivation and study methods do produce interesting but patchy results: low motivation is a stable symptom for men, poor study methods predict failure in arts, and good study methods are associated with success for science men.

Despite the different numbers of indicators and symptoms, and the different cut-off points, the sub-group analyses give approximately equal results. With the exception of science women, the results for the prediction of success are rather better than for the prediction of failure, and the accuracy increases between first-year and degree result for the former and decreases slightly for the latter. This confirms previous findings that good students are more predictable than weak or fail students. But in neither of the analyses do women appear consistently more predictable than men.

The level of accuracy in predicting the performance of the entire intake is encouraging. It should be recalled that the distinction between merit and non-merit performance is a fine one, yet a correct prediction is made for two students in three. In the fail prediction, ratio scores indicate that just under half the intake is at risk. This is not unrealistic when one recalls (Table 6.1) that 48 per cent failed or encountered some failure over their course. The dichotomised ratio scores have identified a high percentage of students who failed (80 per cent in the first year, 70 per cent over the course as a whole) and a relatively low percentage of those who passed. A correct prediction at degree level was made for three students in five. At the same time it should be recognised that these are 'best' predictions rather than true predictions. Each variable was fitted to the data and dichotomised to give the highest value of chi square. Distributions of ratio scores were also dichotomised in this fashion. As has been mentioned some of the predictive variables are probably random, while the usefulness of variables such as headteachers' estimates and entrance qualifications has been shown to change over time. If similar data were collected for a comparable group of students, and the same symptoms and indicators applied (that is, variables dichotomised at the same points) it is extremely unlikely that the present level of accuracy would be repeated. To obtain a true prediction on the present data the population must be randomly divided into control and validation groups. The indicators and symptoms derived from the control group would then be applied to the validation sample. Such an analysis would be possible on the present data, but the small sample would rule out controls for sex and faculty, and there would be problems in handling data which had been collected with different instruments in the arts and science faculties.

An alternative approach to combining dichotomised variables was also attempted by the use of a simple form of cluster analysis. Sophisticated computer-assisted techniques are described in Chapter 10, but the Aberdeen data were not coded for computer analysis, and sorting was done by hand. A prediction of first-year failure for arts women (the largest group) was undertaken with four symptoms with the highest value of chi square in the following order: (1) Head's estimate of student's capacity to take an honours degree, (2) number of SCE passes at the first sitting, (3) student's level of aspiration (honours or ordinary degree) and (4) extraverted personality. The cluster with all four symptoms (estimate ordinary degree, poor entrance qualifications, aspiration ordinary degree and extraverted) consisted of thirty two students of whom eight failed and seven were weak. In the cluster with none of these symptoms ($N = 30$) there were no fails and only four weak students. In all, 28 per cent (98/344) of arts women were weak or fail in the first year. While this pattern of symptoms is interesting, again it should be remembered that no control and validation was attempted.

Headteachers' estimates

Our results so far have confirmed the usefulness of headteachers' estimates as predictors of success and failure. At present, however, these estimates are little used by university selectors who place most weight on the examination performance of the applicant. Pupils are often forced to retake examinations in subjects they have already passed to improve their grade if they wish to be accepted. This practice was deplored in the report of a Scottish working party on the secondary school curriculum (SED Curriculum Paper 2, 1967) and it was argued that more weight should be given 'to the recommendation of head teachers, who could report on the progress made by their pupils in the sixth year'.

In this section evidence is presented on the validity of estimates *only for those students who proceeded direct from school to university*. Students who delayed coming to university, or who qualified through further education, were excluded. It was anticipated that the most reliable estimates would be for pupils who were about to leave school, or (in the case of the check list) who had just left. There were 825 direct entrants (81 per cent of the intake) and estimates were available for the great majority. The study also checked on whether reports by heads in the university's catchment area (local heads) were in general superior to those by heads in other parts of the county. First we look at the data from the standard application form in Tables 6.7 and Appendix B2.

Table 6.7 Headteacher's estimate of class of degree and outcome of course, by sex

End of course result	Headteacher's estimate						
	Hons or poss. Hons		Ordinary degree		Poss. Ord/ doubtful		
	Men N (%)	Women N (%)	Men N (%)	Women N (%)	Men N (%)	Women N (%)	Total (100%)
Honours degree							
First class	12 (50)	10 (42)	1 (4)	-	1 (4)	-	24
Upper second	58 (56)	29 (28)	13 (12)	2 (2)	1 (1)	1 (1)	104
Lower second	72 (40)	46 (26)	29 (16)	18 (10)	10 (6)	3 (2)	178
Third class	10 (36)	5 (18)	4 (14)	8 (28)	1 (4)	-	28
Ordinary degree							
No failure	8 (9)	42 (47)	7 (8)	25 (28)	2 (2)	5 (6)	89
Some failure	35 (17)	45 (21)	32 (15)	73 (35)	12 (6)	13 (6)	210
No degree							
Unsatisfactory (U/S)	46 (33)	22 (16)	29 (21)	20 (14)	10 (7)	13 (9)	140
All	241 (31)	199 (26)	115 (15)	146 (19)	37 (5)	35 (4)	773

Table 6.7 shows that heads' estimates of the class of degree likely to be obtained by the student are best for honours graduates and poorest for students who are unsatisfactory. In all 306 students took first- or second-class honours degrees and 227 of these (74 per cent) were reckoned to be 'capable or possibly capable' of honours. On the other hand 140 students failed to graduate (the great majority for reasons of academic failure) but only twenty-three (16 per cent) were rated as poor risks (i.e. 'possibly ordinary or doubtful').

The table shows very clearly that heads are too optimistic about their pupils' abilities and/or motivation. Sixty-one per cent of the men (241/393) and 52 per cent of the women (199/380) were reckoned to be capable of honours, but only about two in three of the former (152/241) and half the latter (90/199) actually took honours degrees. The results for women also confirm research on Scottish students by Flett *et al.* (1971) in showing that many girls of honours calibre, especially in arts, appear to underachieve. Heads underestimate the number of students who will encounter difficulties. They saw only 9 per cent (72/773) of the group as 'possibly ordinary or doubtful' although almost twice that percentage failed to graduate. A supplementary analysis found that local headteachers identify more fails than headteachers in other parts of the country. Seventy-eight per cent of pupils rated as poor risks by local heads subsequently failed or encountered some failure in taking ordinary degrees, compared with 35 per cent so rated by other heads.

Appendix Table B2 reports results by sex, faculty of study and area of home residence for students rated as 'not hard-working', or for whom 'reservations' were expressed in the head's letter or general report. Heads identify only a small number of fails—46 out of 151 (30 per cent) on the rating for hard work, and 32 out of 127 (25 per cent) on reservations—and the proportion of fail to passing students is low. Just over one in three (37 per cent) of 'not hard-working' students fail, the percentage being slightly higher for men and science students than for women and arts students. Ratings by local heads are better only in arts. An interesting finding is that women are seen to be more hard-working than men (especially arts women compared to science men)— 39 out of 394 (10 per cent) of women were 'not hard-working' compared to 87 out of 420 (21 per cent) men. In the results from the letter a similar sex difference is found. The percentage with 'reservations' who fail is slightly smaller, and the most accurate reports are written for science women from outwith the university region.

We turn now to the results from the check list. Tables B2 and B4 in the Appendix show *for the entire intake of students* the distribution of ratings on the check-list items and means and standard deviations of check-list scores, by sex and faculty against levels of first-year performance. The number of students rated on the various items ranges from 5 per cent (lack of good health, science men) to 43 per cent (lack of a mature outlook, arts men), and 71 per cent are considered to have one or more handicaps. Fewer women are rated than men. Ratings for seven items are related to first-year performance. 'Lack of perseverance' and 'lack of capacity to work independently' discriminate for arts and science men and science women. Only one item—'lack of adequate intelligence'—is significant for arts women.

The mean scores from the check list discriminate better for men than for women: the mean score for women who fail is lower (i.e. they are seen to possess fewer handicaps) than for women who are 'weak'. This suggests that heads can predict men better than women at the lower levels of performance. In each of the four sub-groups, too, (arts men, arts women, etc.) there is a significant difference between the check-list scores of (*a*) good and weak performers, and (*b*) good and fail performers.

Appendix Tables B5 and B6 show how well check-list items and dichotomised scores predict the performance of students in the restricted group who came straight from school and who did not graduate. The number and percentage of unsatisfactory students identified varies considerably on each item. The rating, 'lack of a mature outlook', identifies half of all the fails for whom data were available (72/153). The most accurate rating is for perseverance, however, where 33 per cent of those rated were unsatisfactory. On most items about one student in four is unsatisfactory. Local heads' ratings are slightly superior on all items except home background and perseverance. As has already been indicated, fewer women are rated as having handicaps than men, and the accuracy of the ratings for arts women is consistently poorest.

The distribution of check-list scores for each group of students was dichotomised into high and low categories at the point which best discriminated unsatisfactory students from the rest. For arts men a low score (i.e. few items rated) fell in the range 0-2, while for other groups the range was 0-1. On this basis just under half the sample (382/801 or 48 per cent) had high scores. Two-thirds of all fails had high ratings (100/153), but the percentage was higher for men (69) and science students (70) than for women (60) and arts students (62), and the percentage of unsatisfactory students correctly identified was also higher for these groups. Only one in four of the students with high scores subsequently failed. Local heads' ratings were generally superior, but again the prediction for arts women was poorest.

Do the dichotomised check-list scores give a better prediction than the letter of recommendation? Since the check-list score combines a number of specific ratings the question is not inappropriate, but it is not easy to draw conclusions. A high check-list score identifies two fails in three, but also suggests that half the sample is 'at risk'. The letter identifies only a quarter of the fails, and puts 15 per cent of the sample 'at risk' (112/724). In short, the check list identifies more fails, but a correspondingly larger number of students who succeed. Perhaps the check-list ratings are more realistic in view of the amount of failure experienced by the intake. A supplementary analysis suggested that the check list was a better discriminator for science men, and the letter was better for women. Local heads give more accurate ratings on both measures for all groups except science women.

Two final analyses, confined to arts men, examined the effect of combining the head's report and the rating for hard work for (*a*) predicting degree exam performance and (*b*) discriminating between forty-seven students with minimum entrance qualifications (SCE grades of less than B average). In the first of these only six out of thirty-nine unsatisfactory students were adversely rated on both estimates, while the combined estimates for those with minimum entrance qualifications gave a poorer prediction than the rating for 'hard work' by itself.

On these results heads give women better reports and ratings than men. But heads were better able to predict men who will do poorly in first-year and degree examinations than women. Heads also predict good students better than weak or fail students. They overestimate the number who will graduate with honours and underestimate the number who will fail. The most accurate of the specific ratings is that for 'hard work', while on the check list the rating for 'perseverance' is best. The application form ratings and global report identify only a small percentage of fails; check-list items and dichotomised score identify a high percentage, but also a large number of students who pass. Local heads identify weaker students (particularly arts women) more successfully than other heads, and their general reports and check list dichotomised scores are generally superior, but other heads give more accurate ratings on hard work. The only group for which other heads consistently give a more accurate prognosis is science women.

While the study has shown that head's estimates are associated with performance, they are hardly very accurate. One important explanation, undoubtedly, is the effect of attenuation, for only the estimates for students admitted to university were considered and not those for all applicants. A second reason is that the heads may have made their estimates casually, taking the view that admission is decided almost entirely on entrance qualifications. However, one did not get this impression from reading the reports, although a number were written perfunctorily. A third possibility is that heads made generous estimates to help their pupils succeed in a competitive entrance situation. Certainly heads are optimistic about their pupils' prospects of graduating, particularly the girls, for whom a 'halo' effect seems to operate, but this may simply reflect their difficulty in distinguishing among candidates of similar capacity and potential. Nevertheless our results suggest that estimates could make a larger contribution to effective selection, and we return to this theme in Chapter 11 when we discuss the practical implications of the research.

Personality, motivation, study methods and performance

One of the main purposes of administering the third-year questionnaire was to collect additional data on personality, motivation and study methods to relate to degree performance. Appendix B7 shows that high scores on the scales of motivation and study methods were associated with good performance for both sexes, with the result on motivation for women just failing to reach significance. Combining the scales, so that students have 'high scores on both scales', 'high scores on one', or 'low scores on both' also produced the expected association and substantially reduced the number of 'misfits'; that is, students with high scores on either motivation or study methods, but with poor performance. For example, the number of misfits using the motivation scale alone is 113 out of 265 (40 per cent) for men; the combined scales reduce this to 55 out of 265 (21 per cent).

Personality, at least on these measures, is not related to performance. Even when the extraversion and neuroticism dimensions are combined to form four personality groups—stable extravert, unstable extravert, stable introvert, unstable introvert—no relationship is observed. Also when motivation and study methods scores were related to personality group, only the relationship with study methods was statistically significant. Introverts (and particularly stable introverts) were more likely to score high on the study methods scale, while unstable extraverts were more likely to score low. When motivation and study methods scales were combined unstable extraverts were again the largest group with low scores on both, but the largest group with high scores was unstable introverts for men and stable introverts

Table 6.8 Combined motivation and study methods scores of different personality groups in relation to degree results: all students.

Degree result	Unstable extravert Motivation and study methods scores			Stable extravert Motivation and study methods scores			Unstable introvert Motivation and study methods scores			Stable introvert Motivation and study methods scores		
	Both high	One high	Both low	Both high	One high	Both low	Both high	One high	Both low	Both high	One high	Both low
	N (%)	N (%)	N (%)	N (%)	N (%)	N (%)	N (%)	N (%)	N (%)	N (%)	N (%)	N (%)
Good	23 (27)	32 (37)	31 (36)	26 (24)	41 (38)	40 (38)	38 (43)	36 (40)	15 (17)	32 (49)	23 (35)	10 (16)
Poor	6 (10)	17 (28)	38 (62)	9 (16)	15 (28)	30 (56)	12 (31)	12 (31)	15 (38)	11 (32)	11 (32)	12 (36)
All	29 (20)	49 (33)	69 (47)	35 (22)	56 (34)	70 (44)	50 (39)	48 (38)	30 (23)	43 (43)	34 (34)	22 (22)

Personality group

for women. The inter-relationship of these variables with degree performance is shown for all students in Table 6.8. In the table, academic performance has been described as 'good' (i.e. good honours and honours/ordinary) and 'poor' (poor ordinary /fail). The interaction is statistically highly significant.

It is clear that the percentage of introverts scoring 'both high' on the combined motivation and study methods scales is twice as great as amongst extraverts. Twice the percentage of extraverts, on the other hand, score 'both low' on the scales. In other words introverts tend to score high on these scales, and extraverts to score low. It is also the case that the percentage of introverts with high scores on both scales who have good academic performance is twice as great as among extraverts, while the percentage of extraverts with low scores on both scales who have poor academic performance is considerably greater than introverts. There is another important finding, however, when the table is read vertically. Within each personality group approximately the same percentage of students who score 'both high' and 'both low' have good and poor academic performance. Amongst unstable extraverts 23 out of 29 students (79 per cent) with high scores have good performance; amongst stable introverts the corresponding figures are 32 out of 43 (75 per cent). Amongst low scorers 55 per cent of unstable extraverts (38/69) have poor performance, exactly the same as amongst stable introverts (12/22). In short, extraverts who endorse 'good' study methods and motivation responses achieve just as well as introverts, while introverts who choose 'poor' responses do as badly as extraverts. This result raises some intriguing questions about the relationship between personality, motivation and study methods which will be explored more fully in Chapter 11.

Questionnaire findings

The final section of this chapter briefly reports findings from the remainder of the questionnaire data. Probably the most interesting and yet disturbing finding was provided from the students' ranking of the typologies which represented four points of view about the purpose of being at university. Table 6.9 shows the students' choice of 'best' and 'worst' views.

Forty per cent of the students (210/522) ranked the vocational attitude best, that is they endorsed the view that they were at the university primarily to get a degree qualification useful for a career. A further 36 per cent endorsed the collegiate viewpoint which stresses the importance of the social side of college life. Arts men who subscribed to this attitude were significantly more likely to have a poorer degree performance than those who endorsed other attitudes. Only 10 per cent put the academic or subject-interest view first. The table shows that more men and fewer women than expected chose the academic viewpoint, and most of those who did so had good degree performance. A surprisingly high percentage of students (and more in arts than in science) endorsed the non-conformist viewpoint. The academic view-

Table 6.9 Student attitudes to university

Best statement of my view	Men N	(%)	Women N	(%)	All N	(%)	Arts N	(%)	Science N	(%)
Vocational	105	(50)	105	(50)	210	(100)	116	(55)	94	(45)
Collegiate	82	(44)	104	(56)	186	(100)	111	(60)	75	(40)
Non-conformist	37	(51)	36	(49)	73	(100)	51	(70)	22	(30)
Academic	32	(60)	21	(40)	53	(100)	29	(55)	24	(45)
All	256	(49)	266	(51)	522	(100)	307	(59)	215	(41)
Worst statement of my view										
Academic	77	(38)	123	(62)	200	(100)	134	(67)	66	(33)
Non-conformist	101	(52)	93	(48)	194	(100)	91	(47)	103	(53)
Vocational	40	(53)	36	(47)	76	(100)	50	(66)	26	(34)
Collegiate	38	(73)	14	(27)	52	(100)	32	(62)	20	(38)

point was also most rejected (by 38 per cent of students) especially by women. By contrast only 10 per cent rejected the collegiate view (especially men) and 15 per cent the vocational view.

The questionnaire had also collected relevant information about the extent of student participation in organised clubs and societies, and found that 76 per cent (409/537) had played for no university sports team, and 67 per cent (359/537) had not participated as a leading member in any of the university societies or activities, over their first three years at university. Altogether 58 per cent had participated in neither kind of activity.

Putting these two results together it would appear that most students see themselves at university primarily to secure a marketable qualification, while they participate in an undemanding social life—presumably consisting of parties, record sessions and extended coffee chats—outside of clubs and societies. The replies suggest that the overwhelming majority of students are basically uninterested in academic study for its own sake, and most do not participate in formal student activities on the campus. It would seem that there is a discrepancy between the major goals of the university, as defined for example in the Robbins and Hale reports, and those held by students in this study.

Other findings of interest came mainly from replies to open-ended questions. One-third of the students reported problems in making the transition to university (mainly study problems, examinations, etc.) and arts women with such problems were more likely to do badly ($p < 0.05$). Thirty-five per cent admitted that they had doubts about whether they ought to have come to university.

Universities (and schools) are regularly criticised for offering students poor guidance on the courses they should study. Just over half of the respondents wished to change some aspect of their course. In science, men who wished to change were more likely to have poor performance ($p < 0.05$). The largest number (171/295) wished to change 'outside' or optional subjects, a further 56 their level of degree (mainly from ordinary to honours), while 60 wished they had studied in a different faculty. Two-thirds of these were science students, most of whom wished to transfer to arts.

Students were also asked about the deficiencies they observed in university teaching, libraries etc. While 85 students reported 'no deficiencies', 87 reported several. Most students reported a few. These in rank order were (*a*) quality of teaching (easily the most common), (*b*) lack of informal staff-student contact, (*c*) lack of adequate guidance and (*d*) inadequate student facilities, but there was no association with performance. Separate analysis of the replies to two of the questionnaire items showed the university in a more positive light. Ninety per cent of the students *agreed* with the statement that 'There is at least one member of staff I could ask if I need help or advice', and 84 per cent *disagreed* with the suggestion that 'My life at university has been intellectually unstimulating'.

This chapter began with a statement of the academic record of the Aberdeen student intake, and reported the results of the predictions of first-year and degree performance, and the variables associated with success and failure. The validity of heads' estimates and of measures of attitude and personality have also been considered. The chapter has concluded with the student viewpoint. One of the functions of a university is to encourage students to be critical and an open-ended questionnaire provides a convenient vehicle, but questionnaire data give at best an impressionistic account. There is no doubt that many of the respondents were prepared to be critical of university teaching, organisation and guidance. Yet they did not show themselves to be an academically minded or participant group, and in the former respect at least their academic record bears them out. In the next chapter we continue with the student perspective by looking more closely at what happened to the students who failed the first year and who were required to discontinue at university.

Chapter Seven

Explanations of Failure

In Chapter 2 it was suggested that case studies might be used to supplement and help interpret findings derived from mass testing and statistical analysis. The Aberdeen study employed such an approach with 119 students who were unsatisfactory at the end of the first year. This chapter compares passing and failing students on background data and test scores, and reports the replies of failing students to two postal questionnaires—the first sent out immediately they were informed that they had to discontinue attendance, and the second fifteen months later. Response rates were 90 and 85 per cent respectively. Information about the students' attitudes and abilities was also obtained from university staff who acted as their Regents (or moral tutors) in science, and Advisors of Studies in arts.

The 'committee anent students' of Aberdeen University publishes in October the names of students whose academic progress in the previous session has been unsatisfactory through failure in examinations. In 1968 there were 124 arts and science students in this category, but five were considered to have mitigating circumstances and were allowed to continue their studies. The remaining 119 were suspended from their faculty of study for the session 1968-69. This meant that they could not resume classes, but the students had the right to re-sit the subjects in which they had failed in the June and September degree examinations at the end of the session.

To what extent do the background data and test scores collected for the study distinguish between students who passed and failed? Although many significant differences emerge in the results shown in Tables 7.1 and 7.2 probably the most striking finding is the extent of overlap between the groups of any of the predictive measures selected. Entrance qualifications and the headteacher's rating for hard work are the best predictors, distinguishing between students in both faculties; the degree aimed at and the headteacher's report discriminate only for arts students, while social class is unrelated to performance. The arts/science differences reflect the fact that there are many more women in arts than in science, and that arts women are less likely than men to aim for honours. Only two variables discriminate in Table 7.2: extraversion in arts and motivation in science.

Supplementary information on the failing students was first requested from their Advisors of Studies or Regents. They were asked to indicate (*a*) if the student had attended for consultation when requested to do so, and (*b*) whether any circumstances were known to have affected his performance. Replies were received for all but four of the students. Most students (approximately six out of seven) were described as 'good attenders', and in just over half of the cases staff

Table 7.1 Pass and fail students: background data.

Variable	Arts				Science			
	Pass		Fail		Pass		Fail	
	N	%	N	%	N	%	N	%
Three or more SCE 'H' passes at first attempt.	346	89.6	40	10.4	131	87.9	18	12.1
Two or less SCE 'H' passes at first attempt.	95	80.5	23	19.5 **		29	61.7	18	38.3 ***
Grade of SCE 'H' passes 1.0—2.4 (Good)	308	90.6	32	9.4	117	90.0	13	10.0
2.5—3.0 (Poor)	129	81.1	30	18.9 ***		37	69.8	16	30.2 ***
Entrance Qualifications By 5th Year	301	91.8	27	8.2	110	88.7	14	11.3
By 6th Year	140	79.6	36	20.4 ***		50	69.4	22	30.6 ***
Degree aimed at: Honours	294	92.2	25	7.8	2238	86.2	38	13.8
Ordinary	273	86.1	44	13.9 *		57	82.6	12	17.4
Headmaster's Report No Reservations	436	92.8	34	7.2	254	87.9	35	12.1
Some Reservations	58	76.3	18	23.7 ***		45	79.0	12	21.0
Headmaster's Rating Hardworking	505	90.3	54	9.7	258	89.0	32	11.0
Not Hardworking	53	79.1	14	20.9 ***		60	76.0	19	24.0 ***
Social Class Non-Manual	214	91.9	19	8.1	167	87.4	24	12.6
Manual	96	87.3	14	12.7	81	91.0	8	9.0

Significance of χ^2 test: *** $p<0.01$, ** $p<0.02$, * $p<0.05$

Table 7.2 Pass and fail students: test data

Variable	Arts				Science			
	Pass (N=310)		Fail (N=33)		t	Pass (N=249)		Fail (N=32)		t
	Mean	S.D.	Mean	S.D.		Mean	S.D.	Mean	S.D.	
Neuroticism	11.8	4.6	10.6	3.5	1.76	4.3	2.4	3.6	2.6	1.45
Extraversion	12.0	4.5	13.8	3.7	2.54*	4.8	2.0	4.9	2.2	0.46
Motivation	7.4	2.6	6.6	2.9	1.51	5.5	2.1	4.6	1.8	2.58*
Study methods	10.0	2.9	9.7	2.9	0.63	4.4	2.2	4.4	2.2	0.06
Ability	75.2	11.7	73.2	10.3	1.05	22.0	5.2	21.6	5.4	0.38

* *t* test significant at 0.02 level.
Note: Neuroticism and extraversion for arts students were measured on the EPI (Form A). Arts motivation and study methods scales contained 16 and 17 items respectively; science neuroticism, extraversion and study methods scales contained 10 items, and the motivation scale 11 items.

suggested special factors or circumstances. These can be classified as (*a*) lack of motivation (18 students), (*b*) personal problems (16 students) and (*c*) lack of ability (15 students).

The next stage was to make contact with the students themselves. Earlier researchers have commented on the problems involved. Both Kendall (1964) and Wankowski (1969) reported only a 50 per cent response rate. In Kendall's case this was a reasonably good result since he was trying to contact fails of ten years before by means of a postal questionnaire, but Wankowski was seeking to interview students who had just learned that they had been discontinued. The Aberdeen study also used postal questionnaires (Appendices A4 and A5). It was relatively easy to trace the home addresses of the students, and in November 1968 the first questionnaire was dispatched. Replies were received from 107 students (90 per cent). Eighteen of these indicated that they had been allowed to transfer to a different course and/or faculty within the university. Accordingly they were excluded from the inquiry. In February 1970 a second questionnaire was sent out to the 101 students who had discontinued. On this occasion 85 students replied, including three who had not replied to the first questionnaire. If we exclude the unlikely explanation that Aberdeen students are by nature more co-operative than other students, there appear to be three possible reasons for this good response. The first is the strong university-community identification in the Aberdeen area at this time. Most of the students had been educated in the university's traditional catchment area and their attitudes may have been influenced by this factor. The second reason is the persistence of the investigator, who sent two reminder letters on each occasion; the third is the wording of the accompanying letters and the fact that they were signed by the Professor of Education. The students were never of course referred to as 'failures', but simply as individuals who had encountered difficulties, confidentiality was assured, and stress was placed on the potential usefulness of the information given for guiding future university entrants. The letter accompanying the second questionnaire also offered a copy of a preliminary report of the inquiry and most of those who replied requested it.

While it is always interesting, and frequently illuminating, to hear the authentic voice of the student, two caveats must be emphasised in interpreting the questionnaire data that follow. The first is that the students' views were sought after they had been required to disconti-nue: hence their explanations of their performance cannot necessarily be accepted as *causes*—they may merely represent conventional rationalisations, or the operation of defence mechanisms, because the acceptance of the real reasons for failure would be stress-inducing or even humiliating. The second caveat relates to the inevitable subjectiv-ity in the writer's classification of the replies, and the consequent dangers of distortion and over-simplification. Nevertheless the ques-tionnaire data are frequently illuminating, and it is undeniably important to obtain the students' versions of their difficulties, and to find out their reactions to failure and their future plans.

Table 7.3 Fail students—first questionnaire.

Item	Fail Students				
	Men (N=67)	Women (N=40)	All (N=107)	Arts (N=62)	Science (N=45)
Future Plans (All Students)					
(a) Readmission to university.	33	15	48	28	20
(b) Full-time education elsewhere.	5	8	13	10	3
(c) Permanent employment.	12	9	21	15	6
(d) Transfer within university.	13	5	18	4	14
(c) Other.	4	3	7	5	2
Do you now feel you should not have come to university? (Students who had left university)	(21)	(20)	(41)	(30)	(11)
(a) Yes.	6	6	12	8	4
(b) No.	12	13	25	21	4
(c) Don't know.	3	1	4	1	3
How do you feel about dropping out? (Students required to withdraw)	(54)	(35)	(89)	(58)	(31)
(a) Mainly relieved.	9	9	18	13	5
(b) Mainly depressed.	23	16	39	26	13
(c) Other.	22	10	32	19	13
Main reason for difficulties at university* (All Students)	(67)	(40)	(107)	(62)	(45)
(a) Lack of motivation/hard work.	29	9	29	17	12
(b) Study difficulties/adjustment to teaching.	16	12	28	19	9
(c) Lack of guidance/wrong subjects.	15	8	23	14	9
(d) Other.	16	11	27	12	15

*The first or predominant difficulty was classified.

Replies to the first questionnaire are summarised in Table 7.3. Transfers were mainly from the science to the arts faculty, and within arts from an M.A. to a B.Ed. course at the local college of education. Information was obtained on the subsequent progress of only two of these students: one had no award, and the other graduated with a lower second in sociology. Of 89 who discontinued, 48 said that they wished to return to university, the proportion being greater in science (20/31) than in arts (28/58). Most of the women who continued in full-time education had transferred to a Diploma course in a college of education. Those who had entered permanent employment had commonly taken up posts in banking or insurance. They would require to obtain professional qualifications at, or close to, ordinary degree level if they were to progress in their careers.

By November 1968, 41 of the students had abandoned the idea of returning to university, and twelve said that they felt it had been a mistake to come in the first place. Replies to the following question were given by all students who had dropped out, irrespective of whether they intended to re-sit: 'Dropping out of university affects people differently. Some feel relieved to escape from a stressful situation, others feel depressed and anxious. How has it affected you?' One in five (18/89) of the students said that he was 'mainly relieved' to be dropping out. Students whose replies were classified as 'other' expressed annoyance at themselves, and occasionally at the examination system and academic staff.

Replies to another open-ended question, 'What do you think was the main reason for your difficulties at university?' have been grouped into three main categories which accounted for the major difficulty of 80 students: (*a*) lack of motivation/hard work, (*b*) study difficulties/adjustment to teaching and (*c*) lack of guidance/wrong choice of subjects. Though it is arguable that some of the categories may be inter-related, (wrong choice of subjects could be one reason for lack of motivation), the replies provide a useful profile of the students' reasons for their difficulties. A fourth category (*d*) includes 'personal problems', which were reported most frequently by women students.

The second questionnaire was sent out to discover how many students had actually attempted to return to university, and what they were now doing if they had been unsuccessful. Respondents fell into three categories: *non-sitters* (*N* = 47) who had not attempted to gain readmission, *non-passers (N* = 18) and *re-entrants* (*N* = 20). Both the latter groups had attempted to secure readmission, but only re-entrants had succeeded and were in the spring term (of their second year) when they received the questionnaire.

Appendix B8 shows that the decision whether or not to re-sit was made by the great majority of respondents free from parental pressure. A majority of non-sitters (33/47) said they had made up their minds by the end of October 1968. All those who regarded their year at university as a 'waste of time' were non-sitters. For some students, especially in science, failure had adversely affected relationships with parents.

Half of those who had not returned to university had already enrolled in a new course in another institution, which nearly all were confident of completing successfully, and which over half regarded as 'more congenial' than their university course. Half of the group described their year at university as 'useful, beneficial or enjoyable'.

Half of the students who attempted to return to university encountered special problems (such as finding energy, time and a suitable place to study while working and living in 'digs') in preparing for the re-sits. Just under half kept in touch with a member of staff in their year away, either their Regent or Advisor or a member of staff they had known in a teaching capacity. But some re-entrants had maintained no such contacts, and claimed that facing up to problems on their own had made them more capable of independent work.

Re-entrants were more pessimistic about their prospects of success than was warranted. In their replies to the questionnaire only five were 'confident' of passing the second-year degree examinations, and only seven were confident of ultimately getting degrees. In the degree examinations in June and September 1970, twelve of the students were making good progress, six were still weak, and two appeared to be in serious difficulties once more. A follow-up to graduation showed that these two in fact failed to graduate. Of the other re-entrants five took honours degrees (two arts and two science men and one science woman), and thirteen took ordinary degrees.

An additional analysis found no significant differences between re-entrants and other unsatisfactory students on any of the background measures and test scores.

Student comments

This study illustrates one aspect of the 'cooling-out function' in a Scottish university (Clark, 1960; McPherson, 1970). Though the door to re-entry was still open, just under half of the students who replied to the first questionnaire had already decided not to re-sit the following year, or quickly abandoned the idea. Of forty-eight who did wish to return only thirty-eight re-sat, and only twenty were successful, with more in arts than in science despite the fact that more science students originally wished to return. Fifteen months later, two in three of those who had not returned had enrolled or were about to enrol at other institutions, where they were confident of success in courses which many felt were more congenial than those they had followed at university. In all, therefore, 61 of the 85 students for whom information was available were continuing with their education at university or at institutions of similar, or slightly lower, academic standing. Most of the remainder had taken up permanent employment.

Students' reactions to failure fell into three categories—equanimity, resentment and guilt. In the first group were students—including all of those who considered their year at university had been 'a waste of time'—who were dissatisfied with what the university had to offer, and who were glad to be out of an uncongenial atmosphere, or to be free from subjects which had bored them. Some said they had only come to university to please parents or teachers, and two claimed that staff persuaded them to stay for their degree examinations, but they had planned to leave irrespective of their results. One girl remarked, 'From the first day I knew I had made a mistake, but when I went to see someone about leaving I got a good talking to, being told that the Senatus knew better than to pick someone they did not think fit.' Another girl summed up the feelings of many of the students in this category: 'I treat my year as a year of learning which came my way by mistake. It was not entirely wasted, but, as I discovered, the life of learning was not for me.' A similar case—a female science student—was confirmed by the Advisor of Studies, who reported that the student had, 'By January 1968, decided that she did not wish to stay on in the university. She did not know why she was here . . . she is not unintelligent.' Most such students were not downhearted at their performance, although some had found the university atmosphere (and even the buildings) depressing. As one put it, 'I didn't in the least feel that it was the "end of the world" for me, and have started afresh—new job and new town to live in.'

A small number of students felt depressed or annoyed at their failure, and harboured feelings of resentment against the university. They felt that their failure could be at least partly explained by bad teaching, unreliable and invalid examining, inadequate guidance and generally unsympathetic attitudes on the part of the staff and administration.

An older student, who had sold his electrical business before coming to university, complained bitterly of a lack of advice—'I desperately need to talk to someone who really knows the subjects that are important to me, and who can guide me along the right lines ... all I needed was someone to keep me on the right track—I had nothing else to do whilst in exile in lodgings in Aberdeen. Lodgings—that is a sore point also—it is a wonder I am still sane!' His Advisor saw things rather differently: 'Partly because of his history, and partly because of his temperament, [he] never really came to grips with his own lack of knowledge, preparation and intellectual power.' One or two students seemed emotionally scarred by their experiences. An older woman, who transferred to a College Diploma, described her year as a 'nightmare' which had left her unable 'to shake off this feeling of indifference, of not really worrying about anything'. Two students felt that the committee anent students should have given more weight to medical reports. A man, who had suffered concussion in a car accident, had his appeal rejected on the grounds that there was no evidence of physical injury, although he claimed that his powers of 'assimilation, retention and memory' had been affected, that he could remember little of his first term at university, and that, until nearly the end of the second term, he had but a hazy recollection of lectures and tutorials. A girl, who had been unwell while she sat the June examinations, and who was unable to take the re-sits because she had spent the summer convalescing, complained—'I do feel a certain amount of frustration since I feel I still could do well at university, but it appears one is only given one chance regardless of circumstances.'

Most fails felt guilty at their failure and described their year at university as either 'useful, beneficial, enjoyable', or 'a missed opportunity'. They blamed themselves for being inadequately prepared for their courses, or for lacking the ability or will-power to study effectively. Some had studied subjects which had quickly lost their appeal. Others had done passably at school with little effort, and had attempted to continue in this fashion at university. Failure had come as a rude awakening, and the problem of securing employment with prospects was an important factor in making them try for readmission to prove that they could 'make the grade'. Thus, the main reason for the difficulties of a male arts student with a good school record taking a two-language course was, 'Not realising the amount of work required until too late—making excuses to go out, instead of working', while a male science student admitted to 'Lack of interest in some subjects leading to insufficient work'.

Some detailed comments indicated the difficult personal and domestic circumstances which many students had experienced in their year at university, or were experiencing as they prepared to re-sit. One girl commented, 'My failing the exams is not wholly for academic reasons. My home life is very distressing and becoming more so.' Another, a regentee of John Wilson and a vivacious, attractive but impulsive extravert, had a disturbed family background, and had made what seemed a highly unstable marriage. Her mother was dead, and she had been living with her father and her younger sister. She left school at the end of her fifth year, but then returned for a sixth year and was made head girl. She left again, however, in mid-session to marry an unemployed salesman who had been disowned by his parents, and the couple came to Aberdeenshire. In addition she had a lengthy illness in her second term. Clearly this student could not do herself justice. A third student—a married lady with two children—had been deserted by her husband, and attempted to prepare for the re-sits while conducting a legal battle over custody and alimony.

Casualness was an important factor in the failure of at least two students, an arts man and a science woman. Both required to pass only one subject in the September re-sit to qualify for second year. But the arts student said that he mistook the date of the re-sit, and presented himself the day after the examination had been held; the science student spent the summer vacation working in the United States, and arrived back in Scotland only the day before the examination, and consequently did not prepare herself.

The questionnaire data indicate the variety of reasons or excuses students advance for their performance, and the variety of reactions to 'failure'. Indeed they suggest that this emotive label, with its emphasis on the institutional interpretation of the student's performance, is inappropriate for a number of these students. Failure, as much as success (Stott, 1950), must be related to the individual's personal values, and clearly, for some of these students, satisfaction lay in abandoning their university careers and turning to something more congenial.

One weakness of a case-study approach is that one can almost always find some factor which can be advanced to 'explain' the performance of the student. In the absence of a control group of successful students who were exposed to similar factors it is impossible to draw any definite conclusion. Many students, even with such serious handicaps as blindness or unstable mental health, have performed brilliantly at university. The intelligent or highly motivated student can often triumph against all the odds. Nevertheless such factors as personal illness or difficult family circumstances may present too great a burden for many other students. Whether the burden is in reality too great, or whether it is simply imagined to be so, may depend on the individual's tenacity and self-image. It is difficult to interpret the effect of such factors in individual cases, and it is certainly not suggested that the personal factors cited here can be held to have *caused* the failure of the students or to be the sole factors in failure. Nevertheless these case studies do raise questions about the extent of the university's responsibility for its students, and particularly for those who fail, the effectiveness of its guidance system, and the arrangements for transfer from school to university. The fact that so many students—both fails and successful students (as reported in Chapter 6)—criticised the advice they were given at both school and university, and wished to change their course, suggests that even greater efforts are needed to make students aware of the implications of curricular choices. We return to these questions in Chapter 11.

PART THREE
The Rowntree Project

Chapter Eight

Background and Methods

The study reported here is part of a larger investigation initiated by the trustees of the Joseph Rowntree Memorial Trust. They were anxious to sponsor research at Lancaster which might provide a factual basis from which to plan changes in the existing system of higher education in Britain. The situation, as they saw it in 1967, was that:

'Universities and colleges in the higher education sector are stressing the importance of more accurate selection criteria to prevent student "wastage". This emphasis tends to divert attention from the logically prior question of the objectives of higher education and the difference in objectives between universities, colleges of education and polytechnics. Any re-examination of the whole purpose and structure of higher education would involve asking again the question which the Robbins Committee examined, and deciding first of all whether the present divisions in the system are strictly necessary. Then the emphasis on improving methods of placing students in the most appropriate type of course would follow.'

The trustees suggested that this broad problem be approached on two fronts:

(*a*)   through an analysis of the educational aims and objectives of the different sectors of higher education; and
(*b*)   through a follow-up study of students who entered the different sectors with approximately equivalent qualifications.

This section describes that part of the follow-up study which involved students in universities. Preliminary analyses of the comparisons between universities, polytechnics and colleges of education have already been reported (Entwistle, Percy and Nisbet, 1971; Entwistle and Percy, 1971). Subsequent reports will cover analyses of interviews with students (being prepared by Jennifer Thompson) and a discussion of aims and objectives across the three sectors of higher education. Keith Percy will bringing together historical, philosophical and sociological analyses of higher education, relating these to what lecturers said in interviews about their aims and to the processes which the lecturers apparently used to achieve those aims.

91

Research design

The trustees' memorandum indicated one approach to the follow-up study, but it emphasised contrasts between students entering different types of institution with equivalent entry qualifications. In the planning stage it soon became clear that this limitation could not be imposed on the research design. Universities are still 'first-choice' institutions for most courses in higher education. They are thus able to select students with the highest levels of school attainment, effectively minimising the overlap in entry qualifications between universities and the public sector.

The overall aim of the follow-up study had thus to be modified to examine the characteristics of students who were successful in different courses across the three sectors. In addition, factual information was to be sought about the methods of study adopted by students in different institutions on different courses and with different personality traits. This first report concentrates on contrasting the characteristics of successful university students in six areas of study and also in a number of major disciplines.

The research design was initially limited to a large-scale longitudinal study over four years (to allow for industrial experience or a year abroad for linguists). Psychological characteristics would be measured early in the first year and again in the final year. The study would examine changes in these characteristics during the course and the first-year measures would be used to predict degree performance. Subsequently it was decided to interview a sub-group of students whose first-year performance appeared to be difficult to understand from the psychometric measures available by that time. The number of potential intervening variables which might have confounded the analyses was so great that it seemed to be essential to control some of these as part of the research design. It was decided to exclude foreign students and mature students from this study and to restrict the areas of study to those offered in at least two of the three sectors of higher education. This limitation removed subjects such as medicine and law from consideration.

Hypotheses

The review of theoretical ideas and empirical investigations, together with our own pilot studies, had confirmed the likely importance of certain variables, such as introversion, motivation and study methods, in prediciting academic motivation. But as we were particularly concerned in this project with differences between institutions and between areas of study, previous studies could not provide definite hypotheses. The review did however provide a firm basis from which to explore this new sphere of interest. Previous work indicated the way in which the data should be analysed and the type of explanations to be anticipated. It thus guided the form in which the analyses are presented in the following chapter and restricted, if it did not eliminate, the need for *ex post facto* explanations.

Sampling

Financial, organisational and 'political' considerations affected the initial sampling frame and the actual sample obtained. It was necessary, for organisational reasons, to limit the size of the sample to a maximum of 2,500 university students, preferably to less than 2,000. (There was only one full-time research officer working on the whole follow-up study.) As several visits to each institution would be required, geographical limitation was also necessary. The vice-chancellors, directors or principals of thirty-three institutions in the North of England and the Midlands were approached and twenty-one, seven from each sector, finally agreed to allow access to their students. The seven universities in the sample were Birmingham, Durham, Lancaster, Liverpool, Newcastle, Nottingham and York. The names are given to indicate the nature of our sampling frame, but no analysis is presented by institution, as the sub-groups would produce misleading information. Two universities controlled our access to students and, after discussions at other institutions, we were forced to accept another, more serious, restriction. We were to be allowed initially only one attempt to contact students; those who did not respond immediately were not to be reminded of our request, as this implied 'pestering'. Thus, at an early stage, the compromise of a self-selected sample without follow-up was necessary to allow the study to begin at all. Inevitably the nature of our sample was affected by this restriction.

The next stage in the sampling procedure was to arrange for letters to be sent, or given, to all students entering the faculties of arts, social science, science and engineering in October, 1968. The letter outlined the aims of the project and encouraged the students to participate. Those agreeing to take part returned a brief questionnaire from which the next stage of the sampling was carried out. In the five universities where we were allowed free access, 63 per cent of the year-group volunteered. The true proportion was much higher than this figure because we discovered that some departments intercepted and 'blocked' the letters we had asked to be distributed to the students. In institutions where we knew that letters had reached all the students, the response rate was nearly 80 per cent.

3,468 questionnaires were returned, from which 2,569 were selected as fulfilling the conditions we had decided to impose (age, nationality and area of study). Initially students were included only if they had registered in one of the following departments: mathematics / physics, chemistry, biology or zoology / electrical or mechanical engineering / psychology, economics, politics, sociology or social studies / history, philosophy or religious studies / English, French, German and Russian. (The oblique lines define the six areas of study subsequently used in the analyses.) Because of subsequent changes in registration a slightly wider range of subjects was represented in the sample by the time of graduation.

As one of our main concerns was study methods, we decided not to arrange our test sessions until the beginning of the second term. (More than one set of test sessions was impracticable.) By that time students were, of course, less likely to be enthusiastic volunteers and further self-selection in the sample was inevitable. Attempts to minimise further attrition were made by sending a letter and a post-card reminding students of the times of the test sessions, but as we were only able to arrange two test sessions at each institution (except Lancaster) students who wished to volunteer were often prevented from doing so by time-table clashes. In the end 1,536 students (60 per cent of the defined sample) attended the test sessions and complete data was obtained from 1,531 of them.

Recognising the danger of having obtained, by repeated self-selection, a seriously unrepresentative sample, attempts were made to compare the school attainment of our sample with national surveys. Comparison was only possible with the NFER survey (Choppin *et al.*, 1972) of some 10,000 university entrants and even here the 'A' level scales used were not identical. The best comparison we can make is that on our scale (which put an 'A' grade at 6 and an 'O' level pass at 1), the NFER sample would have had a mean 'A' scale score of 13.2 (the equivalent of grades BCC) whereas our sample with complete data in 1968 had a mean of 12.7 (which approximates to CCC). Most of the analyses in the following chapter are based on those students from whom complete data were obtained over the *whole* project. This group was closer to the NFER mean (12.9).

The overall mean of the sample will be affected by the balance between arts and science students, as the latter tend to enter with lower mean 'A' level grades. Using only the areas of study included in the Rowntree study, the NFER survey contained 50.8 per cent of scientists, whereas among the students in our study who had complete data there were only 44.5 per cent of scientists. The conclusion must be that the average level of school attainment in our sample was below what would be expected in the population. The omission of prestigious universities such as Oxford, Cambridge and London from our sample would be certain to produce this effect.

It was also possible to examine within our own sample the characteristics of responders and non-responders in one university. As expected the self-selected sample was better qualified. The non-responders had an 'A' level score of 11.3 equivalent to CCD, or one grade lower than the responders. The difference is not large, but it is statistically significant. There was a similar, but larger, difference in academic performance by the end of the first year. In other ways, there were few differences between responders and non-responders. There were no differences in area of study, secondary school attended or social class. The non-responders did, however, have rather lower motivation and study method scores.

This evidence suggests that our sample is not seriously unrepresentative, but that it contains smaller proportions of the best qualified and of the weaker entrants. As a result our sample is homogenous compared to the population. Relationships are thus likely to be weakened and analyses of extreme groups will suffer from depletion of numbers. It appears unlikely that the sample is sufficiently distorted to affect the *pattern* of results reported, but the proportions of students found in various sub-groups cannot be accepted as being representative.

Predictive measures

The review of the literature had suggested not only which variables to include, but also some of the instruments which would be appropriate. Thus the Eysenck Personality Inventory was an obvious choice. Although it provides less information than many other personality scales, for example those of Cattell and Guilford, Eysenck has developed his inventory from a firmer theoretical basis and his two main dimensions are found to underlie most of the other scales.

With the on-going validation of the test of academic aptitude for the Committee of Vice-Chancellors and Principals it appeared sensible to obtain permission to make use of this test. The working party responsible for the Investigation of Supplementary Predictive Information for University Admissions (ISPIUA) generously made available, and arranged for a special printing of, half of the second version of their test of academic aptitude. The half of the test used provided a 45 minute series of items, first on verbal and then on mathematical skills. The original development work on the test was reported by Sainsbury (1970) and the introduction to one of the NFER reports (Choppin *et al.*, 1972) describes it further. Essentially the verbal aptitude items related to comprehension of prose passages and to the understanding of words. The mathematical section emphasised understanding of mathematical reasoning rather than basic knowledge.

The development of British scales of motivation and study methods was described in Chapter 4, but it was recognised that, if differences between areas of study were to be investigated, it would be important to include variables which might be predictive in one or other of these areas. The review of the literature did not produce definite evidence about which variables might be predictive, but it seemed probable that the domain of social attitudes and values would be important in defining differences between areas of study. Eysenck's questionnaire of social attitudes was mentioned in Chapter 4. The other instruments chosen to tap this domain were a series of self-rating scales and the Allport-Vernon-Lindzey 'Study of Values'.

In the self-rating scales students were invited to rate themselves on a seven-point scale. They were asked to use 'objective introspection' to compare themselves to their idea of the average university student in terms of such characteristics as 'sociable', 'hard-working', and 'ambitious'.

The Study of Values aims to measure the relative importance of six basic interests or motives in personality: the 'theoretical', 'economic', 'aesthetic', 'social','political', and 'religious'. The classification is based directly upon Eduard Spranger's *Types of Men* (1928), a work which defends the view that the personalities of men are best known through a study of their values or evaluative attitudes. Although Spranger's value types have an 'armchair' rather than an 'empirical' basis, and although the Study of Values may in some instances fail to distinguish between 'value' and 'interest', there is considerable supportive evidence on the usefulness of the test as a research instrument, primarily with college and university students or with adults who have had some form of higher education. Not the least appealing feature of the scale is its 'practical' nature. It is self-scoring: students tend to show an interest in their own scores, and feel that the classification of the six kinds of value is useful to them. Details of scoring are given in the manual (Richardson, 1965). Since every student obtains the same total score over the six values, the scores are ipsative* and are thus artificially inter-correlated. High scores on one value reduce the possibility of high scores on other scales. The test has satisfactory reliability for group use, but validity data in the manual consist mainly of showing that educational and occupational groups have the expected value patterns.

Initial test sessions

The test sessions took place under examination conditions, except for a small number of sessions which had to make use of tiered lecture rooms. The sessions lasted up to three hours with a twenty-minute coffee break after the third test. The arrangements for the sessions and the order of presentation of tests had been piloted in an institution not included in our sample. At one stage we had discussed offering payment to the students, but the sum we could have offered would have been derisory. Instead we prepared an introductory talk in which we attempted to demonstrate the potential value of the project. As only five students who stayed long enough to start the tests actually failed to complete all of them, it appears that this approach was successful.

The tests were presented in the following order:

1. A questionnaire asking for background details, information about study habits, self-rating scales, and containing the Student Attitude Questionnaire.
2. One half of the verbal scale from the Test of Academic Aptitude (Sainsbury, 1970). (Each scale is produced in two parallel parts each lasting 45 minutes.)
3. The Eysenck Personality Inventory, Form B (Eysenck and Eysenck, 1964)
      — Coffee Break —
4. One half of the mathematical scale from the Test of Academic Aptitude.
5. The Study of Values (Richardson, 1965; adapted from Allport, Vernon and Lindzey, 1960).

---

*The term 'ipsative' is used to describe a scoring system in which a fixed number of 'points' is distributed among the scales following a forced-choice ordering of responses to each item.

Follow-up phase

Additional data were collected on three subsequent occasions (excluding the detailed interviews which are not reported here). After the end of the first year departments were asked to provide ratings on a seven-point scale, or marks, for each of the students. In three universities it was possible to scale and sum these marks, otherwise the ratings themselves were combined to provide the measure of first-year attainment.

In March 1971 a further series of questionnaires was sent out to the students, so as to obtain repeat measures of most of the first-year variables (excluding the timed tests). By this time there had been 'natural' wastage from the sample. Fifty-five students had withdrawn for academic reasons; 53 had other reasons for leaving. 1,125 students returned the questionnaires; 26 questionnaires were returned without reaching the student. The response rate by those students who, to the best of our knowledge, actually received the envelope was thus just over 80 per cent. The sample with complete data shrunk to 1,087 due to incomplete questionnaires and the inability to obtain the degree results of a small number of students. This final sample with complete data was so similar to the initial sample that it has been used for most of the subsequent analyses, except where predictions are being made from first-year measures in sub-groups.

The final piece of information collected was the degree results. As the normal degree classification represents a rather coarse grading of a crucial variable, departments were asked to indicate whether students had been 'high', 'middle' or 'low' in the degree class awarded. Most departments supplied this information, but in its absence students were placed in the 'middle' category. This fine grading allowed analyses to compare the characteristics of students who had a near upper-second performance or better, with those whose performance was nearer third-class or worse. The degree result was coded on a 16-point scale which incorporated the fine grading of honours degrees, general and pass degrees, with a zero indicating failure.

Data collection

The logistic problems associated with collecting data, of coding, checking and producing punched cards and of analysing cannot be discussed here. An account of the problems (which included research officers and data firmly stuck in a snowdrift overnight) has been given elsewhere (Entwistle and Nisbet, 1972, Chapter 4). Figure 8.1 does, however, provide an indication of the various steps by which the research design was implemented.

List of variables

The variables derived from the various tests mentioned earlier and used in the subsequent analyses are summarised below within approp-

Figure 8.1 Flow diagram of follow-up study (from Entwistle and Nisbet, 1972)

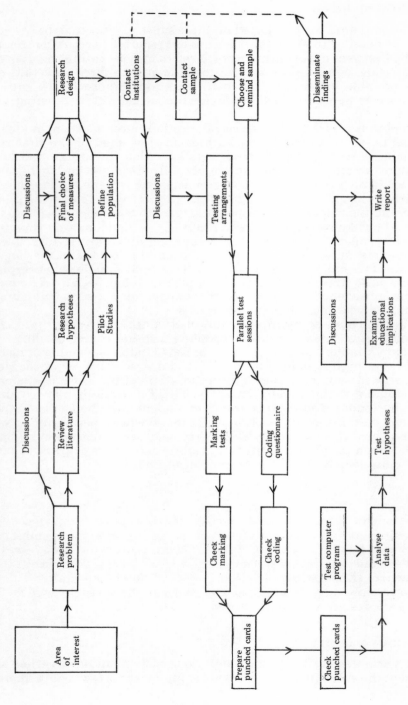

riate educational or psychological domains. Variables marked with an asterisk were included only in the cluster analyses.

Criterion measures

Academic performance

1. Degree result on a scale which gave a score of 9 to a 'middle' lower-second.
2. Total first-year assessment grade.

Self-ratings in third year

The questionnaire in the follow-up phase asked students to rate themselves on a five-point scale 'compared with other students at your college or university'.
3. Concentrating efforts on studying.
4. Feeling satisfied with the content of courses.
5. Having an active social life.
6. Making use of sports facilities.*
7. Developing aesthetic interests.*

Predictive measures

Attainment and academic aptitude

8. Number of 'O' level subjects passed.
9. 'A' level total (CCC = 12).
10. Verbal aptitude (as raw score).
11. Mathematical aptitude (as raw score).
12. Good at mathematics (self-rating in first year—see below).

Motivation and study methods

13/14. Motivation (from the SAQ completed in both first and third years).
15/16. Study methods (from SAQ).
17/18. Number of hours spent in private study during previous week.
19. Syllabus-boundness (third year only).
20. Syllabus-freedom (third year only). (Scored in opposite direction to syllabus-bound items.)
Self-ratings completed in first year on a seven-point scale 'compared with an average university student':
21. Hard-working.
22. Ambitious.

Personality

23/24. Extraversion from the 'Eysenck Personality Inventory'.

*Used only in the cluster analyses.

25/26. Neuroticism.
First year self-ratings:
27. Serious-minded.
28. Sociable.
29. Likeable.*
30. Self-confident.*

Values and attitudes

31/32. Social values from the 'Study of Values'.
33/34. Political values.
35/36. Economic values.
37/38. Theorectical values.
39/40. Aesthetic values.
41/42. Religious values.
43/44. Radicalism from 'Student Attitudes Questionnaire'.
45/46. Tender-mindedness.

In addition a number of self-explanatory categorical variables, such as sex, area of study, main discipline being studied and father's occupation, were used in several of the analyses.

Chapter Nine

Academic Performance and Area of Study

In reporting a study of this magnitude some limitations have to be imposed on the analyses carried out, and again both the review of the literature and the pilot studies prevent *ex post facto* decisions being taken. Starting from the main purposes of the enquiry and drawing on previous research findings, it is possible to select, in advance, appropriate analyses and particular groups of variables to include in them. The presentation of results must also have an inherent logic. Here the starting point is a discussion of simple means and standard deviations which describe various sub-groups of our sample. Simple correlations with academic performance follow; and finally multivariate techniques, such as regression and factor analysis, are applied to the data.

Another problem in presentation concerns the sample. Complete data over the whole degree course had been collected from 1,087 university students, but full first-year data combined with degree results (or knowledge of earlier academic failure) were available for another 391 students. As it was useful, on occasions, to compare first- and third-year scores on tests and as few differences in relationships were found between the two samples, most of the analyses were based on the sample with complete data. Any variation in sample is noted in the description of the analysis.

To avoid the inclusion of the same sub-group totals in tables, the sizes of the main groups which were analysed are shown in Table 9.1.

Student 'drop-outs' and non-responders

The main purpose of the enquiry was to identify those characteristics which distinguished between academically successful and unsuccessful students in different areas of study. The small number of drop-outs (5 per cent) from our self-selected sample precluded any detailed analysis by area of study. But the mean scores on selected predictive variables shown in Table 9.2, allow comparisons to be made between various sub-groups and the total sample, which give a flavour of results from later analyses.

The first point to note is that the sample with complete data was closely similar to the total sample, except on variables measuring academic performance. Again self-selection left a slightly superior group, but without affecting heterogeneity. The next step is to look at

101

Table 9.1 Numbers of students with complete data in various sub-groups

Area of study*	Men	Women	Total
Languages	71	158	229
Humanities	59	68	127
Social sciences	133	106	239
Pure science	203	112	315
Applied science	60	4	64
Mathematics	64	41	105
Total	594	493	1,087

Honours disciplines** Total only	
English	111
French	53
History	93
Economics	35
Sociology	76
Biology	82
Chemistry	97
Physics	59
Engineering	45
Mathematics	68

* The departments included in each area of study are shown on page 93.
** Only those disciplines containing 35 or more students have been included in the analyses.

the non-responders again. The students who did not return the follow-up questionnaire were higher on extraversion, aesthetic values and radicalism, but lower in first-year marks, mathematical aptitude, study methods and religious values than students who continued to co-operate with us.

When we turn to 'drop-outs', those who left for personal reasons showed only one significant difference from the total sample. They had been below average in academic performance by the end of the first year. On the other hand students who had been required to leave because of their poor attainment were clearly an atypical group. Their low verbal aptitude and, to a lesser extent their poor 'A' level grades (CDD), are in part attributable to a higher failure rate in the science departments. But their scores were in fact much lower than even those science students who subsequently obtained rather poor degrees (see Table 9.3). Again this group had low motivation and study methods scores combined with short working hours. Their sixteen hours per week compares with an average of twenty-three hours in the full sample. Among scientists (who have less time for private study because of practical classes) the average is still twenty hours. The first-year failures have high extraversion scores, but average levels of neuroticism. They also have high economic and low religious values compared with other students, but these differences are only just statistically significant.

This first simple analysis provides immediate confirmation that at least some of our predictive variables have been effective. Thus 'A' level grades, motivation, study methods, hours studying and extraversion all show the expected relationships with academic success. The only surprise is that the test of verbal aptitude, which came out so

Table 9.2 Mean scores and standard deviations of students with complete and incomplete data

Selected variables	Complete sample N = (1531)		Complete data (1087)		Incomplete but degree (336)	Academic withdrawals (55)	Non-academic withdrawals (27)	No degree (reason unknown) (26)
	Mean	(S.D.)	Mean	(S.D.)	Mean	Mean	Mean	Mean
Degree results	8.7	(3.8)	(**) 9.5	(3.2)	(**) 9.2	—	—	—
First-year marks	12.3	(3.7)	** 12.7	(3.5)	* 12.0	(**) 6.8	** 10.3	11.7
'A' level grades	12.7	(2.8)	* 12.9	(2.8)	12.6	** 10.2	12.8	12.1
Number of 'O' levels	8.1	(1.2)	8.1	(1.2)	8.0	7.9	8.0	8.0
Verbal aptitude	32.5	(8.1)	32.8	(8.1)	32.2	** 28.4	31.7	31.8
Mathematical aptitude	19.5	(6.8)	19.9	(6.8)	** 18.3	20.1	18.3	19.0
Motivation	8.1	(2.2)	* 8.3	(2.1)	8.0	** 7.1	7.1	* 6.9
Study methods	7.1	(2.5)	7.3	(2.5)	* 7.0	** 5.9	6.2	6.8
Hours studied	22.7	(9.6)	23.0	(9.7)	23.2	(**) 16.2	21.2	21.0
Neuroticism	13.4	(4.3)	13.3	(4.2)	13.7	13.1	14.2	14.0
Extraversion	13.7	(4.0)	* 13.4	(4.0)	* 14.2	** 15.5	14.5	15.0
Radicalism	8.2	(2.9)	8.1	(3.0)	** 8.7	8.3	8.0	8.3
Tendermindedness	7.2	(2.6)	7.3	(2.6)	7.1	* 6.5	6.5	7.2
Social values	39.8	(6.3)	39.7	(6.3)	40.3	40.0	40.3	39.8
Political values	25.9	(7.0)	25.7	(7.0)	26.3	26.6	25.6	24.9
Economic values	29.7	(6.8)	29.8	(6.8)	29.1	* 31.8	29.1	28.9
Theoretical values	32.8	(6.3)	32.8	(6.5)	32.5	33.5	32.1	33.9
Aesthetic values	28.2	(7.7)	27.7	(7.6)	** 29.4	27.8	29.8	29.5
Religious values	22.8	(12.4)	23.3	(12.7)	21.7	* 19.5	22.5	22.1

*   significant difference between this mean score and that of complete sample ($p < 0.05$)

** ($p < 0.01$)

(*) significant F ratio indicating differences in variances contributing to significant t value poorly in the NFER validation study, does discriminate effectively in this analysis. However our test was given at university, while the validation exercise involved testing sixth-formers. A gap of another eighteen months or so is bound to decrease the predictive validity.

Students taking different courses

The next analysis compares the mean scores of students in the six areas of study previously defined in Chapter 8. Not only is it possible to compare first-year scores, but differential changes over a two-year period can also be examined. Detailed results have been relegated to Appendix C1 and even there some simplification has been necessary. Mean scores on all self-rating scales and tests of statistical significance have been omitted, but indications of the levels of significance have been included in the text.

To facilitate the graphical presentation of contrasting profiles, standard mean scores* were used to convert each variable on to a common scale. As different proportions of men and women were found in the various areas of study, differences attributable solely to the composition of the sub-groups had to be eliminated. Standard mean scores for each area of study were thus calculated separately for men and for women. Although there had been differences in the raw scores, no sex differences were found in the standardised scores and so an average standardised mean is reported for each area of study.

In subsequent discussions of these standardised scores it it is important to recognise that comparisons are made only within the sample and not against population norms. For example, when a group is described as having 'high religious values' this should be taken to mean 'high compared with other students in the sample' and not as 'high compared with the norms presented in the manual' (although this might also be true).

The mean raw scores showed sex differences on a number of variables. Women had consistently lower scores on mathematical aptitude and on political and economic values. They had higher overall scores on neuroticism, tendermindedness and religious values. Women also tended to work longer hours than men.

The next analysis focused on one of the main questions of the study. Are there any differences in the personality and attitudinal characteristics of students who choose to read different disciplines at university? Perhaps we should let C. P. Snow set the scene with the controversial views he expressed in the 1959 Rede Lectures. He was in no doubt from his own experience as both an author and a scientist that there were, at least in the years preceding the last war, *two cultures*.

*Standard mean score = $\dfrac{\text{(mean of sub-group)} - \text{(mean of sample)}}{\text{standard deviation of sample}}$

Thus a score of zero indicates that the sub-group has the same mean as the sample, while positive scores show that the sub-group has a higher mean.

'Constantly I felt I was moving among two groups—comparable in intelligence, identical in race, not grossly different in social origin, earning about the same incomes, who had almost ceased to communicate at all, who in intellectual, moral and psychological climate had. . . little in common. . . Literary intellectuals at one pole—at the other scientists, and as the most representative, physical scientists. Between the two a gulf of mutual incomprehension—sometimes (particularly among the young) hostility and dislike, but most of all lack of understanding. They have a curious distorted image of each other. Their attitudes are so different that, even on the level of emotion, they can't find much common ground' (Snow, 1964, pp. 2-4).

Our research cannot probe Snow's claims about the way in which scientists perceive linguists or investigate the existence of problems in communication, but it can show the extent to which students in the various areas of studies differ in terms of those attitudes, values and personality traits, which were included in this study. Appendix C1 shows detailed scores by area of study for all students and by discipline for honours students (Appendix C3) but the clearest way of presenting the results is using the bar diagram in Figure 9.1.

Following Snow's lead the first comparison is between honours students reading English (literary intellectuals in the making) and the most characteristic group of science students—physicists. The remaining eight honours subjects included in the analysis are paired off randomly to illustrate possible differences. The visual impact of Figure 9.1 is immediate. At first sight it appears as if Snow must have been right about the 'two cultures'. In several of the comparisons between arts and science students the profiles appear as mirror images— opposites in almost every respect. English students are on the opposite side of the sample mean in all but two of the dimensions and on one of these two there is a large, and statistically significant, difference. Almost the same degree of difference is found between sociologists and mathematicians, and here it may be helpful to indicate levels of statistical significance. The 't' value (indicating the difference in mean scores) on radicalism is 5.81 (p <0.001), on social values it is 3.94 (p <0.001), while even the smaller difference on extraversion still reaches statistical significance (2.23, p <0.05). The differences on motivation, religious values and tendermindedness are nonsignificant.

Naturally, with relatively small self-selected groups, the differences between the individual honours disciplines must be interpreted with caution. But there are consistent differences between students in the much larger groups formed by the areas of study. Pen pictures derived from the mean scores shown in Appendix C1 suggest that in at least some respects students taking different courses are, in Snow's words, 'poles apart'.

Students in language departments tended, as we might expect, to have very high verbal aptitude and aesthetic values; they also had high 'A' level grades, but a rather low level of motivation together with a syllabus-free orientation to studying. In social attitudes they were radical and, in personality, predominantly emotionally unstable. Their values showed below average scores on the political, economic and theoretical scales of the 'Study of Values'.

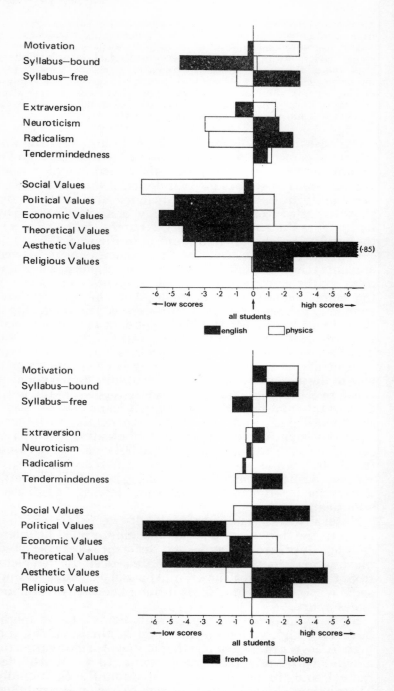

Figure 9.1 Comparisons of mean scores of students taking different courses

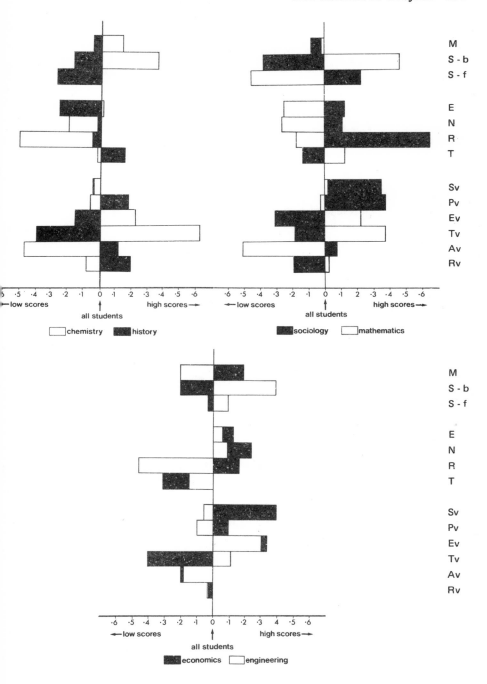

Pure scientists showed opposite characteristics almost without exception. They had high mathematical aptitude, but rather poor 'A' level grades. Low aesthetic values were combined with high economic and theoretical values, high levels of motivation, and a syllabus-bound orientation. Scientists were emotionally stable and in social attitudes they were distinctly conservative.

These pen pictures, and the profiles shown earlier, might imply, as Snow suggested, mutual misunderstanding and the existence of 'two cultures', but our research was not designed to investigate that possibility. In any case the differences reported, although often quite large, only represents *trends*. There is a considerable overlap between groups, with scientists having the characteristics of arts students and vice-versa. The profiles do present an exaggerated impression of isolation. Nevertheless the trends are marked and their implications are worth considering.

While the pen pictures describe differences between areas of study, there were also some differences between honours disciplines within area of study, although only on a few variables. Students taking English were an intellectually outstanding group, while historians spent five or six hours longer in private study than other arts students. Historians were also much more introverted, having scores similar to those of mathematicians. Sociologists showed distinctive social attitudes. They were toughminded radicals whose syllabus-freedom (demand for autonomy) was associated with unstable extraversion. They had high political and low religious values. It is interesting to note that this profile is atypical of students in our sample and yet corresponds closely to the sterotype presented by the 'selective photography' of the mass media.

Other social scientists showed rather different characteristics. Economists, for example, were altogether more conventional in their outlook. Their political values decreased during the course, while, not surprisingly, their economic values increased.

Among the scientists, students taking physics and biology had the highest levels of motivation, physicists were the most stable, chemists the most conservative and engineers the most syllabus-bound. However these inter-disciplinary differences may be largely sampling fluctuations, and without independent verification cannot be treated seriously.

Looking at changes in scores between first and third years, some consistent changes were found. As final examinations loomed up there were the expected increases in study methods scores and hours spent in studying (an extra five hours per week). On the other hand motivation scores dropped, perhaps as students of average ability accepted the futility of striving after unattainable academic goals. All students become more radical in their social attitudes, with sociologists, who started with the highest mean score, moving even further ahead. Sociologists were also one of the few groups to increase their political values. There were overall increases in social, aesthetic and theoretical values and lower scores in economic and religious values.*

The pattern of changes in attitudes only rarely suggests an effect of the course of study. It may be that studying sociology increases social awareness and leads directly to a more radical outlook and political commitment. The increased economic values of economists may also be related to their academic training. But the general changes in attitudes seem to be more a reflection of the strength of the 'student culture', with its emphasis on radical social values and its rejection of economic values, rather than a direct result of attending lectures and tutorials at university.

On theoretical grounds no general changes in personality were expected over the two-year period and, on the whole, the relative differences between the areas of study remained constant. However, there were consistent reductions in the neuroticism scores and in some cases, for example among applied scientists, these changes were quite large (13.0 down to 12.3). It would be interesting to know if the first-year scores represent an abnormally high level of anxiety induced by the transition from school to university, which decreases as students become familiar with their environment and adjust to the demands made on them. As the second testing came shortly before finals it is possible that even lower scores might have been obtained in the second year.

Academically successful students

The next analysis overlaps more directly with results from the Aberdeen study. Using the fine grading in degree class it was possible to compare the characteristics of students who obtained a 'high' lower-second degree or better, with those who obtained the bottom category of lower-second or worse. Again this analysis was carried out by area of study, but the sample size was not large enough to allow analyses separately by sex. Comparisons of mean scores and standard deviations on variables expected from the review of the literature to be useful predictors are shown in Table 9.3.

The best predictor of degree class is of course first-year marks. Of the other variables, 'A' level grades, hours studied, study methods and the aptitude tests provide the best indication of future performance, although motivation and extraversion show consistent, but smaller, differences between the two groups of students. These results parallel those reported in the Aberdeen study, although there is a greater tendency for introversion to be associated with high class of degree.

Earlier it was suggested that one weakness in the method of comparing extreme groups was that students of average attainment were ignored. In this analysis only one category of degree class (average

*Changes in scores derived from the study of values must be treated with caution as the scoring is ipsative. High scores on one dimension thus artificially depress the other scores.

Table 9.3 *Mean scores and standard deviations of selected variables for groups of students with contrasting levels of degree performance*

Selected variables	Languages		Humanities		Social sciences		Pure sciences		Applied sciences		Mathematics	
	Hi	Lo	Hi	Lo	Hi	Lo	Hi	Lo	Hi	Lo	Hi	Lo
	(N = 61)	(36)	(31)	(14)	(50)	(37)	(101)	(79)	(19)	(12)	(35)	(29)
First-year marks	14.4** (3.0)	11.4 (3.1)	14.9** (3.4)	9.3 (2.4)	13.7** (2.8)	10.6 (3.4)	15.0** (3.5)	10.8 (3.5)	17.7** (2.4)	9.3 (2.3)	16.6** (3.3)	10.7 (3.1)
'A' level grades	14.6** (2.4)	12.8 (2.8)	14.0* (1.9)	12.1 (2.2)	13.3 (3.4)	12.5 (2.2)	13.8** (2.8)	12.1 (2.7)	14.4** (2.3)	11.3 (2.3)	15.4** (2.1)	12.0 (2.7)
Verbal aptitude	37.9* (6.9)	34.8 (7.6)	36.0** (7.0)	28.4 (5.8)	35.1 (7.7)	32.3 (7.6)	30.8 (7.8)	32.5 (8.5)	31.0 (9.7)	31.3 (8.7)	32.5 (8.7)	28.4 (7.4)
Mathematical aptitude	16.4* (4.9)	14.1 (4.6)	17.8** (4.4)	14.4 (3.6)	19.3 (6.2)	20.0 (6.5)	23.0 (5.3)	23.2 (4.9)	26.1 (5.0)	24.8 (5.5)	29.1** (3.9)	26.2 (4.5)
Motivation	8.4 (2.1)	7.7 (1.9)	9.0 (1.9)	8.3 (1.7)	8.3 (2.0)	7.6 (2.0)	8.8 (2.0)	8.2 (2.3)	8.1 (1.9)	7.8 (2.3)	8.9* (1.9)	7.7 (1.9)
Study methods	7.7 (2.3)	6.9 (2.1)	8.9* (2.0)	7.1 (3.0)	7.5 (2.5)	6.6 (2.1)	8.1* (2.4)	5.8 (1.7)	6.8* (2.2)	4.8 (2.4)	7.0 (2.7)	6.5 (2.4)
Hours studied	27.8* (8.3)	23.4 (9.7)	32.1** (9.5)	23.4 (8.8)	26.2* (8.2)	22.0 (9.2)	21.7** (9.1)	17.7 (8.2)	19.0* (7.4)	12.3 (5.6)	21.7 (10.2)	22.1 (7.0)
Extraversion	12.2** (3.6)	14.8 (3.9)	11.5* (4.9)	14.9 (5.0)	13.8 (4.5)	14.2 (4.0)	13.1 (3.8)	13.9 (4.3)	12.6 (3.6)	14.2 (4.3)	13.2 (3.8)	13.2 (3.9)
Neuroticism	14.5 (3.6)	14.8 (4.2)	11.9 (3.8)	13.6 (4.2)	14.0 (4.3)	13.7 (4.0)	11.8 (4.4)	11.9 (3.9)	12.8 (4.5)	13.8 (2.9)	11.8 (4.4)	13.8 (4.3)

* Significant difference between Hi and Lo groups ($p < 0.05$)

** $p < 0.01$

The Hi group included students with a top lower-second or better; the low group had bottom lower-seconds or worse.

lower second) has been omitted and so correlational analyses are almost certain to show the same pattern of results.

Correlations with degree results

In the literature, relationships between predictive measures and academic performance are usually reported as simple product-moment correlation coefficients, and typically the values obtained are low. The results reported in this section follow this all too familiar pattern in spite of attempts to avoid some of the problems described in Chapter 2. We did, of course, fail to avoid self-selection and homogeneity in the sample and there is no way of improving the reliability of the criterion measure. The values of the correlation coefficients reported in Table 9.4 indicate that even after analysing separately by area of study and after devising several scales appropriate to the British academic setting, prediction of academic performance from *single* variables is weak. No strong relationships were found which were characteristic of individual areas of study. There were, however, recurring patterns which suggested the existence of some general relationships. Consistent, and mainly statistically significant, correlations in line with previous research findings were found between degree results and 'A' level grades, motivation, study methods, hours studied, introversion and the self-ratings of 'hard-working' and 'sociable'. The aptitude scores showed correlations comparable with 'A' level grades among students taking languages, humanities and mathematics. There can be little surprise that verbal aptitude is a useful predictor of performance in languages. What is more surprising is that it also relates to degree results in mathematics. One explanation may be that students in languages have uniformly high linguistic abilities (or at least the range of scores is small) while their mathematical skills are more widely spread. As mathematical items involve reasoning they may thus be an effective indicator of 'general ability'. Appendix C2 provides confirmatory evidence of such differential ranges of verbal and mathematical ability for male linguists, but not for women.

From the Eysenck Personality Inventory and from the self-rating measures there was clear evidence of the consistent superiority of introverts, although no correlation exceeded 0.2. On the whole stability was associated with higher degree classes; there was little indication of high performance by 'neurotic introverts' at least in terms of the general relationships reported here. It is, however, possible that a separate analysis by 'personality type' would produce such a finding. This possibility will be examined in a subsequent report.

Looking at variables measured on two occasion, the test-retest correlations on both personality and study methods over a period of two years are reassuringly high (Appendix C7), with the personality dimensions, as expected, being the more stable. There is also no improvement in the predictive validity of the personality scales between first and third years. Both motivation and study methods scales do, however, show substantial increases in correlation with the

Table 9.4 Correlations of predictive measures with degree results, by area of study

Selected variables	Languages Year 1	Languages Year 3	Humanities Year 1	Humanities Year 3	Social sciences Year 1	Social sciences Year 3	Pure sciences Year 1	Pure sciences Year 3	Applied sciences Year 1	Applied sciences Year 3	Mathematics Year 1	Mathematics Year 3
First-year marks	39		57		34		53		74		71	
Number of 'O' levels	16		-07		08		10		19		22	
'A' level grades	16		19		11		29		53		49	
Verbal aptitude	26		22		11		-03		-04		29	
Mathematical aptitude	22		15		-01		-01		11		29	
Motivation	16	15	28	09	15	24	16	30	22	39	35	26
Study methods	17	20	26	29	09	18	23	35	31	28	18	39
Hours studied	13	17	31	33	14	16	17	21	38	16	24	21
Syllabus-bound		10		-15		04		-01		-05		-11
Syllabus-free		-08		-10		-18		-08		04		-10
Self-ratings of:												
Good at maths	08		10		00		07		25		24	
Hard-working	23		37		12		14		49		33	
Ambitious	-10		07		-01		03		13		01	
Sociable	-25		-09		-02		-10		-05		-12	
Seriousminded	11		08		-02		11		06		04	
Extraversion	-19	-17	-16	-11	-01	-05	-11	-12	-09	-18	-13	-03
Neuroticism	01	-08	-15	-15	-05	-04	-05	-01	-03	-03	-13	-10
Radicalism	11	04	02	09	-06	08	07	03	11	06	01	19
Tendermindedness	08	18	-06	-05	03	02	-10	-04	-05	00	13	08
Social values	06	06	10	07	-03	-04	02	06	14	14	-06	-01
Political values	-09	-08	13	08	04	08	-03	-03	03	-08	10	08
Economic values	-10	-15	01	-01	-06	-06	02	-02	09	05	-02	-05
Theoretical values	-13	-14	-06	09	-07	01	11	09	00	04	00	03
Aesthetic values	-12	-15	-18	-20	06	01	-04	-08	-12	-03	-07	-10
Religious values	18	23	00	01	04	01	-04	00	-05	-05	-02	05
Statistical significance $p \leq 0.05$ if $r \geq$	13		18		12		11		25		19	

Decimal points omitted

criterion. We are thus able to say that there are changes in these measurements over the two years (lower test-retest reliability) and that these changes increase the association between scores on these scales and degree class. The most likely explanation is that these scores are directly affected by knowledge of previous examination marks, but this possibility will be examined more closely in Chapter 11.

It is worth drawing attention, finally, to the utility of the self-rating scales. 'Hard-working', based on a student's own perception of the first-year work habits, related as closely to degree performance as did the scales of motivation and study methods. No doubt this relationship would be much smaller if the scale was applied by a student's own tutor, a situation in which the less 'transparent' attitude scales might be expected to retain their effectiveness. In the present study 'hard-working' showed correlations of 0.34 with motivation, 0.43 with study methods and 0.48 with hours studied (see Appendix C6). The self-rating on 'sociability' also appeared to be a good index of extraversion (0.55).

As there might still be strong relationships within particular types of department, it was decided to analyse the data separately by the ten most populous honours disciplines in our sample. The results are shown in Appendix C4 but again there are few noteworthy correlations. Most of the variations in levels of correlation between different disciplines are small enough to be attributed to chance sampling fluctuations. The only really striking relationships were found in the science departments. There, correlations of up to 0.7 between first-year marks and degree performance will be found. This level of agreement in the assessments of students is reassuring, implying a much higher inter-marker reliability than is normally assumed in higher education. Others may not find this situation 'reassuring', but find in it an indication that tutors 'label' their students in the first year and retain those labels thereafter. The nature of marking schemes in the sciences makes such an argument rather weak, and correlations of up to 0.5 between degree class and 'A' level grades put even more strain on the credibility of what might be called the 'conspiracy theory' of university assessment.

As some departments pay particular attention to 'A' level grades in a particular subject, another analysis isolated groups of students taking an honours course who had all taken the same 'A' level subjects. There was some improvement in the correlations produced between degree performance in an honours discipline and 'A' level grade in the equivalent school subject, in, for example, French (0.20), economics (0.30), biology (0.51) and physics (0.51), but on the whole the sum of 'A' level grades was the more effective predictor. However, it might still be useful, with larger samples, to examine the way in which 'A' level performance in two or more subjects might be combined most effectively. For example, 'A' level economics is a useful predictor (0.30) of degree class in sociology and the addition of another subject, such as history, in an appropriate weight might well boost this correlation substantially. But even this information may not be of direct use to an admissions tutor, who has to decide at what level to pitch a 'conditional

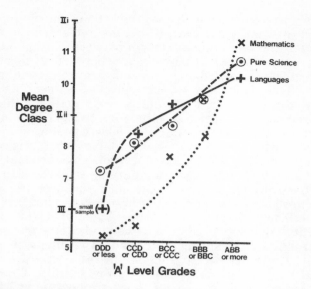

Figure 9.2 Relationship between 'A' level grades and degree class in three areas of study

offer'* of a group of 'A' level level grades, say CCC. Specific demands, perhaps for a 'B' in history, are possible, but specific combinations would be unlikely.

Prediction from groups of 'A' level grades

Admissions tutors will be concerned mainly with the level of academic performance reached by students admitted with differing groups of 'A' level grades. Some evidence has been provided already in UCCA statistical supplements, but only in terms of the distribution of degree class. The data collected in the present study allowed us to analyse the mean class of degree by entry qualifications and area of study. In order to produce larger numbers in the cells, the complete sample with degree results (or early failure) were included in the analysis. The detailed results are shown in Appendix C5 and it is apparent that the correlations previously reported have not been severely distorted by varying admission requirements for different faculties.Figure 9.2 shows the pattern of results from three contrasting areas of study—languages, pure sciences and mathematics. The close correlation between 'A' level grades and degree class in mathematics is clear from the steep ascent of the graph. In languages the slope is much less marked and the dotted line which suggests a sharp drop-off for poor 'A' level grades is derived from a small sample.

---

*Within the UCCA system departments make conditional offers. If the student subsequently achieves the required grades, he will be offered a place.

In mathematics it appears that unless a student enters with grades of ABB or better he has less than an even chance of obtaining a good second-class degree. Students with grades of CCD or CDD obtained, on average, a weak third-class degree. In most arts departments such students could expect to receive a second-class degree.

The different predictive validities of 'A' level grades so clearly illustrated in Figure 9.2 take on more significance when it is realised that it is in just those faculties where 'A' level grades provide the *worst* indication of subsequent degree performance that selection based on those grades is, at present, the most rigorous. Admittedly the results from the present analysis may not be as clear-cut as they appear at first sight. Information about admission to honours and general degree courses and about the different distributions of degree classes would be necessary to understand the situation fully. But the possible implications of Figure 9.2 are surely sufficiently disturbing to warrant more detailed investigation by those responsible for the admissions policies of universities.

Inter-relationships between variables

Appendix C6 presents, by sex, the correlational matrix of the inter-relationships between variables* mentioned in previous analyses. It is presented partly for the sake of completeness, but also as the basis of the subsequent multivariate analyses. While many of the inter-relationships may be of general interest, only a few are directly relevant to our main theme.

In the pilot studies it had been found that students with high study methods scores tended to be stable introverts. In this main investigation the scale of study methods showed correlations of –0.05 with extraversion and –0.32 with neuroticism (–0.27 for women). Equivalent values for the motivation scale were 0.07 with introversion and –0.26 (–0.24) with neuroticism. In other words 'good' study methods and high motivation are firmly linked with low levels of neuroticism. But perhaps we should be cautious in this interpretation. 'Good' study methods and high motivation may have been defined as that behaviour exhibited by stable students, leaving open the question of how to measure effective study methods and high motivation for anxious students.

So far we have examined only simple correlations and yet it is clear that in a complex social situation variables will interact. No straightforward explanation of human behaviour in a social setting is likely to be convincing. Multivariate techniques of analysis which bring together the effects of several variables simultaneously are more likely to provide appropriate statistical models for explaining differing levels

---

*Where tests were applied on two occasions only the scores in the first year have been used. The study of values scales have also been omitted because their ipsative scoring scheme distorts the inter-correlations.

of academic performance. In the remaining two sections of this chapter the use of multiple regression analyses and factor analyses are reported. In Chapter 10 cluster analysis is discussed.

Multiple regression analyses

This technique allows a number of variables to be taken together and weighted in such a way as to obtain the highest possible multiple correlation with a criterion variable. The computer program used a step regression technique in which variables are added into the calculation in order of their ability to improve the overall correlation with the criterion. The result of this calculation is a series of 'beta coefficients' indicating the weighting given to each variable in maximising the correlation with, in this instance, degree results.

The main strength of this method for our purposes is that it is directed specifically towards prediction. The main weakness is that it capitalises on chance characteristics in boosting the value of the multiple correlation. As a result analyses with repeated samples from the same population may produce large variations in the pattern of beta coefficients. Small samples are particularly likely to create 'bogus' weightings. For this reason the analyses reported below were restricted to the three areas of study in which substantial samples were available—languages, social sciences and pure sciences. Two separate analyses were run for each area of study. In the first the four intellectual measures were used to predict degree performance. In the second the main non-intellectual scales which had been identified as useful predictive measures in the literature review were added to the intellectual measures in an attempt to improve the level of prediction. The beta weights and multiple correlations are shown in Table 9.5, but the improvement in prediction is not uniform. Among linguists the simple correlation of 'A' levels with degree results was low (0.16). Adding the other intellectual variables did double this value, with verbal aptitude being given the highest weighting. Using all the variables pushed the final correlation up to 0.42 and it is interesting to note that introversion and both aptitude scores had high beta weights.

Among social scientists the addition of the aptitude test had rather less impact. The simple correlation of 0.11 with 'A' level grades was raised only to 0.17 and the remaining variables failed to reach even a moderate level of prediction. In the final equation verbal aptitude and hours studying were given the highest weightings.

As already mentioned 'A' level grades are a much better predictor in the sciences (0.29) and adding the aptitude test had almost no effect on this relationship (0.31). The non-intellectual variables allowed the final correlation to reach 0.38 with 'A' level grades and study methods dominating the weightings.

The particular values of the beta coefficients shown in Table 9.5 must be treated with caution, particularly where several similar variables are included. There will be a large chance element in deciding which of a number of similar variables is given the highest weighting. For

Table 9.5 Beta weights and multiple correlation coefficients for three areas of study

Predictive variables	Languages		Social science		Pure science	
	Intellectual variables only	All variables	Intellectual variables only	All variables	Intellectual variables only	All variables
Number of 'O' levels	11	10	07	07	07	07
'A' level grades	10	06	10	10	29	24
Verbal aptitude	19	18	09	10	-06	-07
Maths aptitude	14	14	-05	-04	-03	00
Motivation		10		10		05
Study methods		13		01		17
Hours studied		02		12		06
Extraversion		-18		00		-09
Neuroticism		08		-04		03
Constant in regression equation	2.84	2.03	6.37	4.57	4.39	2.46
Multiple correlation	0.33	0.42	0.17	0.25	0.31	0.38

Decimal points omitted from beta weights

example, the reversal in the importance of study methods and hours studied between languages and social science samples is almost certainly a chance effect. On the other hand the low weightings given to extraversion in the social sciences and to verbal aptitude in the pure sciences are in line with findings in previous studies and are less likely to be chance characteristics of the samples.

The uncertainty in multiple regression analysis prevents firm conclusions being reached. In factor analysis the technique is not so clearly relevant to the purposes of this study, but using the sample divided into groups of men and women consistent patterns of relationships between variables emerge and these in turn provide insights into the observed variations in academic performance.

Factor analyses

As it is impossible to interpret all the inter-relationships present in a correlational matrix some method of simplification must be used. Factor analysis (or principal components analysis to be more precise) extracts the similarities between groups of variables and creates factors which replicate the relationships between the variables. Thus a small number of factors can explain the variance among a much larger number of variables. After an initial extraction of the principal components these axes are rotated in an attempt to simplify the interpretation of the factors. Rotation can be done by computer using objective, but psychologically 'blind', statistical criteria, or the axes may be rotated graphically. Both procedures were used here. Appendix C8 provides the details of the computer rotation for men and women separately. The factor structure was closely similar in both analyses and the factors were readily interpretable:

Factor　　I — academic performance
Factor　 II — motivation and study habits
Factor　III — mathematical aptitude (science bias)
Factor　IV — ambition (linked with 'hard-working' in men and 'neuroticism' in women)
Factor　 V — verbal aptitude and syllabus-freedom (arts bias)

There can be little surprise in these factors: the dimensionality is decided by the variables initially selected. The main interest is in the sex difference shown of Factor IV. The link between ambition and neuroticism for women, but not for men, may link in with the analyses of study habits and personality already reported (Entwistle, Thompson and Wilson, 1974).

One disappointment was that the computer rotation had been too effective in separating motivation from the other factors. It was thus decided to examine the most important unrotated factors with a view to graphical rotation. The first factor, which always explains the most variance, had high loadings on hard-working, hours studying and degree results. The second factor described an arts/science split in

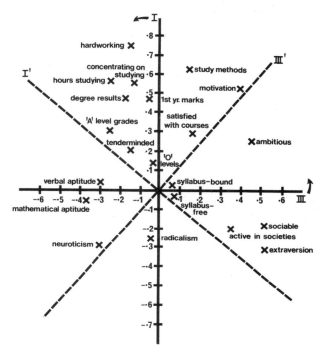

Figure 9.3 Position of variables in relation to two of the unrotated factors for the sample of women

terms of verbal aptitude and syllabus freedom, while the third factor was related to personality, describing a dimension of sociability and motivation—high drive and high activity. As this third factor, combined with the first, appeared to cover areas of particular interest in this investigation, the positions of the variables in relation to these two factors were plotted in Figure 9.3 using data from women. The axes were then rotated anti-clockwise through some 50° to create two distinct personality/study habits dimensions. Picking out the highest loadings which were not also loading highly on the arts/science factor, these rotated factors make sense. The pattern using data from men was similar, but not identical. For example, there was still an arts/science division on Factor II between verbal and mathematical aptitude, but syllabus freedom and radicalism loaded negatively on Factor I, while syllabus boundness had high negative loadings on Factor III. However it appeared that there was an arts/science division within Factor III for men and it makes the interpretation of the loadings less clear-cut than for women. Figure 9.4 summarises the pattern of loadings derived from the rotated axes (I' and III') shown in Figure 9.3.

The position of degree result and first-year marks within the axes created by I' and III' places them with high positive loadings on both dimensions. Relating back to the Aberdeen study, the variables which

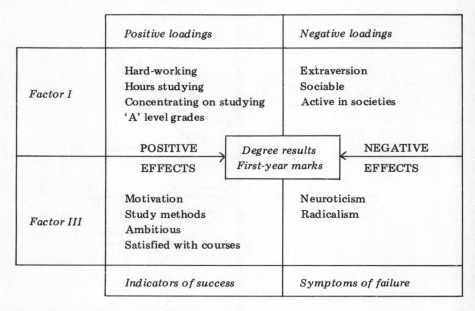

Figure 9.4 Academic performance in relation to graphically rotated factors (from Figure 9.3)

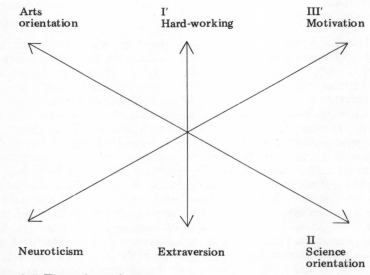

Figure 9.5 First three factors

also have high positive loadings on these factors may perhaps be taken as 'indicators of success', while those with substantial negative loadings become 'symptoms of failure', although the derivation of these 'indicators' is of course quite different. The particular variables picked out in this way are shown in Figure 9.4. These measures appear to be independent, to a large extent, of area of study. Figure 9.5 shows the pattern created by the first three factors and the third factor brings back an area of study. From this diagram two formulae predict academic success in the two areas of study:

Hardwork + motivation + mathematical aptitude = success in science
Extraversion + neuroticism + low mathematical aptitude = failure in science

But as in all correlational analyses, even multivariate ones, the attempt to produce only one formula each for success and failure, even in a single area of study, is over-simplistic. It represents little advance on a lesser known formula from Albert Einstein:

'If A equals success, then the formula is $A = X + Y + Z$, with X being work, Y play, and Z keeping your mouth shut.'

Alternative methods of analysis are necessary to avoid naive and unsatisfying conclusions about differences in levels of academic performance.

Chapter Ten

Types of Students*

The analyses reported in the previous chapter made use of traditional statistical techniques for investigating the accuracy of prediction. All of these rely on what Torgerson (1965) has described as the 'dimensional' approach. The relationships we have described are between variables and refer to people only indirectly. Correlational analyses, and their multivariate extensions, average out relationships across the whole sample or sub-sample, leaving out the possibility of students arriving in the 'successful' category by a variety of different 'routes'. Thus the successful students come to be described as having high aptitude, high scholastic attainment and good study methods combined with high levels of motivation and introversion. But the very weakness of the relationship suggests that what the analyses are hinting at is that *some* students have high ability, while *others* are introverted or have good study methods. The different groups of attributes will coincide for some students, but not for *all* of them. The 'paragons' implied by the correlational averaging process will occur, but presumably rather infrequently. The Aberdeen study bears out this idea. Most successful students had *some* of the indicators of success, but very few scored on every measure which predicted high degree performance. What the Aberdeen analysis could not do was to give differential weights to the indicators or to suggest whether some students showed particular *combinations* of symptoms. In this chapter we report attempts to identify groups of students who have similar profiles of scores. To simplify the description such groups are called 'types' and it is possible to contrast the academic performance of several different types of student. In this way it is possible to pick out a variety of patterns of indicators which seem to be linked to academic success or failure.

Two different statistical techniques have been explored, cluster analysis and automatic interaction detection (AID), and both seem to provide useful insights in trying to understand variations in academic performance.

*This chapter was written in collaboration with Dr Tim Brennan, who carried out most of the analyses.

122

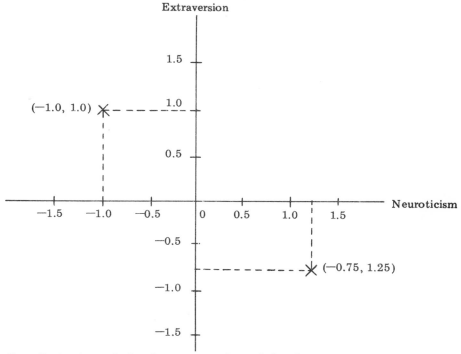

Co-ordinates (scores) of each person are shown in brackets.

Figure 10.1 Graphical representation of standardised scores of two individuals on two tests

Identification of student types by cluster analysis

The statistical bases for profile analysis have been available for many years, but only with the advent of large high-speed computers have the techniques become available for data processing. Cluster analysis has now been applied in a variety of scientific disciplines, but until recently little use had been made of this method in educational research. Yet it seems, at least at the conceptual level, that this technique should be ideally suited to many of the models of human behaviour which underlie research on students. In essence the aim of cluster analysis is to group together *people* whose profiles of scores show a high degree of similarity. It can perhaps best be understood by comparing this approach with factor analysis. There the aim is to condense many *variables* into a few factors which summarise the inter-relationships between those variables in an accurate, but parsimonious, manner. Tests which have elements in common are replaced by a single factor. In cluster analysis *people* who have attributes in common are placed together into groups. Clusters are thus used to describe profiles of scores which have a high degree of similarity. In this way clusters are analogous to factors.

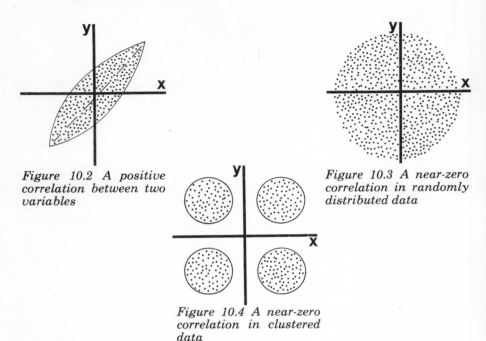

Figure 10.2 A positive correlation between two variables

Figure 10.3 A near-zero correlation in randomly distributed data

Figure 10.4 A near-zero correlation in clustered data

In bivariate analysis the scores of any individual may be shown graphically as a point between the axes formed by the two tests. The position of the point (its co-ordinates) being determined by the person's scores on the tests. An example is shown in Figure 10.1.

If a whole sample is plotted in the same way a swarm of points is produced which indicate the relationship between the variables. Figure 10.2 shows a strong positive correlation, while Figure 10.3 has a random distribution, created by a zero correlation. But a zero correlation would also be found with the symmetrical distribution shown on Figure 10.4. In other words correlational analyses could not distinguish between the relationships shown in Figure 10.3 and Figure 10.4, but the psychological meaning of the two distributions of points is very different. If a relationship like that shown in Figure 10.2 exists, a correlation coefficient would summarize it effectively. However, if the data has fragmented, as in Figure 10.4, only a form of cluster analysis would provide a useful description of the distribution of the data.

In multivariate analyses it is again possible to conceptualise, if not to visualise, a sample as a swarm of points in a hyperspace of any number of dimensions created by tests as axes. The distribution of these points will again determine which method of analysis will be most appropriate. If the swarm takes the form of the multidimensional equivalent of an ellipse, factor analysis or multiple regression analysis may be applied with confidence. If the swarm varies in density without this type of symmetry, cluster analysis may produce more meaningful results.

An analogy in three dimensions may help to visualise how clustered data in three dimensions might look. Imagine the swarm of points to be stars which are, of course, not evenly distributed across the universe. Stars are held together within galaxies of varying shapes and sizes separated by vast distances of space containing very little matter. It is possible that in studies using a variety of cognitive and non-cognitive measures, where there are interactions between variables, distributions of points in this psychological space may vary in density from place to place in a asymmetrical way. For example, in the present study, the combination of good 'A' level grades, high motivation and high degree class would be an area of relatively high density. Another area of high density might be described by high neuroticism, introversion, syllabus-boundness, high aptitude and good degree results. But extraversion, neuroticism, radicalism, and high academic attainment might be rather thinly populated. The task of a computer program designed for cluster analysis is to pick out dense areas and to draw boundaries around the clusters where the density drops below a predetermined level. The centroids (central points) of these clusters will then provide a picture of the data quite different from that obtained through factor analysis.

Relocation procedures in cluster analysis

A variety of cluster or classification methods are now available, together with a bewildering array of similarity or dissimilarity coefficients which provide quantitative estimates of the closeness of two profiles of scores. A summary of these methods has already been produced (Brennan, 1972), and Everitt (1974) has recently published a simple introduction to cluster analysis.

The procedure used in our analyses has been the 'k-means' method of relocation analysis following a computer program developed by Wishart (1969). The starting point is to decide how many clusters (say 'k') are required in the first solution to be printed out. The computer program begins with the 'k' centroids positioned randomly throughout the data space. Individuals are then allocated to the cluster nearest to them. The program then proceeds iteratively to reposition the centroids to provide a better description of the *real* distribution of the data—seeking areas of greatest density. The program excludes from the analysis individuals not close to any cluster centroid, thus forming a 'residue group'. Eventually a stable or optimal solution is reached for this cluster level and the co-ordinates of the 'k' centroids are printed out as mean standards scores of the defining variables. F values are also calculated to provide an indication of the heterogeneity of the cluster. The cluster will then be described in terms of variables on which it has high standard mean scores and low F values (greatest homogeneity). The program then merges the two most similar clusters and relocates points iteratively to produce a solution for $(k-1)$ clusters. The $(k-2)$ solution follows and so on until only two clusters remain.

As this analytic technique is still in its formative stage there are no

Table 10.1 Standard mean scores‡ of cluster centroids for 444 split-half sample

Variable	Year	1‡‡	4	5	6	9	11	12	14	15
		(N=49)	(23)	(40)	(52)	(58)	(44)	(29)	(53)	(32)
Degree result	3	8	3	4	1	5	3	-1	-12*	-7*
First-year marks	1	8	4	0*	-1*	5*	0	-4*	- 6	-7*
Satisfied with courses	3	5								-7*
Active social life	3		-6			-4	8*			6
Using sports facilities	3				-4				4	
Aesthetic interests	3	-5*	-6*	6			6			6*
'A' level grades	0	5							-6*	
Verbal aptitude	1	-4		5					-4	6
Maths aptitude	1	8*		-5	-7				7	
Motivation	1	6	4	5	-9*	4	5	-7*		-8
Motivation	3	6		5	-7	5	4	-6		-10*
Study methods	1	5	5	5				-6		-6
Study methods	3	6	6	6		4		-7*	-4	-10
Hours studied	3	-5		8	5	5*			-7	-8
Syllabus-bound	3			-6	4		-6			-8*
Syllabus-free	3			5	-6*		6			7
Extraversion	1		-10		-6*		9	5*		
Neuroticism	1	-7*			8					
Sociable	1		-6				8*	6		
Likeable	1				-5*		5			
Self-confident	1		-9*		-5*		6			
Social values	1						5*			4
Political values	1		7*			-5*				
Economic values	1	8				-7	-5		8	-6
Theoretical values	1	9	7*			-10			4	
Aesthetic values	1	-5		9		-6	5		-5	8
Religious values	1	-5	-7			15				-6
Radicalism	1	-7*	7*				6		-5	8
Tendermindedness	1	-5*	-5			12*		-6		

*   Indicates *F* ratio $\geqslant 0.7$
‡   Scores are shown to one decimal place ($\times 10$). Scores below 4 have been omitted.
‡‡   Cluster numbers refer to the summary table (l0.2).

established traditions to guide the presentation of findings. In these analyses only one cluster solution has been reported, chosen as a stable solution in which a minimum of information has been lost by merging clusters, but where the cluster sizes are still large enough to represent identifiable 'types' of students.

Table 10.2 Summary of size and degree results of student types

	Cluster number and brief description	Split-half 444	Split-half 443	Langs.	Human.	Soc Sci.	Science
1	Stable, high ability, high motivation, good study methods	49 Very high	47 Very high				
2	High ability, syllabus-bound introverts				24 High		33 Very high
3	Sociable, syllabus free, radicals with adequate motivation		37 Average			38 Above average	
4	Radical, political introverts with good study methods	23 Above average		8* Average			
5	Aesthetic, syllabus free, conscientious	40 High	52 High				20 Below average
6	Neurotic introverts with low motivation, but work long hours	52 Average	22 High				
7	Conventional introverts, syllabus bound, with adequate motivation			12 Above average		31 Average	
8	Low ability, high motivation, good study methods					28 Above average	24* High
9	Religious, tender-minded, hard-working	58 High	30 Above average	26 High	23 Average		
10	Religious, tender-minded, syllabus-bound, unambitious		47 Low			29 Average	20 Average
11	Sporty, sociable stable extraverts with adequate motivation	44 Above average	44* Average		17 Average	18 Average	41 Low
12	Toughminded extraverts with poor study methods	29 Average	40 Very low	28 Average			
13	Toughminded neurotic extraverts				35 Below average		28 Above average

table continues overleaf

	Cluster number and brief description	Split-half 444	Split-half 443	Langs.	Human.	Soc Sci.	Science
14	High numerical ability, low motivation, poor study methods	53 Very low	28 Very low				
15	Aesthetic radicals with low motivation and poor study methods	32 Very low	53* Above average	24 Below average		45 Below average	26 Low

* Cluster does not fit clearly into assigned category.

Split-half relocation analyses

Previous analyses (Entwistle and Brennan, 1971; Brennan, 1972) using data obtained in the first year had provided evidence of clear-cut and replicable student 'types' associated with different levels of academic performance. Using complete sets of data available early in 1972 these analyses were repeated and extended. 887 students from all seven universities were included in these analyses and this sample differed from the main follow-up sample only in under-representing the foreign linguists and other students on four-year courses.

Rather than using the whole sample for the main analysis, as had been done earlier, the sample was divided into two (444 and 443) on a random basis and each half was clustered separately. This strategy gives a useful indication of the extent to which clustering has been affected by chance. On the whole there is encouraging consistency in the clusters produced. The nine and ten cluster solutions produced the most satisfactory level for interpretation and comparison. Of these, eight clusters were identifiably common to both samples, while the remaining two clusters in the 443 sample overlapped clusters in the 444 sample. The defining variables for equivalent clusters in the two samples were by no means identical, but the main characteristics were sufficiently similar to allow clear identification. Table 10.1 presents the standard mean scores of the centroids of the various clusters found in the 444 sample. The equivalent table for the other sample has been placed in Appendix C9.

The clusters proved replicable not only in terms of the defining variables, but also in their association with degree performance— Cluster 15 was the only marked exception. High or low degree results are repeatedly associated with particular sets of characteristics. While the realism of the clusters is no doubt restricted by our particular choice of variables, and by inaccuracies of measurement, the clusters which emerge do not give the impression of being random combinations of the variables. The recurrence of identifiably similar patterns of scores within these two equivalent samples emphasises that the data space does contain areas of varying density which this cluster program is delineating consistently. The main emphasis of this study is on prediction, so the following pen-pictures of the centroids have been grouped into low and high attainment categories. Further details, but not complete information, about the defining features of the clusters can be obtained by examining Table 10.1 and Appendix C9. Table 10.2 shows the sizes of the various clusters and their degree performance.

High attainment clusters

Highly motivated, stable scientists

Cluster 1 represents by far and away the most successful group of students. Due to the higher percentage of scientists and mathematicians who obtain first-class degrees both these clusters formed from the two halves of the sample contained a preponderance of scientists.* Cluster 1 contained students with high 'A' level grades who were satisfied with their courses. These students had not had a particularly active social or sporting life, nor had they concentrated on developing aesthetic interests. In common with scientists as a whole, this group spent rather less than average time in private study, presumably due to the demands of laboratory classes. However, they were highly motivated and had good study methods. In personality they were emotionally stable and had high scores on theoretical and economic values, linked with a tendency towards toughminded conservatism. This combination of characteristics suggest a rather cold and ruthless individual, governed by rationality and spurred on by competition to repeated demonstrations of intellectual mastery.

Hard-working syllabus-free arts students

Cluster 5 contains the most successful arts students with a rather different combination of attributes from the successful scientists. These students did not have outstandingly high 'A' level grades, although their verbal aptitude scores were well above average. High motivation, good study methods and long hours of study were linked with syllabus-freedom. There was no defining characteristic in terms of personality, but high aesthetic values were associated with radical attitudes. Another striking feature of this group was the high proportion of students whose fathers had professional or managerial occupations. Presumably a 'cultured' home, which would be found more frequently among students from the higher social classes, represents a considerable advantage to students studying languages or the humanities.

*The clusters were cross-classified in terms of area of study, proportion of men and father's occupation; details of these measures have been omitted from the tables.

Two other arts-based clusters were found only in one or other of the samples. Cluster 3 contains sociable, syllabus-free radicals with adequate levels of motivation whose academic performance is just above average, while Cluster 4 contains introverts who are radicals with high political values. This combination of radical attitudes with political values is associated with good study methods and fairly good degree results.

Anxious students who work long hours

Although Cluster 6 is identifiable in both samples, there were some differences in the composition of the two groups. In the 444 sample a large, mainly arts-based, group with average attainment was produced. The other analysis produced a small group of scientists obtaining a fairly high proportion of good honours degrees. The main defining features of both groups were high scores on neuroticism and syllabus-boundness, and low scores on both extraversion and motivation. Their self-ratings were uniformly negative. They saw themselves as neither likeable nor self-confident. They had no active social life and had few aesthetic interests. Both groups had low motivation and study methods, and yet the scientists in the 443 sample obtained good degree results. It is tempting to see these students as motivated mainly by 'fear of failure' and it is also interesting to note the contrast between these students and the other successful scientists of Cluster 1 who were highly motivated and stable. The two clusters both have a majority of men, but the Cluster 6 scientists have a higher social-class background. The possibility that neurotic introverts with low motivation and poor study methods might be almost as successful as highly motivated stable students was noted in a preliminary analysis of the interview data (Entwistle, Thompson and Wilson, 1974).

Hard-working students with high religious values

One of the surprising features of these analyses was the relatively large number of students, both men and women, whose main defining feature was high religious values linked with tenderminded attitudes and long hours of studying. Cluster 9 presents a flat contradiction to the stereotype student of the mass media. The atypicality of the score on religious values produces negative scores on other values, but this is mainly an artefact of the method of scoring in the 'Study of Values'. Cluster 9 is made up of arts students who work long hours; while their scores on both motivation and study methods are not outstanding, their degree results are above average. A second cluster with high religious values was found in the 443 sample. Cluster 10 contained a majority of women taking science, who did rather badly in their degree examinations. It is apparently the effectiveness of the study methods which distinguishes two similar clusters with differing levels of degree performance.

Stable extraverts with adequate motivation

Cluster 11 is not well defined and barely merits being included in the 'high attainment' category at all. In the 444 sample the main characteristics of this cluster are extraversion and an active social life. In the 443 sample, the extraversion is only implicit in sporting activities, but in both samples the students see themselves as either motivated or working reasonably hard. In these groups of students participation in extra-mural activities does not appear to be unduly deleterious to academic performance.

Low attainment clusters

Toughminded extraverts with poor study methods

The toughmindedness of Cluster 12 goes with a tendency towards conservative attitudes which is particularly strong in the cluster created from the 443 sample. The students do not consider that they have put much effort into studying, but in the 444 sample their examination performance is only just below average. In the other sample there is a preponderance of scientists who obtain very poor degrees and who had low 'A' level grades on entry.

Science students with low motivation and poor study methods

Cluster 14 contains science students who came up to university with below average 'A' level grades, but their numerical ability appeared to be equivalent to the highly successful scientists (Cluster 1). This group showed a marked deterioration in performance after the first year and, in the 443 sample, had very low motivation and study method scores in first and third years. In both samples these students show themselves as dissatisfied with the courses. They spent little time on studying and rather more on leisure pursuits. The 444 sample does not show particularly low motivation, but this group contains a majority of students from lower social class backgrounds and their theoretical values are low for science students.

Arts students with low motivation and poor study methods

The two samples create a contradiction in mean criterion score on Cluster 15. The 444 sample produces the smaller and better defined cluster. Although entering university with average 'A' level grades and having relatively high verbal ability, these students have such a succession of negative standard scores in the motivation and study methods domain, combined with highly radical attitudes, that poor academic performance is an understandable outcome. The probable explanation of the above-average degree performance of the 443 sample lies in differences in personality. The 444 sample is extraverted, while the other group contains a majority of students with high neuroticism scores who are not extraverted. Admittedly these students still have low motivation and study methods scores, but we have already seen among science students that anxiety combined with low motivation can be associated with good examination results. It seems probable that the 443 sample contains a mixture of Cluster 15 and Cluster 6, who have been allocated to Cluster 15 in the 443 sample by virtue of their arts bias and radical attitudes. Subsequent analyses by area of study confirmed this interpretation.

Relocation analyses by area of study

It was clear from the two initial relocation analyses that clusters were being formed partly on the basis of area of study membership. For example, a relatively short working week on private study could mean science orientation or a lack of industry. It was important to clarify this type of difference by re-examining the clusters within area of study. Unfortunately the sub-groups taking engineering and mathematics were too small to apply cluster analysis successfully. For example in mathematics only the three-cluster solution had groups large enough to interpret with confidence, but these three clusters appeared to be a mixture of cluster-types identified previously. Appendices C10—C13 present the standard mean scores for the four remaining areas of study and Table 10.2 summarises the characteristics of the clusters compared with those formed in the 'split-half' analyses. It should be noted that the same students have been included in both the 'split-half' and the area of study analyses. Similar clusters are thus to be expected, but there will be some reassignment of students between clusters, or redefinition of clusters, because the profiles are now being compared to area of study norms, rather than to those of the whole sample.

There is evidence that some of the clusters previously identified have been 'contaminated' with area of study differences. For example neither Cluster 1 nor Cluster 14 have exact parallels in the areas of study. It appears that the stability of Cluster 1 and the high numerical ability of Cluster 14 were science-related characteristics. Within the areas of study Cluster 1 disappears and three new clusters (2, 7 and 8) emerge which have some of the charactersitics of the previous cluster, but which have differing levels of ability. Students previously in Cluster 14 appear to have been reassigned to Clusters 11 and 15.

Most of the other clusters fit into the definitions already presented in the 'split-half' analyses, often improving the clarity of the earlier definitions. There were several clusters of particular interest. The sample of linguists (mainly taking English) created two clusters (4 and 12) which showed patterns of deteriorating performance not previously identified. Although Cluster 4 is small it could be important. Students entered university with high 'A' level grades, being a full standard deviation above the mean for linguists. By the end of the first year their academic performance was less outstanding (0.5) and two years later their degree results were only average. No doubt statistical regression towards the mean explains some of this decrease in performance, but the deterioration in performance is also clearly associated with a complete reversal of their motivation in relation to other students. Their scores change from +0.6 to –1.0 over the two-year period. Again in the first year these students put an average amount of time into private study but by the third year they were almost a full standard deviation below the mean. These students 'opted out' of their academic work, but showed no more than an average interest in any other sphere of university activity.

Cluster 15 is more clearly defined in the areas of studies where it occurs, than in the 443 split-half sample. The cluster contains radical students who are dissatisfied with their courses, but who have had an active social life and have developed their aesthetic interests. Their poor degree results are again associated with low scores for motivation and study methods, but these students started with such low motivation scores that poor subsequent performance would have been predicted.

Cluster 15 is found in the science faculties and poor degree results can be explained by ineffective work habits. But Cluster 5 also shows below-average degree results from students who are conscientious. Here a possible explanation of poor performance is that they chose to study the wrong discipline. These students had very high verbal aptitude, were syllabus-free, radical and had high aesthetic values— and yet they were studying science. Their poor performance may thus be a result of a mismatch between the students' abilities and interests and the courses they were studying.

Cluster 2 represents the most successful students in pure sciences and humanities. They were able introverts who did not have an active social life. They worked hard and had good study methods combined with a syllabus-bound orientation.

Cluster 8 also contains successful students in both social science and pure science faculties. Lack of aptitude did not appear to hamper these students. Their academic attainment was consistently above the level implied by their aptitude scores and was linked, in both first and third years, with high levels of motivation, long hours of work and good study methods. The social science group was clearly atypical of the area of study profile. Its students had conservative social attitudes and rejected aesthetic values. It is interesting to contrast the successful academic performance of this cluster, with the rather poor degree results of the atypical scientists in Cluster 5.

Automatic interaction detection

The previous analyses have been based on the relocation procedure which Brennan (1972) had found most appropriate for these data. Relocation analysis aims to produce clusters which most accurately depict areas of high density. An alternative method of classifying students was applied to the first-year data—automatic interaction detection (AID). As its name suggests this statistical technique is designed for data in which interactions between variables are anticipated. AID is also a clustering analogue of multiple regression. The basic aim is to achieve accurate prediction of a criterion by splitting the sample into a number of sub-groups which differ maximally in terms of the criterion. The splitting is carried out using a small number of explanatory variables on which appropriate threshold values are calculated. These values allow repeated dichotomous splits to be made in the sample. The computer program starts with the whole sample and chooses that variable and that threshold value which produces a maximum difference in mean criterion scores between the dichoto-mised sub-samples. Each sub-sample is then taken separately and dichotomised on the same basis. The process of successive sub-division is continued until further splits would improve the prediction only marginally. The analysis is then terminated.

As the area of study differences had been recognised, the AID analyses were carried out separately for arts and science students on the first-year data. No more specific analysis by area of study could be attempted as large samples are necessary to allow repeated divisions to be made in the sample. The simplest method of presenting these findings is in the form of hierarchical tree diagrams which indicate the variables on which the various splits have been made. It is also possible to look at the mean scores of the terminal groups. The methods and purposes of this type of analysis are so different from relocation analysis that close similarity in profiles between these groups and the relocation clusters was not anticipated.

Figures 10.5 and 10.6 show the tree diagrams derived from 378 science students and 497 arts students, being the same group who were included in the first relocation analyses (Entwistle and Brennan, 1971; Brennan, 1972). The AID analysis apparently worked effectively for science students. Eleven terminal groups were created, of which eight contained twenty students or more. The terminal mean criterion scores for these larger groups ranged from 7.5 up to 15.2. The analysis was less effective with the arts students as 'fragmentation' occurred after the first few splits. Subsequent divisions produced a series of sub-groups varying in size between 5 and 1, leaving the main group almost unchanged. However, the six terminal clusters still produced criterion scores ranging from 8.9 up to 14.6.

With science students the importance of 'A' levels in predicting subsequent academic performance becomes clear (Figure 10.5). 'A' level grades are chosen to make the first split; students with very high grades are successful, except for a small group who have low motiva-tion. In the remaining group with average or low 'A' level grades the self-rating on 'hard-working' produces the next division. Of the stu-dents who see themselves as not hard-working, only those with high theoretical values reach an average level of performance. This self-rating occurs again to produce a group (1) with the lowest criterion value (7.5) who have low theoretical values and rate themselves very low on 'hard-working'.

Among the hard-working scientists ($N = 183$), those with the low 'A' levels form a terminal group (4) with below-average attainment. The

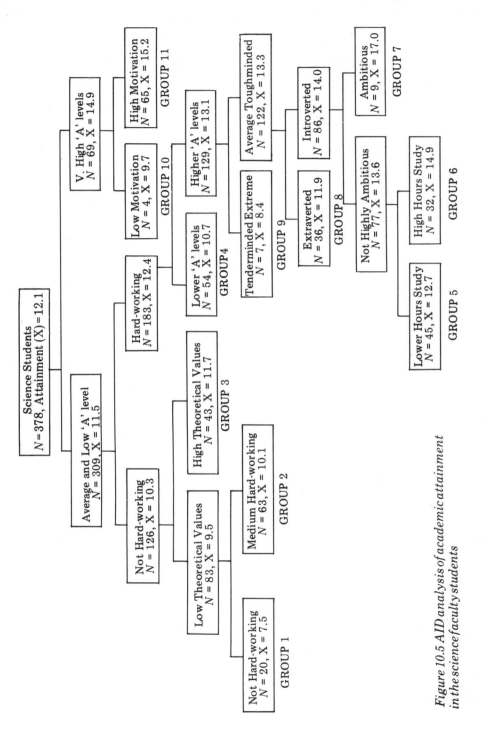

Figure 10.5 AID analysis of academic attainment in the science faculty students

Figure 10.6 AID analysis of arts student sub-sample

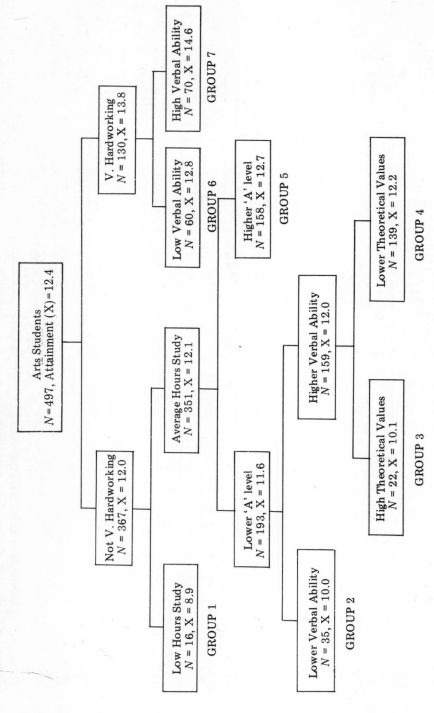

next major division of the remaining students with average 'A' level grades is such that introverts show well above average performance: a small group of ambitious students (7) have the highest criterion score of all, while those with lower ambition who put in long hours of studying still do well (6).

'A' levels do not show the same importance in defining groups of arts students (Figure 10.6). The only outstandingly successful group (7) see themselves as very hard-working and also have high verbal aptitude scores. Hard-working students with lower verbal ability show average levels of attainment (6). Of the students who rate themselves lower on 'hard-working', the terminal group (1) with the lowest criterion score also admit to having done rather few hours of studying in the previous week. The majority of the students, not surprisingly, do an average amount of work, but three further splits help to differentiate their levels of performance. Above average 'A' level grades create a large terminal group (5), which leads only to very small splinter groups (not reported). This large terminal group has no defining features other than high 'A' level grades.

Students with average or below average school attainment allow two low performance groups to be created: those with low verbal ability (2) and those with high theoretifal values (3). These two characteristics are more typical of science students and here again poor performance may follow from a lack of match between students and courses. In most other ways these students appear to be unexceptional, although Group 3 have above-average scores on radicalism.

When the characteristics of the terminal groups are examined in more detail (see Brennan, 1972), some overlap with the relocation clusters can be seen. For example, Science Group 1 represents students from working-class backgrounds with high mathematical ability, but poor study methods. These students have the lowest level of academic performance in both methods of analysis. Hard-working, less able, introverts, and conventional students with good study methods and high 'A' level grades, are both successful groups which emerged from the relocation analyses. The analysis of the arts students does not create sufficiently clear types to allow comparisons with relocation clusters. Low verbal ability, few hours of study and radicalism are all related to poor performance, but the combinations of these values are not equivalent to the clusters reported earlier.

The AID method does seem to offer an interesting alternative to relocation analysis, but there is no apparent improvement in predictive accuracy over relocation analysis. The standard mean criterion scores differ between relocation clusters to much the same extent as they do between the terminal groups of the AID analysis. At first sight this result may seem surprising, as prediction of the criterion is the specific aim of AID. the most likely explanation of this anomaly lies in certain weaknesses of AID. Once the major splits have been made, no re-allocation of individuals between groups is possible. The procedure dichotomises each sub-group in isolation ignoring similarities between adjoining sub-groups created from different parent groups. Again the

particular variables chosen for the early splits will be affected by
chance characteristics of the sample, but have a decisive effect on the
groups created. As with regression analysis replication studies are
unlikely to lead to close similarity in the values of the defining
parameters. In AID even small differences early in the analysis could
create large differences in the characteristics of the terminal clusters.

The utility of the AID method lies mainly in its ability to identify a
small number of variables which are highly predictive of the chosen
criterion. From these two analyses only a few variables create differences in criterion scores between major sub-groups. In order of importance these are:

'A' level grades;
Self-rating on hard-working;
Hours spent studying;
Verbal aptitude (arts only);
Introversion (science only).

Scores on theoretical values also created useful discriminations,
although the direction differed between arts and science samples.
However, as the difference is in the expected direction, this variable
could be accepted as a useful predictor.

There is nothing surprising, or informative, about this list as it
stands, but certain facets of the AID findings could be important. For
example, the verbal scores from the test of academic aptitude appear
twice in the analysis of arts students, being of comparable importance
to 'A' level grades among science students. Of course this result may be
a chance attribute of this particular sample but, if replicated, it might
indicate that this part of the aptitude test has a greater utility as a
predictive instrument than was apparent in most of the correlational
analyses.

PART FOUR
Synthesis and Conclusions

Chapter Eleven

The Academic Achievement Game

So far the Rowntree and Aberdeen studies have been kept separate, but if they are truly complementary, relating the two sets of findings should take us further than any of the previous chapters. The findings reported in Chapters 6 and 9 indicated which factors were associated with success and failure in higher education. How much agreement was there? Are we any closer to understanding the causes of differing levels of academic achievement?

Synthesis of findings

The major problem in comparing the results is that the two studies were planned separately and overlap is to some extent accidental. There are differences both in the method of sampling and in the measuring instruments applied. While the pure science samples in both studies are essentially similar, the Aberdeen 'arts' sample contained students grouped under 'languages', 'humanities' and 'social science' in the Rowntree study.

None of the instruments used in the two investigations was exactly the same, but several of the underlying dimensions were intended to be identical and measures were closely similar. Thus results derived from the Eysenck Personality Inventory are comparable, as parallel forms of the same scale were used in some analyses. The scales of motivation and study methods overlapped considerably, with many items in common. The measures of school attainment are tapping the same dimension, but at different ages and in different school systems. The verbal reasoning test used for students in the arts faculty at Aberdeen overlaps with the verbal aptitude test included in the Rowntree study, but the types of item in these tests did differ markedly.

The studies also differed in the way the data were treated. The Rowntree study employed sophisticated statistical tools to carry out multiple regression and factor analysis of the data over the whole range of performance; it also combined variables by means of cluster analysis. The Aberdeen study on the other hand kept close to the data and employed very simple statistics. The analysis was straightforward, with clearly defined criteria, and although it is possible to criticise the approach, to disagree over where dichotomies should be drawn, and over how many symptoms to include in a prediction, nevertheless what is happening is transparent. By contrast the Rowntree study dazzles by its statistical sophistication, and there is a danger of forgetting that the reliability and the validity of the results are only as good as the data on which they are based. In this respect it was important that the sample could be shown, despite the problems of collecting data, to be reasonably representative. On the other hand the sample size, though large overall, was still too small to enable analyses to be reported separately by sex or area of study within institution.

In Chapter 3 the literature review identified a series of factors commonly associated with success or failure in higher education. Most of these variables were subsequently included in one or other of our studies. Here we summarise our results, indicating where sex or area of study differences may be expected, under the following headings:

Entry qualifications
Intellectual aptitude
Headteachers' reports
Age and social background
Social attitudes and values
Neuroticism and extraversion
Academic motivation and study methods

The best indicators of success over the degree course are, however, not included in this list. First-year examination results, and in the Aberdeen study the award of merit certificates for class work, showed the closest relationships with degree class, but for most purposes this prediction comes too late.

Entry qualifications

Both studies found that previous scholastic attainment was the best pre-entry predictor of subsequent academic attainment. Significant relationships were obtained in all areas of study with the exception of social science. Nevertheless the correlation coefficients reached 0.5 only in engineering and mathematics. Graphs corroborated the impression that 'A' levels predicted better in science than in arts or social science.

In the Aberdeen study the most consistent indicators of excellence were a large number of SCE 'H' grade passes obtained at the first attempt, and a bursary competition place. Failure was predicted most consistently by having obtained entrance qualifications at the second attempt.

Intellectual aptitude

The Moray House verbal reasoning test did not emerge either as an indicator of success or as a symptom of failure in the final year, although it was related to merit performance in the first year. The vocabulary score showed just one significant relationship with success—for science men. This string of insignificant relationships fits in with other recent findings.

The Rowntree study found a higher correlation between the test of academic aptitude and degree result than did the NFER study (Choppin *et al.*, 1973), but this may simply reflect the difference between testing in the first-year sixth and at university. The most interesting results are probably the differences between subject areas. In languages and humanities verbal aptitude correlated more highly with degree result than did 'A' level grades. In the multiple regression analyses of data from language students, verbal aptitude obtained the highest weighting of the combination of intellectual variables and the multiple correlation (0.33) represented a substantial improvement on the simple correlation with 'A' level grades (0.16). Verbal aptitude was also an important variable in the AID analysis of arts students.

Headteachers' reports

The Aberdeen study showed that specific ratings by headteachers were consistently included among symptoms of failure. The heads' reports were less often found among the indicators of excellence, although first-year merit was consistently related to the rating on honours degree potential. The check list used by the headteachers produced significant relationships with both first-year and final-year failure for both men and women in arts and science, and was the only variable to show such consistency in the prediction of failure. Lack of perseverance, lack of maturity and lack of independence showed the strongest relationships with failure among the separate items of the check list, while lack of intelligence was predictive for women in arts subjects.

Age and social background

These variables were included only in the Aberdeen analyses although social class was used to cross-classify the Rowntree clusters. In the Aberdeen study there was just one significant result with age. Male students aged twenty or more at entry were more likely to fail science courses than younger men, and this was also true of those who had not come direct from school to university. This finding is in line with previous results reported in Chapter 3.

Place of home residence, social background and parents' education were also related to performance for some groups of students, although there were few stable relationships. Residence in the university region was associated with final-year excellence for science men, but was a symptom of failure in both first and final year for arts women. Having professional parents did appear as an indicator of excellence among arts students, and this pattern reappeared in one of the Rowntree clusters, but parents' education proved an unstable variable showing no consistent pattern of results.

144   *Degrees of Excellence*

Social attitudes and values

Although these dimensions were useful for describing differences
between students entering different areas of study, few significant
correlations with attainment were recorded. In the absence of predicted
relationships some of the significant correlations which did occur
might well have been chance characteristics of the particular sample.
Only in the language area were there sufficiently strong relationships
to be worth mentioning. Tendermindedness and religious values were
associated with above-average degree performance. Low economic,
theoretical and aesthetic values were apparently also an advantage,
but the ipsative nature of the measurement instrument might have
caused distortions in the patterns of relationships. The safest
conclusion appears to be that, in themselves, social attitudes and
values are unrelated to academic performance. There was certainly no
consistent indication that radicalism was associated with poor degree
results, although in combination with other variables it is linked with
poor degree results (Chapter 10).

Neuroticism and extraversion

The review of the literature had indicated that no simple relationship
between neuroticism and degree results was to be expected. There was
a suggestion from the Aberdeen study that stability was a consistent
symptom of failure among women, but not men. Correlations between
neuroticism and degree performance were uniformly low across all six
areas of study and neuroticism also had low weightings in the multiple
regression analyses. In all, our findings are in line with the inconsistent previous results, but are not helpful in clarifying the reasons for
those inconsistencies.

Extraversion was expected to be a symptom of failure and introversion to be a correlate of high achievement. In the first year, high levels
of extraversion did predict failure among Aberdeen arts students, but
there was only one significant relationship with degree performance,
and that was for science women. Introversion appeared only once as an
indicator of success. There were, however, consistent relationships in
the Rowntree analyses between introversion and academic performance; in some of the honours subjects relatively high correlations
were found (0.35 in history; 0.29 in English). In the multiple regression
analysis of language students and in the AID analysis of scientists,
low extraversion scores were clearly associated with good honours
degrees.

Taking the two sets of evidence together it does appear that the
rather low overall correlations may disguise a number of closer relationships within individual disciplines (mainly in Wankowski's 'theoretical subjects'—see Chapter 3). There may also be some non-linearity
of relationship, with high scores on extraversion being more consistently related to poor degree results than are low scores associated with
outstanding performance. It is hoped to examine this possibility
further in subsequent analyses.

Academic motivation and study methods

These variables had been selected as likely concomitants of academic performance, and both studies confirm these expectations. Again the average level of correlation was by no means high, but maximum values of 0.39 were recorded with both motivation and study-methods scales in the follow-up questionnaire. In the Aberdeen study motivation and study methods appeared as both indicators of success and symptoms of failure, but not for every sub-group. Motivation appeared to be a better predictor than study methods, particularly for men, but correlations tended to be rather higher for study methods.

Perhaps the most striking finding with these variables in the Rowntree study was the change in relationship between first- and third-year questionnaires. Across subject areas the median correlation with motivation in the first year was 0.19, rising to 0.25 in the third year. Equivalent values for study methods were 0.18 and 0.29. While it is usual to expect closer relationships between variables measured in the same year, the increases are larger than had been anticipated. Additional evidence of instability in these scores comes from the rather low test/re-test reliability coefficients (Appendix C7). The clusters (Appendix C10) in which there were extreme changes in motivation and study methods paralleling, rather than preceding, changes in academic performance, suggest moreover that the idea of using either motivation or study methods as an *explanation* of success or failure is doubtful. Changes in attainment might equally well be affecting the level of motivation. Should we thus ignore the effect of motivation as a possible explanatory variable? Before doing so, we should remember that low correlations are the norm, not the exception. For example the median correlation between 'A' level grades and degree results was only 0.24, compared with the 0.19 between *first-year* motivation scores and final-year attainment. There is also another way of looking for evidence of causality—by adopting what has been termed 'cross-lagged' panel analysis (see, for example, Crano *et al.*, 1972). Which is the closer correlation, first-year motivation with degree results or first-year attainment with third-year motivation? If one of these were substantially higher than the other, a predominating direction of causality might be inferred. Taking the various indicators of motivation and study methods, only one—number of hours studied—shows any clear-cut difference. It appears that first-year attainment has little effect on hours worked in the final year (0.07), but there is a much closer relationship between hours worked in the first year and degree results (0.21). As other measures of motivation and study methods show only a slight tendency for the direction to imply that they might cause changes in performance, we must accept that causation has not been clearly demonstrated. Certainly motivation will *explain* the subsequent academic performance of some students, but there is no uniformity and the direction of causality may well be reversible. Where there is a direct connection between any predictive variable and attainment, the interaction between these variables will produce feed-back effects which complicate attempted explanations of observed correlations.

If we accept that the academic motivation scale measured a form of intrinsic motivation related to the maintenance of self-respect through academic achievement, it becomes clear that we should have expected such a two-way interaction. Presumably high-drive individuals who fail to obtain satisfaction from their academic performance will look for achievement in other areas of activity. Birney, Burdick and Teevan (1969) came to a similar conclusion in their study of *Fear of Failure*. Indeed, teachers often use the interactive nature of this relationship intuitively, for example, by awarding 'encouraging' marks to pupils with an expectation that motivation will increase. It is strange to find little comment on the phenomenon of changing directions of causality in the literature of education research. There must be other important variables which interact directly with attainment and so complicate explanations. Such variables would consistently be found as concomitants of succes and failure, but, before explanations could follow, more would have to be known about the conditions under which these traits *cause,* rather than simply reflect, changes in academic performance.

Personality and study methods

In Chapter 9 it was shown that there werę consistent relationships between emotional stability and both study methods and motivation. In the pilot study stable introverts had been found to have the higher scores in the study methods scales both in university and in college of education. However, in the Aberdeen study one simple, but revealing, analysis threw considerable doubt on the interpretation of the correlation. Table 6.8 reported a zonal analysis which presented combinations of motivation and study methods scores in relation to personality type. The table again showed a clear relationship between stable introversion, study habits and motivation, with 43 per cent of the students in this personality type having study attitude scores in the top category, compared with 39 per cent unstable introverts, 22 per cent stable extroverts and 20 per cent unstable extraverts. But it also showed that students with similar study attitudes had comparable levels of performance, irrespective of their personality type. Thus while 75 per cent of unstable introverts with good study attitudes had good academic performance, 79 per cent of unstable extraverts were equally successful.

It appears then that while extraversion scores may be related to poor performance, this will depend on the way in which the extraversion is exhibited (cf. Eysenck, 1972). Only where extraversion leads directly to poor study methods will the predicted low degree class materialise. For students with high motivation, extraversion is presumably kept under control and does not affect their academic performance. This type of finding reinforces the necessity of adopting methods of analysis (like symptom or cluster analysis) which allow profiles of scores to be used in explaining academic performance. Overall relationships based on correlations may lead to incorrect conclusions.

The methodology of prediction

In Chapter 2 we criticised various weaknesses of previous prediction studies in higher education. Have our studies been any better? In some ways they have been disappointing. There are still major weaknesses in the samples used; self-selection prevented the samples from being fully representative of university students in general. However, the checks on non-responders and comparisons with national samples in other studies do indicate that the relationships reported are unlikely to have been seriously distorted. By comparing results between the two studies and by relating findings back to the previous literature, the effects of sampling errors can be minimised.

The two studies used a wide range of measures, many of which showed relationships with academic performance. Again the correlations, both simple and multiple, were too low to claim much progress on this front, but these low correlations do seem to be misleading. Both studies show that alternative methods of analysis can provide more insight into the concomitants of students success and failure.

The symptom approach used in the Aberdeen study owes much to McClelland's (1958) concept of threshold effects, and to Small's (1966) discussion of the usefulness of dichotomised variables. It takes into account the fact that, while many variables may predict success or failure, few students will show all the characteristics of success or failure. Chapter 6 shows clearly that the *number* of indicators of success, or symptoms of failure, is a much better predictor of academic performance than any single variable. The ability to utilise appropriate threshold values in combination and the simplicity of the statistical procedure are important advantages of this method. One weakness is that each variable was given an equal weighting (although this is not a necessary feature of the method) and that the effect of particular combinations of variables could not be identified.

The cluster analyses reported in Chapter 10 grew out of the work of Walton, Drewery and Philip (1964). These analyses have the advantage of producing varying *combinations* of attributes which are related to academic performance. Yet the statistical method is far from transparent, and it is too early to be sure that statistical artefacts are not interfering with the interpretations. The crucial importance of both methods is that they direct attention to the way different combinations of variables may lead to the same level of academic performance. Once this is recognised more complex explanations of success and failure should follow.

What did these methods show? At first sight the results may not seem to take us much further. In the Aberdeen study failure was related mainly to scholastic attainment, particularly to re-sit examinations, to headteachers' ratings on the check list and, to a lesser extent, to low motivation, poor study methods and, for women, stability. Reversing the directions of these variables, and omitting stability, would provide a useful set of indicators of success. In the AID analyses of the Rowntree study, dichotomised variables were used to maximise the

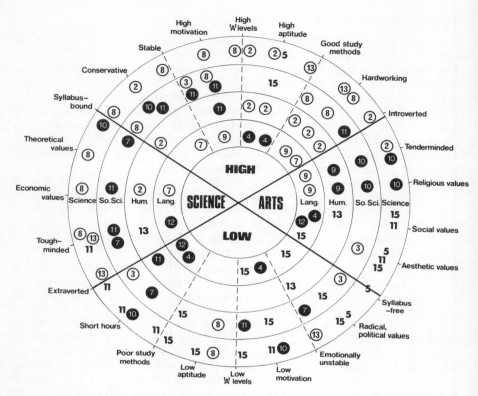

Figure 11.1 Circular representation of main defining characteristics of clusters within four subject areas.

Note: numbers refer to cluster notation given in Table 10.1. High attainment clusters are circled; average attainment clusters are shown as white numbers on black; the remaining cluster numbers relate to low levels of attainment.

prediction of academic performance. Similar predictive variables were found here. 'A' level grades, verbal aptitude (arts only), hard-working, motivation, hours studied and introversion (science only) distinguished between students with high and low criterion scores.

When it comes to summarising the relocation cluster solutions, no simple structure can be seen at first sight. But if the clusters are described in terms of their main defining variables, a pattern emerges. Figure 11.1 presents the main defining characteristics of the clusters created in the four area of study analyses. The main variables are shown around the circumference of the outer circle and the concentric bands represent the various areas of study with numbers of the clusters (see Table 10.2) shown in different lettering to indicate high, average or low levels of performance. The variables have been ordered, partly in terms of factor structure reported in Chapter 9 and partly through the consistent patterns which emerged. Again the idea of indicators of

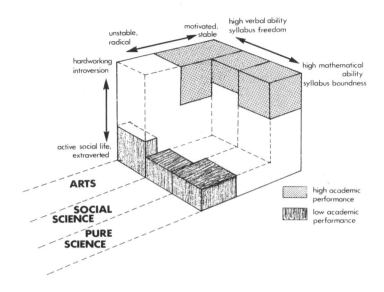

Figure 11.2 A factor-analytic model of academic performance for three areas of study

success and symptoms of failure reappears. The resultant structure seems to indicate that some variables (or poles) are characteristically associated with success or failure. Other variables are neutral, being associated with success or failure depending on other characteristics of the cluster. In these 'neutral' variables there is, however, an area of study bias; a theoretical, economic and toughminded orientation is found mainly among scientists, while social and aesthetic values predominate, as we found in earlier analyses, among arts students. Although the defining characteristics are not totally separate, there are only two low-performance clusters showing any indicator of success. There are more successful groups with symptoms of failure, but each cluster has at least one opposite characteristic which would indicate high performance. Figure 11.1 represents our first attempt at developing a model of academic attainment.

Another way of summarising the relationships found in the analyses is to return to the factor analyses reported in Chapter 9. One of the main factors was arts/science-related and contrasted verbal aptitude and syllabus-freedom with mathematical aptitude. The other two dimensions, after graphical rotation, became stable motivation/unstable radicalism and hard-working introversion/sociable extraversion. Again a simple descriptive model can be devised to show where, within this structure, successful or failing students are most likely to be found for three main areas of study (Figure 11.2).

This model shows that for a set of moderate 'A' level grades success will be associated with motivation, hard work and stable introversion, in different degrees in the three main areas. Instability is less of a hindrance in arts than in science, while hard work counts for more in arts.

For students with higher 'A' level grades the volume of the 'successful' area at the top of the model would increase, particularly in the sciences, while the 'poor performance' at the bottom would shrink accordingly, indicating the proportion of good and poor degree results to be expected with those entry qualifications. The reverse effect would be expected for students with weak 'A' levels on entry. The relative changes in the 'poor' and 'successful' areas would be largest for science and smallest for social science, indicating the extent to which 'A' level grades are related to performance.

Both the two models so far described have attractive features. They summarise earlier research findings in a simple manner, which aids the description of factors associated with success and failure in higher education. But they have major weaknesses. They do not, for example, help us a great deal towards *understanding* the processes involved in success and failure. They emphasise the elements which are predictable and ignore chance effects—the error variance, which in human terms, may have its own significance. And finally both models are static, while the results showed that students changed in their levels of motivation, attitudes and attainment over the three-year period. Neither the cluster model, nor the cube, could represent changing patterns of performance. So we must look for a dynamic model which incorporates chance, as well as predictable, aspects of academic performance.

It was not easy to see how to produce a model with characteristics of both chance and movement. The most obvious analogy was with the Grand National. The horses are engaged in a race in which they face obstacles. Their ability to clear these obstacles depends on predictable factors, such as strength, timing and speed, but also on chance factors, such as slippery ground or fallen horses. This analogy proved helpful in formulating our final model, which is presented as a type of 'parlour game'. At first sight it may seem to trivialise our research findings, but TAAG—the academic achievement game—does bring together more features of our research than the other models, and also allows the chance factors to be described—although here we have to rely on intuition as much as on our research.

The course is shown in Figure 11.3. There are three tracks, or faculties, representing arts, social science and science, and along each track are a variety of 'hazards', 'bonuses' and 'chance' elements in the form of squares which either assist or retard progress in a way which will be described shortly.

The players (students) are presented with different starting conditions. First they assign themselves to different intellectual levels (perhaps this might eventually be done by a test of conceptual ability). Each player is given a die representing intellectual ability. There are three different types of dice numbered 1 - 6 (low ability), 2 - 7 (medium

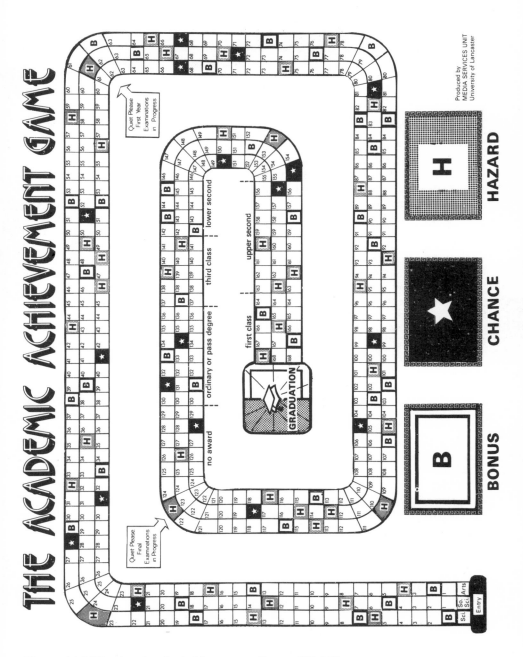

Figure 11.3 The Academic Achievement Game (TAAG)

ability) and 3 - 8 (high ability). The next starting condition is based on 'A' level grades. In science, 'high' 'A' level grades (better than BBB) allow two free throws; in arts, 'high' and 'medium' grades both allow one extra throw; while 'A' level grades do not produce differential starting conditions along the social science 'track'. An additional starting condition for each track represents the probable advantage of independence in studying being fostered in secondary school (see Thompson, 1976): students who have been trained to work by themselves are allowed one free throw.

The final starting condition depends mainly on the cluster analyses. Players are assigned coloured 'counters' according to four student 'types'; stable and motivated (orange); anxious, fear of failure (black); extraverted, syllabus-free (green); idle and unmotivated (brown). It would, of course, be possible to use questionnaires to assign players to appropriate 'types', but this starting condition (and that of ability) is not irrevocably fixed thereafter. A further dynamic feature of the model is provided by the 'chance' squares (stars). A player landing on one of these squares draws a 'chance' card which may lead to him changing the 'type' to which he was originally assigned (in line with the changes found in the research findings). A player whose counter lands on a 'hazard' or 'bonus' square picks up a card from the appropriate pack, which assigns a penalty or an advantage respectively.

Our research showed that student types might well be affected differentially by events encountered in higher education. For example, extraverts would be more likely to be distracted by social 'hazards', and unmotivated students by almost any potentially distracting event. Thus the cards carry different penalties and bonuses for each student type, and players choose the appropriate penalty or advantage according to the colour of their counter. Our psychometric research did not indicate which of these 'chance' factors would affect academic performance, but interviews with students (Entwistle, Thompson and Wilson, 1974; Thompson, 1976) and the follow-up of Aberdeen 'drop-outs' did provide some indications of which events to include. The contents of the various packs of cards, together with notional penalties and advantages are shown in Figure 11.4. The rules for the game are shown in full in Appendix D.

The object of the game is to get a good degree. The player(s) with most free throws start first, and the other players then throw their dice in turn. There can be several players in each faculty and each track finishes separately. When the first student in a faculty gets to 'Graduation' the results for the other students in that faculty are then read off from their position on the board. The winner must get a score which takes him the exact number of moves into 'Graduation', and he cannot move closer than the lowest number on his dice. However, after waiting three throws, a player may proceed to 'Graduation' on the fourth throw irrespective of whether he has got the exact number of moves or not.

TAAG was first played in June 1975 with senior pupils at Craigmount High School, Edinburgh. A more sophisticated version was included in the Minus One (Pre-Sessional) programme offered to

Figure 11.4 Chance elements in TAAG (contents of card packs)

Chance Pack

1. You are injured in a car accident.   Repeat the year—go back to starting point.

2. You become pregnant (females only!)   If 'black' or 'brown' retire from the game. If 'orange' or 'green' miss three throws.

3. Your study methods are increasingly effective.   If 'moderate' or 'low' ability change to next higher dice. If 'higher ability' take one free throw.

4. You no longer see any point in studying.   If 'orange' or 'black' change to 'brown'. If 'green' miss one throw.

5. You decide you want a good degree.   If 'brown' change to 'orange'. If 'green' take one extra throw.

6. You find student politics more interesting than academic study.   If 'orange' change to 'green'. If 'brown' take one extra throw.

7. You decide on a career.   If 'brown' change to 'orange'. If 'green' or 'black' take one extra throw.

8. Your study methods are increasingly ineffective.   If 'high' or 'moderate' ability change to next lower dice. If 'low ability' miss one throw.

9. You are converted to an obscure religious faith.   If 'green' change to 'orange'. If 'black' or 'brown' take one extra throw.

10. Ignore the next chance card you draw.

11. Ignore the next hazard card you draw.

12. Ignore the next bonus card you draw.

	Number of Throws Missed			
	Stable and motivated (Orange)	Fear of failure (Black)	Syllabus-free sociable, (Green)	Idle and unmotivated (Brown)
13. You are wrongly arrested at a demonstration.	1	2	1	1
14. You settle for a lower second/ ordinary degree.	3	2	1	1
15. Your lecture notes are stolen.	2	4	1	1
16. You mistake the date of a vital examination.	1	2	1	2

Figure 11.4 cont.

Hazard Pack	Bonus and Penalty Scores (Number of Squares Moved)			
	Stable and motivated (*Orange*)	Fear of failure (*Black*)	Syllabus-free sociable, (*Green*)	Idle and unmotivated (*Brown*)
1. Lectures are boring.	–2	0	–2	–4
2. You get a lower essay mark than you expect.	+2	–2	–2	0
3. The course is badly organised.	0	–4	–2	–2
4. Your tutor is very sarcastic.	–2	–6	–2	0
5. You do badly in the class exam.	–4	–4	–2	–2
6. You cannot get the recommended books.	–2	–2	–4	0
7. Your flat mates interrupt your work.	–2	–4	–4	–6
8. You feel you have no friends.	0	–4	0	–2
9. You play for the second fifteen.	0	0	–2	–6
10. You feel sure your friends are talking about you.	0	–4	0	–2
11. You worry about your work.	+2	+2	–2	–2
12. You feel sure you have an incurable illness.	0	–4	0	–2
13. You become Secretary of the Radical Society.	0	0	–2	–6
14. You work in a bar in the evenings.	0	-2	0	–3
15. You get a lead part in the Dramatic Society Play.	0	0	–4	–4
16. Your father dies.	–2	–6	–4	–4
17. You worry about money.	–2	–4	–2	–4
18. You start guitar lessons.	0	+2	–6	–4
19. You have a bad dose of 'flu.	–4	–4	–4	–4
20. You fall in love.	0	+4	–4	–6

'Freshers' to Edinburgh University in October 1975, and 201 students participated. Versions have been used with first-year B.Ed. and College of Education Primary Diploma students at Edinburgh University and Moray House College of Education, and with senior fifth- and sixth-year university-potential pupils at Peebles High School. Preliminary analysis provide an indication of how far the model corresponds to the 'reality' of our empirical data. A more detailed report is being prepared (Wilson, 1977).

Results were available for 188 students, and of those 57 (30 per cent)

Figure 11.4 cont.

Bonus Pack	Bonus and Penalty Scores (Number of Squares Moved)			
	Stable and motivated (*Orange*)	Fear of failure (*Black*)	Syllabus-free sociable, (*Green*)	Idle and unmotivated (*Brown*)
1. You have an inspiring lecturer.	+5	+3	+1	0
2. You find you have covered much of the syllabus at school.	+1	+5	0	0
3. Your tutor is sympathetic.	+3	+5	+1	0
4. You discuss the course with your friends.	+1	+5	+1	+3
5. Your exam results are outstanding.	+5	+3	+3	+1
6. The department is well organised and helpful.	+3	+5	+1	+1
7. Your tutorial group is stimulating and constructive.	+5	+3	+5	+1
8. The Professor agrees to consider you for entry to the Honours class.	+3	+5	+1	+1
9. Your practical work is praised by the tutor.	+3	+5	+1	+1
10. You get 'hooked' on a subject you have encountered for the first time.	+3	+3	+5	+3
11. A friend helps you to get access to the recommended books.	+3	+5	+3	+1
12. You get a broad hint from a tutor as to what will be in the examination.	+3	+5	+1	+1
13. You get better marks than expected for your essay.	0	+3	+1	0
14. Your adviser discusses your career with you.	0	+3	0	+5
15. Your flat mates are conscientious workers.	+1	+1	+3	+3
16. Your parents send you a £10 cheque for your birthday.	0	0	+3	+3
17. You have a quiet place to work.	+3	+3	0	0

were outright winners by getting to 'Graduation', while another 70 (38 per cent) took lower-second-class honours degrees or better. Twenty-two (12 per cent) got third-class or pass degrees, and 39 (20 per cent) got 'no award'. These results are not dissimilar to those reported in the Aberdeen Study (Table 6.1). In the game, too, ability was clearly related to performance, with only 4 per cent of high-ability students, and 46 per cent of low-ability students failing to graduate. Personality type was also related to performance. Stable motivated students (orange) did best, with 82 per cent getting a second-class degree or better, while in arts and science unmotivated (brown) and anxious (black) students did equally badly. When ability and personality were both controlled it became clearer that personality was not a factor in performance amongst students who had rated themselves 'high' on ability: in other words the 'high' die was outweighing the values on the 'bonus' and 'hazard' cards. On the other hand, at other ability levels, the interaction with personality was apparent: low ability students who chose 'black' did worst, with 55 per cent getting 'no award'.

While students found TAAG, like many games, a reasonably enjoyable 'ice breaker' which was interesting and worth playing, almost two in three rated it as 'unhelpful' for thinking about university life. There was evidence that some had unrealistic expectations of the game, but the major reason for this rating was that students did not have an opportunity to discuss the rationale of the game, an omission which several pointed out in their comments. Many criticised TAAG for over-emphasising 'chance' as a factor in student performance, while others felt that TAAG lacked sophistication, giving too little scope for decision-making once the initial ability and personality allocations had been settled.

Reality, of course, is complex, and to mirror it too faithfully may be self-defeating. TAAG already has considerable complexity with its thirty-six different student types (faculty × ability × personality), and it combines both personal attributes and situational variables, as well as coping with predictability, chance and change. No doubt it could be developed further, both by using computer 'games' to establish appropriate parameters in the light of empirical relationships (for example, with 'A' level grades), and by investigating which specific 'hazards', 'bonuses' and 'chances' factors might be expected to occur most frequently. But in its present form TAAG does seem worth serious consideration because it incorporates, admittedly somewhat crudely, many of the components of academic success and failure within a conceptually simple structure. And it appears to reflect, in its outcomes, the patterns of performance which our empirical studies have portrayed.

TAAG also fulfils other functions which should not be forgotten, and which may be even more important in the long run. It makes students reflect on their own capabilities, and the range of factors which affect their success and failure at university. It also communicates some of the academic research findings on student performance which may be highly relevant for the student, and which may make him more conscious of the need to plan his own survival. TAAG, besides being fun to play, is both a means to enlightenment and a vehicle for the dissemination of academic knowledge.

Chapter Twelve

Implications for Action

To end with a *game* for understanding 'degrees of excellence' in academic performance may seem a long way from our starting point. We anticipated the creation of rather more precise models of student achievement out of our psychometric approaches. Such precision proved impossible and, with changes in the research climate, our conclusions are perhaps acceptable. In education there has been a shift away from objective and static measurement—what Parlett and Hamilton (1972) have called the agricultural-botany paradigm—towards approaches associated with social anthropology, for example depth interviews and various forms of observation. The Rowntree project followed this drift to some extent (Entwistle, 1974b) by using fairly open interviews with students in universities, polytechnics and colleges of education (Thompson, 1976). Although the interviews have not been fully analysed, some of the students' comments, together with the responses of the Aberdeen students who failed, have helped to fill out, but loosen, the psychometric evidence into our academic achievement game.

In educational research it is safer to present statistical findings and conclude with 'suggestions for further research'. In this way controversial areas of policy are avoided. But if research is to be useful, possible implications for action must be pointed out by those closest to the data, even though their value judgements may intrude. Charles Carter (1972) has expressed his views forcefully on this issue:

> 'The purpose of research into higher education, for most of us, is a practical one. We do not want merely to describe the quaint or awful things which are going: we want to make things better... So I hope that in planning research, you will... refrain from chasing along familiar paths and surrounding what you find with a spurious appearance of erudition; and see if your colleagues can be helped with some of the simple and obvious faults which have persisted in higher education for too long' (pp. 1-3).

This final chapter represents an attempt to relate our findings back to the general framework described in the first chapter. Selection, guidance and choice were then seen as our prime targets, with implications for teaching as another possibility. With hindsight there are ways in which our studies might have been modified to make the findings more directly relevant to important educational issues. Gaps in our explanations of academic performance make the drawing of inferences hazardous, but the findings of the two studies, the interview data, and the experience of working in this field for some six years do provide a basis from which to discuss educational practice.

The implications we identify go beyond the scope of our statistical analyses, opening up additional questions on which evidence will have to be sought. In choosing, at times, to be bold in our extrapolations, we recognise the danger of losing the strength of implications which rely more directly on evidence. However, research findings in education have a dual function. They stimulate other research workers to seek the missing evidence and they also act as an irritant to 'conventional wisdom', challenging the validity of existing practices which may have become habitual. Education is inherently conservative. Change in higher education, though conspicuous at the institutional level, is almost imperceptible where it relates to teaching and learning. The recent Nuffield survey of innovations in British higher education (Becher *et al.*, 1975) was not called *The Drift of Change* without good reason. The implications of our findings should thus be treated as a challenge to existing practice from a research base, rather than as conclusive evidence for the changes we suggest.

Selection and wastage

It is tempting but quite misleading to see the problem of wastage as basically one of improved selection. Of course there is a connection, but our results confirm other findings that high correlations between school and university measures are rare, and that wastage rates reflect interactions between characteristics of the student and the academic environment he encounters. Let us look first at the implications of basing selection for higher education on school attainment. Correlations between 'A' level grades and degree results rarely exceed 0.5. In mathematics and certain science courses such grades provide a reasonable indication of degree performance, but paradoxically it is in some of these departments where selection is now the least rigorous. In other areas of study, where correlations are too low to be useful, 'A' level grades remain an important selection device. It is not clear, however, how far the implications of this paradox should be pushed. School attainment still seems the logical and most objective (if inaccurate) mechanism for selecting students, but the low levels of relationship, compared with relatively high correlations formerly found at 11+, must surely make us think twice before accepting the existing situation.

What should be done? The first possibility would be to seek supplementary evidence before offering places to students. Our findings suggest that only in certain areas (for example, in languages) would aptitude test scores be useful, but the Aberdeen data did indicate the potential value of rating scales used by headteachers. Even though some schools might resist an apparently mechanistic rating procedure, the combination of report and ratings (including estimated 'A' level or SCE grades) would almost certainly boost the accuracy of selection. More work would, however, be needed on the most appropriate form

such ratings should take, as there are varying estimates of the validity
of this approach (Powell, 1973; SCEEB, 1974) and Nisbet and Welsh
(1966) suggested that such ratings were least helpful where they are
most needed—at the borderlines of admission.

An alternative response to finding low correlations with school
attainment would be to introduce a more open entry to higher education, together with a higher failure rate after one year. This procedure
is, however, known to create dissatisfaction on the Continent where
there is a large failure rate during the course. Besides introducing a
social factor, this would put great weight on the reliability and validity
of university assessments. Instead we should perhaps examine again
reasons for the weak relationships between scholastic attainment and
degree performance. Apart from possibilities already mentioned, such
as homogeneity of sample and unreliability of measures, another
explanation might be a disparity between the education given at
school and in higher education. If school attainment and university
degree results depend on different skills, or if quite different methods of
studying led to high marks in the two sections of education, low
correlations are unavoidable. But *are* the experiences of school and
university so different? Wankowski (1973) argues convincingly on the
basis of interviews with students at Birmingham University that there
is indeed a gulf between methods of teaching and 'reward systems' (the
basis on which marks are rewarded) in school and in higher education.
In the sixth form the teacher-pupil relationship is often close, the
pupil's working habits are controlled by the teacher, there are generally many small pieces of work done on a regular basis and the external
examination syllabuses clearly define what must be known by the end
of the course: teacher and pupil work together in overcoming a 'common enemy'—the external examiners. At university the student may
encounter what seems to be an impersonal, and confusing, situation.
He may find large first-year classes, ill-defined course objectives,
infrequent assessment of progress and many lecturers who do not see
themselves primarily as teachers. In addition students and staff find
themselves on opposite sides of the assessment 'war' in most universities. If the learning environments at school and in higher education are
so different, it cannot be surprising to find that in many subject areas
personality characteristics, allied to conscientiousness and clarity of
purpose, are as important in determining success and failure in higher
education as are marks awarded at 'A' level. Chance too will play a
greater part if students are not being shown how to acquire effective
study strategies and are uncertain of what is required of them.

One possible remedy, both to inaccurate selection and to some of the
causes of student failure, would thus involve matching teaching
methods across this educational watershed. Following Wankowski's
arguments, it seems that the present courses in secondary school may
not provide an effective preparation for the more independent work
demanded in higher education. Unfortunately recent discussions
about new examinations in England and Wales have not taken
account of this problem; the 'N' and 'F' proposals (Schools Council,

1973) would not guarantee any greater independence in studying. Scotland has a more promising development in the Certificate of Sixth Year Studies (CSYS). As Highers are taken by the ablest pupils after five years in the secondary school (entry is at 12+ in Scotland), this sixth year could become a preparation for higher education. To date there is, however, little evidence that the year is being used in this way. For example, McPherson and Neave (1976) have shown that only about one in five entrants to university take CSYS alone in the sixth year, and success in this certificate does not appear to correlate with first-year performance at university. Nevertheless the examination structure in Scotland would allow the sixth year to be used to encourage independent learning.

In England the Schools Council rejected the earlier "Q' and 'F' proposals, mainly because they involved external examinations in three consecutive years. The 'N and F' system (Schools Council, 1973) concentrates on avoiding examinations in the first year of the sixth form, but an alternative approach might be to abandon *external* assessment in the final year. If 'N' levels were externally examined at age seventeen and the final year in school involved higher-level work assessed by teachers with their marks moderated on the basis of 'N' level results for the class (teachers decide the rank order; examination boards decide the standards), the final year could be spent either in school, where independent learning and project work could be encouraged, or in further education, where work experience and appropriate vocational courses would also be available.

Even if it proved impossible to introduce such a fundamental change into the English system, much could still be done within a more traditional examination scheme to smooth the transition from school to higher education. But, of course, universities and colleges would also have to change their approaches. On the whole, they do not make it at all easy for students to recognise, and adapt to, the different educational demands being made in higher education. First-year courses need to be planned with a clear recognition that it is sixth-formers, not fully prepared students, who are entering higher education. Current arrangements for induction are minimal and emphasise social integration, not the starting-point of three or more years of academic study along lines which are very different from school. Courses which started with more structure, with more opportunity for regular advice and assessment of progress, and with clearly specified objectives and syllabuses, might help students to appreciate the value of academic goals, as opposed to the vocational or social benefits which most students in the Aberdeen study were seeking.

A smoother, and more carefully planned, academic transition from school to higher education would avoid many of the initial difficulties, but student wastage cannot be attributed solely to inadequate preparation. Wastage varies from department to department and, as Beard and her co-workers (1962) showed clearly, a departmental ethos can affect students' attainment. Certainly attitudes may depend on staff-student relationships and on the way students perceive the 'academic game'. Interviews conducted as part of the Rowntree studies (Entwistle and Percy, 1971; 1974; Entwistle *et al.*, 1974) throw up similar impressions to those recently reported by Miller and Parlett (1974). Staff and students view academic attainment in contrasting, even opposed, ways, In the Rowntree interviews many lecturers grumbled about a type of student who 'is not very well motivated . . . [and who] takes the courses largely because he likes other courses less. He may even be doing his whole degree on this basis . . . He's only attending university because there's nothing else more intelligent occurred to him to do.' But staff attitudes are not always geared to student realities. Staff seem at times to inhabit a dream world of idealised past experiences and expectations based on a dwindling proportion of exceptional students who share their own enthusiasm for the intellectual life. Yet in our Aberdeen study we found only one student in ten giving academic or subject interest as his main reason for being at university.

It is certainly reasonable for lecturers to find apathy discouraging. But who is to blame? Most lecturers were quick to castigate unmotivated students, but slower to point out a puzzling feature of this lack of concern:

> 'The main trouble is unwillingness to get down to work, but having said this, there is no doubt . . . a paradox . . . in that at some time in the past, in order for a person to have got here presumably he had been willing, and something is going on which diminishes this willingness.'

As far as students were concerned, there was no paradox:

> 'So often are students bored by uninspired teaching or disenchanted by badly taught material. While university lecturers are undoubtedly knowledgeable they are totally untrained and unexamined in the art of communication . . . The completely incorrect assumption is that anyone with a good degree will automatically be able to impart this knowledge to others.'

Our task is not to attribute blame. Students are, of course, responsible up to a point for their own lack of motivation, but inadequate teaching must make their task unnecessarily difficult. The Hale Committee (1964) stressed the importance of training lecturers to teach effectively, but without much avail. There are still few compulsory induction courses. Without doubt there are many talented lecturers who, without any formal training, have inspired generations of students. But presenting a lecture to a large class, or conducting an imaginative tutorial, does involve special skills of which lecturers should at least be aware. Why should we expect all school teachers to spend at least a full year in training and yet allow academics to start teaching without any professional preparation at all? Wankowski (1973) saw poor tuition as one of the basic factors in explaining academic failure. Much could be done to help tutors adopt a more professional approach to teaching and to the planning of new courses (Entwistle, 1977). Induction courses alone, would, of course, have little effect. Incentives are needed to improve teaching and various possibilities (including promotion) have been suggested by Fielden and Lockwood (1973). But, in addition, an investment of time and money is needed for curriculum development in higher education. The coherence of courses developed by the course teams of the Open University shows the kind of pay-off that systematic planning can bring. A funding agency for tertiary education, equivalent to the Schools Council, is urgently needed to encourage a systematic re-examination of curricula and methods of teaching across all the sectors of higher and further education.

So far we have discussed failure at university in terms of discontinuities in teaching methods, lack of student motivation, and standards of tuition. But the definition of failure itself is variable; it is not determined entirely by academic standards. Failure is often defined by individual faculties or departments and may involve inflexible regulations, or even built-in failure rates. Although universities and colleges are becoming more student-orientated, their degree structures are rooted firmly in their historical origins. Requirements which made sense in the last century, or even ten years ago, may no longer be appropriate. Students may still be required to conform to a lock-step formula in which they progress from year to year, fulfilling specific requirements at each stage. Where there is formality and inflexibility, failure may occur for the wrong reasons. Our case studies in Aberdeen produced multifarious explanations of failure, but chance did seem to play an important part in deciding the few who failed outright, out of the large number at risk. Some of these students had apparently been unfortunate in choosing courses with persistently high failure rates, or they may have been handicapped by recurring minor illnesses or by emotional problems. One advantage of the newer universities is that they have been able to devise more humane procedures for deciding whether students are allowed to continue their studies. Some formal requirements are, of course, essential but it seems pointless to eject students according to well-worn procedures which take insufficient account of individual circumstances.

Our point is not to challenge the right of departments to fail inadequate students, but rather to question the practice of 'pushing out' students who are failing to progress at a pre-determined rate. Many of those who are sent down subsequently return to take degrees, or they complete equivalent courses in other institutions. Of course many academics would argue that substantial failure rates in the first year have a purpose—*pour encourager les autres*. The shock of failure can be a necessary stimulus for some individuals, as well as a warning for others. We agree, too, that adequate levels of performance must be maintained, and it *would* be detrimental to make the outcome of the first year a foregone conclusion. But can this argument be stretched so as to justify the harsh penalty of a 'year in the wilderness', no matter what the circumstances? A high failure rate in a degree course is more likely to reflect unexamined assumptions about student progress, or a Procrustean degree structure, than to represent an important force in preserving academic standards. In the Scottish context, for example, the older universities have defined the number of subjects to be taken and the number of passes to be obtained by the end of the first year. It seems to us that students with a relatively poor academic record should be encouraged to tackle fewer subjects in their first year while they adjust to new academic demands. Implementation of this proposal would not mean a reduction of degree standards, but simply the acceptance of a transitional period during which students would be allowed a slower rate of progress. There is little reason to insist on all students progressing at a uniform rate throughout their three or four years in higher education; it is the final standard which is important.

Wastage, then, is not explicable solely in the terms of our original research designs. The results summarised in the previous chapter allowed us to describe the various types of students who were at risk of failure and to identify factors associated with poor performance, but the problem of wastage cannot be dissociated from the total context. The match between teaching methods at school and in higher education, the quality of instruction and the formal requirements which define failure, must all form part of any full explanation of student failure. It is within this total setting that suggestions for change must be presented.

Guidance and choice

Guidance and choice, in a sense, present alternatives to wastage and selection, at least in terms of emphasis. Do we stress the need to improve methods of selection or look for ways of helping students to find the most suitable course for themselves? Do we examine failure rates or consider the provision of adequate counselling arrangements? The questions present false alternatives, but do draw attention to contrasting sets of attitudes. In higher education the traditional emphasis has been on the demands of the institution—*its* entrance standards and *its* degree requirements. In recent years thinking has been related more to the student—*his* choice of courses and *his* problems in adjusting to the demands of the institution. This changing emphasis has led to greater attention being given to counselling.

The responsibility for providing advice and guidance again must be shared between schools and universities or colleges. At school level there is much room for improvement. In Scotland, although a massive guidance system has been introduced in secondary schools (including approximately ten per cent of the entire teaching force), few of the staff have been systematically trained; there is considerable confusion over the aims of the service and wide variation in practice (McDonald, 1974). In England and Wales there are few trained counsellors, and careers teachers often retain substantial teaching commitments. Yet the task of keeping up to date with changes in higher education alone is a full time job. The range of courses is vast and the literature surrounding them is growing rapidly.

Pupils have a right to expect counselling procedures which give full and careful consideration of their own individual interests. They require, if they are to choose wisely, detailed information about the way courses are taught, about entrance standards and about the academic record of departments. Our findings do not simplify the task of the sixth-former; in fact they add to its complexity by pointing to additional considerations. The way personality and values varied characteristically between areas of study suggests that pupils should also ask, or be asked, whether they are temperamentally suited to the courses for which they intend to apply. For many pupils their growing liking of particular school subjects probably means that the matching process is fairly well advanced, but 'all-rounders' and those who look towards non-school subjects in higher education may still have considerable difficulties in making an appropriate choice. The importance of matching students and courses was shown in our cluster analyses, where, for example, scientists with the characteristics of arts students tended to do rather badly. But we are not arguing for psychometric matching procedures; we accept Baird's (1974) strictures on such attempts. All we are suggesting is that pupils should be made aware of the need to examine themselves in relation to the courses they decide to take. Recent work on the psychology of occupational choice (Whiteley and Resnikoff, 1972) has drawn attention not only to the matching process, using for example Holland's (1973) typology of personality and occupations, but also to the evolutionary nature of occupational preferences (Crites, 1969).

Advice would help sixth-formers in making these choices, but we still know all too little about the strategies pupils adopt in dealing with the many alternatives they face. It is not just a matter of which course: the logically prior question is whether to enter higher education at all. Pupils should surely be encouraged to examine carefully their reasons for accepting or rejecting opportunities for continuing their education. At present there are fluctuations in the demand for higher education of an apparently capricious nature. These variations could represent cavalier acceptance of employment prospects and student stereotypes projected by the media. Advice to pupils should bring them face to face with their future. Why are they deciding for or against higher education? Are the reasons based on a full understanding of the consequences? Counselling, to be effective, is more than presenting appropriate information and making suggestions. Watts (1972) has suggested that British schools are inclined to take a fairly directive role in advising their pupils on their choice of education, and quotes Daws (1968) as saying: 'a decision based on a recommendation is not genuinely one's own, for one has not earned it by dint of hours of information processing and self-evaluation, and one therefore cannot feel thoroughly identified with it' (Watts, 1972, p. 213). Watts suggests that pupils and students will choose appropriate courses if they are counselled, rather than merely informed about the alternatives. The counselling approach avoids both categorical recommendations and impersonal presentation of information; it encourages the pupil to come to terms with the emotional factors underlying future choices.

The case for an expanded counselling system in higher education surely does not need to be argued. Although Aberdeen University has a good reputation for the provision of advice, many of the students in our study felt in retrospect that they might have been better to study other subjects or to aim for honours rather than for ordinary degrees. But counselling should not be limited to advice on courses to be studied: even with much improved guidance facilites, students would still make faulty choices—though hopefully less frequently than at present. They would also run into unexpected difficulties. The TAAG model suggests a wide range of events which may influence student attainment, but students themselves are often unaware of factors which may be affecting their progress. The 'personal tutor' system may cope adequately with students with minor problems (the advice they require is generally within the competence of the 'amateur' counsellor), but when students present more serious problems, such as opting out of work, *professional* counsellors are essential. They have the time and experience to understand and sympathise with potential 'drop-outs' and there is evidence (Wankowski, 1973) that counselling facilities do, in fact, reduce wastage.

The analyses presented in earlier chapters should be of value to both counsellors and personal tutors. Besides providing evidence about factors associated with success and failure in higher education, the symptom approach and the descriptions of typical student 'clusters' suggest alternative ways of conceptualising and categorising these factors. Tutors will be well aware that there are different routes towards success and failure: the cluster analyses make the signposting of these routes a little clearer. Counsellors will recognise the dangers of simply using the clusters as convenient labels to categorise problem students. The clusters refer to *groups*; individuals rarely fit into our empirical categories at all closely. However, a discussion of a student's difficulties can be helped by having a general idea of how that student's characteristics fit into the general pattern provided by both the 'symptom' and the cluster analyses. We should like to see TAAG developed into a therapeutic device which might help students to view their experiences of higher education in a more objective way. Advance warning of possible difficulties might prevent problems; retrospective explanation in terms of commonly expected patterns may help a student to work his way out of difficulties already encountered.

It is possible that the scales of personality, motivation and study methods might also form the basis for a diagnostic instrument which would identify different types of study difficulty. These scales could perhaps be developed further by incorporating the more psychiatrically-orientated factors of Crown, Lucas and Supramaniam (1973). While the scales are not sufficiently reliable to provide an accurate indication of an *individual's* level of motivation, an examination of the pattern of item responses would provide a useful starting point to a guidance interview. The clinical situation would allow the counsellor to explore more fully areas of difficulty suggested by the questionnaire and so to identify the precise nature of the individual student's problems.

At present lecturers in higher education are slow to accept any need for systematic instruction in effective methods of studying, and yet many of them complain about the more obvious weaknesses they encounter in students. Although it is clear that students need to develop their own idiosyncratic patterns of effective study, provision of appropriate advice to students in difficulty would help to remove one source of unhappiness for the student and frustration for the tutor.

Styles of studying and methods of instruction

Lecturers can help students to adapt their methods of studying to the demands of the current system, but they should also take seriously the fact that students, when left to themselves, adopt widely different styles of studying. Hudson's description of a 'syllabus-bound/ syllabus-free' dimension has been followed by other similar distinctions. For example, Miller and Parlett (1974) have identified the 'cue seekers' and the 'cue blind' in their recent study of students' attitudes to assessment. In the Rowntree study we also found contrasting types of students which fit into this general pattern:

> 'Some students are stable, confident and highly motivated by hope for success, while others are anxious, uncertain of themselves and haunted by fear of failure, and yet both groups are capable of high levels of academic performance. The interview data take the differences even further. Students of differing personality and motivational types not only tackle their academic work in different ways but, from their descriptions of their university experience, they evidently perceive themselves to be in differing environments' (Entwistle, Thompson and Wilson, 1974, p.393).

What implications do these differences hold for course structures and for teaching methods? The basic essential is that course structures should accommodate these very different approaches to studying. At the moment students are normally required to follow a uniform diet of lectures, tutorials, practicals, essay writing, seminar preparation and so on. But there are now varied ways of presenting information (see, for example, MacKenzie, Eraut and Jones, 1970) and we are beginning to understand why students may learn more effectively with different modes of presentation.

> 'Lecturers should become more aware of the *proceses* of learning in planning courses. As the Nuffield Group (Becher *et al.*, 1975) pointed out, the lecturer is an expert in a subject area and this inevitably directs his attention towards the *content* of the course. The selection of methods of teaching has seemed almost an afterthought. . . .'
> 'If the individual differences of students are taken seriously, the implications are that alternative approaches to learning should be available. The traditional pattern of offering lectures and tutorials may, in part, be a recognition of this need to offer alternatives, but with the innovations in instructional methods now available, a much greater variety could be offered to students . . . If we add to this . . . the availability of learning materials carefully designed to follow principles of learning appropriate to the course and its objectives, perhaps we should be nearing an ideal arrangement. If students themselves were able to vary the mix at least to some extent, the guidelines provided in the research literature would have been followed to the letter' (Entwistle, 1975).

Another problem to be faced in trying to respond to the implications of our research is that of student motivation. In an earlier section contradictory views of staff and students were evident. We also showed that levels of motivation of some students changed drastically while they were at university. Students attributed these changes to poor teaching: staff saw the lack of motivation as a recent phenomenon attributable, perhaps, to a growing lack of purpose among students. As teaching involves communication, such opposed attitudes could prove a serious block. But did our selected comments highlight a non-existent problem? The Nuffield Group (Becher *et al.*, 1975) has also commented on similar difficulties in communication between staff and students:

> 'The "them-us" distinction was often alluded to; and it is not easily resolved. A genuine consensus of view between students and staff (rather than some form of armed neutrality) may in extreme cases prove impossible to achieve, so fundamental being the differences in life-styles and attitudes' (p. 44).

The potential conflict which is seen between staff and students should not be over-stated, but still merits serious thought. Confrontation in terms of barely overlapping frameworks of interpretation would not be conducive to effective teaching or learning. If both staff and students were made aware of the existence of these differing perspectives, the problem might vanish as each 'side' recognised some validity in the other's interpretation of the situation. Of course part of the problem may be a generation gap, exacerbated by the extreme anti-intellectual and irrational values which some students espouse. However, there is a middle ground which encourages imaginative thinking without denying the power of logic or the usefulness of evidence, and here staff and the majority of students might still communicate effectively.

Complementary approaches in research

At the beginning of this chapter we referred to a move towards research methods which emphasised observation and interviewing. This is surely a facet of a general change in intellectual climate, which many students have actively endorsed. Some may see this as a move away from scientific explanation towards 'irrational sentimentality', but that is too extreme a response. What is involved is no more than a redefinition, in more generous terms, of what is accepted as a scientific approach. The shift in emphasis indicates a recognition that one approach to educational research had become so dominant that alternative interpretations were being suppressed. It is easily forgotten that, especially in social science, explanations of human behaviour depend on the perceptions and pre-conceptions of the theorist. Dominant views are thus potentially restrictive, as Hoyle (1972) has pointed out in his own research area:

> 'We must be on our guard against being prisoners of the time-order in which information happens to be stored in our brains ... | and also recognise| that it is

completely useless to attempt to impress the way we happen to think on the world itself. The world is not open to persuasion' (pp. 8, 64-5).

The change in intellectual climate should perhaps be welcomed, albeit cautiously. Perhaps the pendulum should shift, to allow a fresh approach to educational research to emerge. But the reaction should not be extreme. There is no sense in abandoning psychometrics altogether in the search for intuitive certainty from observation. New methods of analyses—such as the symptom approach and techniques of clustering—help objective measurements to match reality more closely. And psychometric measurements allied to careful research design do allow a check to be made on observations which all too readily degenerate into unverifiable introspections and 'selected' supportive evidence. The way forward is surely to try to combine strategies in trying to understand human behaviour. Jaffé (1972) quotes Jung as saying:

'We shall probably have to resort to a mixed explanation, for nature does not give a fig for the sanatory neatness of our intellectual categories of thought' (p. 32).

The two studies we have reported here started with carefully constructed research designs within the psychometric paradigm—although practical constraints introduced some weaknesses into both. The difficulty we found in extrapolating our statistical results into the real world of lecturers and students is not uncommon, but it is an indictment of the traditional preoccupations of educational researchers.

Our solution was to draw on the interview data and inject a dose of intuition. The result was *The Academic Achievement Game* which provides, in some ways, an ideal conclusion. It represents an attempt to provide a potentially sophisticated, dynamic model to represent some of the complex human and social problems found in higher education. It lacks the precision of statistical models, but in its more direct links with students' descriptions of their perceptions of 'reality', it is in keeping with recent trends in research methodology. Finally it contains, in itself, a summary of the main implications we see in our findings. The game has starting conditions, one of which draws attention to the need for more independent work in the sixth form. The selection of appropriate 'tracks' or courses reminds us of help which counsellors may provide. The different coloured counters represent the individual differences between students. The 'hazards' and 'bonuses' around the track indicate some of the effects of teaching and interpersonal communication, besides the many other chance factors which affect student performance. The Academic Achievement Game thus represents our tentative attempt to illustrate and summarise the interwoven, yet changing, patterns of cause and effect which together may explain the varying *degrees of excellence* found among students.

References

ABELSON, R.P. (1952) Sex differences in predictability of college grades. *Educ. psychol. Measur.*, **12**, 638-44.

ALLPORT, G.W., VERNON, P.E., and LINDZEY, G. (1960) *A Study of Values* (third edition). Boston: Houghton Mifflin.

ALPERT, R., and HABER, R.N. (1960) Anxiety in academic achievement situations. *J. abnorm. soc. Psychol.*, **61**, 207-15.

ASTINGTON, E. (1960) Personality assessment and academic performance in a boys' grammar school. *Br. J. educ. Psychol.*, **30**, 225-36.

ATKINSON, J.W., and FEATHER, N.T. (1966) *A Theory of Achievement Motivation.* New York: Wiley.

AUSTWICK, K. (1960) GCE to BA. *Univ. Quart.*, **15**, 64-71.

AUSUBEL, D.P. (1968) *Educational Psychology: a Cognitive View.* New York: Holt, Rinehart and Winston.

BAGG, D.G. (1968) The correlation of GCE 'A' level grades with university examinations in chemical engineering. *Br. J. educ. Psychol.*, **38**, 194-7.

BAGG, D.G. (1970) 'A' levels and university performance. *Nature*, **225**, 21 March, 1105-8.

BAIRD, L.L. (1974) The practical utility of measures of college environment. *Rev. educ. Res.*, **44**, 307-29.

BARNETT, V.D., and LEWIS, T. (1963) Study of the relation between GCE and degree results. *J.R. statist. Soc.*, Series A, **126**, 187-226.

BEACH, L.R. (1960) Sociability and academic achievement in various types of learning situations. *J. educ. Psychol.*, **51**, 208-12.

BEARD, R.M., LEVY, P.M., and MADDOX, H. (1962) Academic performance at university. *Educ. Rev.*, **16**, 163-74.

BECHER, R.A., and co-authors (1975) *The Drift of Change.* London: Nuffield Foundation.

BECKER, H.S., GEER, B., and HUGHES, E.C. (1968) *Making the Grade--the Academic Side of College Life.* New York: Wiley.

BENDIG, A.W. (1960) Extraversion, neuroticism and student achievement in introductory psychology. *J. educ. Res.*, **53**, 263-7.

BIGGS, J. (1970a) Faculty patterns in study behaviour. *Aust. J. Psychol.*, **22**, 161-74.

BIGGS, J. (1970b) Personality correlates of certain dimensions of study behaviour. *Aust. J. Psychol.*, **22**, 287-97.

BIRNEY, R.C., BURDICK, H., and TEEVAN, R.C. (1969) *Fear of Failure.* New York: Van Nostrand.

BLAINE, G.B., and MCARTHUR, C.C. (1971) *Emotional Problems of the Student.* London: Butterworth.

BLOOM, B.S., and PETERS, F.R. (1962) *The Use of Academic Prediction Scales for Counselling and Selecting College Students.* Chicago: University of Chicago Press.

BRENNAN, T. (1972) Numerical taxonomy: theory and some applications in educational research. Unpublished Ph.D. thesis, University of Lancaster.

BROWN, E.M., and MCCOMISKY, J.G. (1955) Ex-National Service and 'schoolboy' undergraduates—a comparative study of academic performance. *Br. J. educ. Psychol.*, **25**, 55-9.

BROWN, W.F., and HOLTZMAN, W.H. (1955) A study-attitudes questionnaire for predicting academic success. *J. educ. Psychol.*, **46**, 75-84.

BROWN, W.F., and HOLTZMAN, W.H. (1966) *Manual of the Survey of Study Habits and Attitudes*. New York: Psychological Corp.

BURGESS, E. (1956) Personality factors of over- and under-achievers in engineering. *J. educ. Psychol.*, **47**, 89-99.

BUTCHER, H.J. (1968) University education. In BUTCHER, H.J. (ed.) *Educational Research in Britain, Volume 1*. London: University of London Press.

CARTER, C.F. (1972) Presidential Address. In *Innovation in Higher Education*. London: SRHE.

CATTELL, R.B. (1965) *The Scientific Analysis of Personality*. Harmondsworth: Penguin.

CHOPPIN, B.H.L., and co-authors (1972) *After A-Level ? A Study of the Transition from School to Higher Education*. Slough: NFER.

CHOPPIN, B.H.L., and co-authors (1973) *The Prediction of Academic Success*. Slough: NFER.

CLARK, B.R. (1960) The 'cooling-out' function in higher education. *Amer. J. Sociol.*, **65**, 569-76.

CLARK, B.R., and TROW, M. (1966) The organisational context. In NEWCOMB, T.M., and WILSON, E.K. (eds.) *College Peer Groups: Problems and Prospects for Research*. New York: Aldine.

CLARK, B.R., and co-authors (1972) *Students and Colleges: Interaction and Change*. University of California, Berkeley: Center for Research and Development in Higher Education.

COHEN, L., and CHILD, D. (1969) Some sociological and psychological factors in university failure. *Durham Res. Rev.*, **22**, 365-72.

COHEN, L., REID, I., and BOOTHROYD, K. (1973) Validation of the Mehrabian need for achievement scale with college of education students. *Br. J. educ. Psychol.*, **43**, 269-78.

COOPER, B., and FOY, J.M. (1969) Students' study habits, attitudes and academic attainment. *Univ. Quart.*, **23**, 203-12.

COWELL, M.D. (1970) An investigation of the reliabilities and a comparison of two instruments measuring motivation and study habits. Unpublished M.A. dissertation, University of Lancaster.

COWELL, M.D., and ENTWISTLE, N.J. (1971) Personality, study attitudes and academic performance in a technical college. *Br. J. educ. Psychol.*, **41**, 85-9.

COX, R. (1967) Examinations and higher education. *Univ. Quart.*, **21**, 292-340.

CRANO, W.L., KENNY, D.A., and CAMPBELL, D.T. (1972) Does intelligence cause achievement ? A cross-lagged panel analysis. *J. educ. Psychol.*, **63**, 258-75.

CRITES, J.O. (1969) *Vocational Psychology*. New York: McGraw-Hill.

CROWN, S., LUCAS, C.J., and SUPRAMANIAM, S. (1973) The delineation and measurement of study difficulty in university students. *Br. J. Psychiat.*, **122**, 381-93.

DALE, R.R. (1954) *From School to University*. London: Routledge and Kegan Paul.

DALE, R.R. (1963) Reflections on the influence of social class on student performance at university. *Sociol. Rev. Monogr.*, **7**, 131-40.

DARLINGTON, R.B., and STAUFFER, G.F. (1966) A method of choosing a cutting point on a test. *J. appl. Psychol.*, **50**, 229-31.

DAVY, B.W. (1960) The sources and prevention of mental ill-health in university students. *Proc. R. Soc. Med.*, **53**, 9.

DAWS, P.P. (1968) *A Good Start in Life*. Cambridge: Careers Research and Advisory Centre.

DREVER, J. (1963) Prediction, placement and choice in university selection. Godfrey Thomson Lecture, University of Edinburgh (reprinted in the Robbins Report, 1963, Appendix 2B, Annex A. London: HMSO).

EASTING, G. (1973) A multiple-choice approach to the measurement of achievement motivation and fear of failure in primary school children. Unpublished Ph.D. thesis, University of Lancaster.

ELTON, L.R.B. (1969) The making of physicists. *Physics Educ.*, **4**, 236-44.

ENTWISTLE, N.J. (1974a) Aptitude tests for higher education? *Br. J. educ. Psychol.*, **34**, 92-6.

ENTWISTLE, N.J. (1974b) Complementary paradigms for research and development work in higher education. In VERRECK, W.A. (ed.) *Methodological Problems in Research and Development in Higher Education*. Amsterdam: Swets and Zeitlinger.

ENTWISTLE, N.J. (1977) Approaches to teaching and learning: guidelines from research. In ENTWISTLE, N.J. (ed.) *Strategies for Research and Development in Higher Education*. Amsterdam: Swets and Zeitlinger.

ENTWISTLE, N.J., and BRENNAN, T. (1971) The academic performance of students II—Types of successful students. *Br. J. educ. Psychol.*, **41**, 268-76.

ENTWISTLE, N.J., and ENTWISTLE, D.M. (1970) The relationships between personality, study methods and academic performance. *Br. J. educ. Psychol.*, **40**, 132-41.

ENTWISTLE, N.J., and NISBET, J.D. (1972) *Educational Research in Action*. London: University of London Press.

ENTWISTLE, N.J., NISBET, J.B., ENTWISTLE, D.M., and COWELL, M.D. (1971) The academic performance of students I-Prediction from scales of motivation and study methods. *Br. J. educ. Psychol.*, **41**, 258-67.

ENTWISTLE, N.J., and PERCY, K.A. (1971) Educational objectives and student performance within the binary system. In *Research into Higher Education, 1970*. London: SRHE.

ENTWISTLE, N.J., and PERCY, K.A. (1974) Critical thinking or conformity? An investigation of the aims and outcomes of higher education. In *Research into Higher Education, 1973*. London: SRHE.

ENTWISTLE, N.J., PERCY, K.A., and NISBET, J.B. (1971) *Educational Objectives and Academic Performance in Higher Education*. Mimeographed Report, (2 vols). University of Lancaster: Department of Educational Research.

ENTWISTLE, N.J., THOMPSON, J.B., and WILSON, J.D. (1974) Motivation and study habits. *Higher Educ.*, **3**, 379-96.

ENTWISTLE, N.J., and WILSON, J.D. (1970) Personality, study methods and academic performance. *Univ. Quart.*, **24**, 147-56.

EVERITT, B. (1974) *Cluster Analysis*. London: SSRC and Heinemann.

EYSENCK, H.J. (1947) Student selection by means of psychological tests—a critical survey. *Br. J. educ. Psychol.*, **17**, 20-39.

EYSENCK, H.J. (1951) Social attitudes questionnaire and scoring key. *Br. J. Psychol.*, **42**, 114-22.

EYSENCK, H.J. (1957) *The Dynamics of Anxiety and Hysteria.* London: Routledge and Kegan Paul.

EYSENCK, H.J. (1965) *Fact and Fiction in Psychology.* Harmondsworth: Penguin.

EYSENCK, H.J. (1967) *The Biological Basis of Personality.* Springfield, USA: C.C. Thomas.

EYSENCK, H.J. (1970) *The Structure of Human Personality.* London: Routledge and Kegan Paul.

EYSENCK, H.J. (1972) Personality and attainment: an application of psychological principles to educational objectives. *Higher Educ.*, **1**, 39-52.

EYSENCK, H.J., and EYSENCK, S.B.G. (1964) *Manual of the Eysenck Personality Inventory.* London: University of London Press.

FELDMAN, K.A. (1972) *College and Student.* New York: Pergamon.

FELDMAN, K.A., and NEWCOMB, T.M. (1969) *The Impact of College on Students* (2 vols). New York: Jossey-Bass.

FIELDEN, J., and LOCKWOOD, G. (1973) *Planning and Management in the Universities: A Study of British Universities.* London: Chatto and Windus.

FINGER, J.A., and SCHLESSER, G.E. (1965) Non-intellective predictors of academic success in school and college. *School Rev.*, **73**, 14-29.

FISHMAN, J.A. (1962) Social-psychological theory for students. In SANFORD, N. (ed.) *The American College.* New York: Wiley.

FLETT, U., JONES, C., and MCPHERSON, A.F. (1971) Women entrants to universities and colleges of education. Paper read to Scottish Section of British Sociological Association at University of Stirling on 11th December, 1971.

FOREHAND, G.A., and MCQUITTY, L. (1959) Configurations of factor standings as predictors of educational achievement. *Educ. psychol. Measur.*, **19**, 31-43.

FORSTER, M. (1959) *An Audit of Academic Performance.* Belfast: Queens University.

FRASER, E.D. (1959) *Home Environment and the School.* London: University of London Press.

FURNEAUX, W.D. (1961) *The Chosen Few.* Oxford: University Press.

FURNEAUX, W.D. (1962) The psychologist and the university. *Univ. Quart.*, **17**, 33-47.

GAMMIE, A.J. (1963) The influence of a sixth year in school on academic performance at university. *Educ. Res.*, **6**, 77-9.

GOULD, E.M., and MCCOMISKY, J.G. (1958) Attainment level on leaving certificate and academic performance at university. *Br. J. educ. Psychol.*, **28**, 129-34.

Hale Committee (1964) *University Teaching Methods.* London: HMSO.

HEIM, A.W., and WATTS, K.P. (1960) An inquiry into the relationship between university career and scores on a high grade intelligence test. *Cambridge Rev.*, **81**, 463-9.

HEYWOOD, J. (1971) A report on student wastage. *Univ. Quart.*, **25**, 189-237.

HIMMELWEIT, H.T. (1950) Student selection: an experimental investigation. *Br. J. Sociol.*, **1**, 50-71.

HIMMELWEIT, H.T. (1963) Student selection—implications derived from two student selection enquiries. *Sociol. Rev. Monogr.*, **7**, 79-98.

HOARE, D.E., and YEAMAN, E. (1971) Patterns of teaching and learning of first-year Chemistry in Scottish Universities. *Scot. educ. Stud.*, **3**, 79-87.

HOLLAND, J.L. (1973) *Making Vocational Choices: a Theory of Careers.* Englewood Cliffs, N.J.: Prentice Hall.

HOPKINS, J., MALLESON, N., and SARNOFF, I. (1958) Some non-intellectual correlates of success and failure among university students. *Br. J. educ. Psychol.*, **28**, 25-36.

HOYLE, F. (1972) *From Stonehenge to Modern Cosmology.* San Fransisco: W.H. Freeman.

HUDSON, L. (1968) *Frames of Mind.* London: Methuen.

JAFFÉ, A. (1972) *From the Life and Work of C.G. Jung.* London: Hodder and Stoughton.

JONES, C.L., MACKINTOSH, H., and MCPHERSON, A.F. (1973a) The associations between various measures of SCE performance, academic achievement and wastage in the first year at Edinburgh University in 1969-70. University of Edinburgh: Centre for Educational Sociology.

JONES, C.L., MACKINTOSH, H., and MCPHERSON, A.F. (1973b) Questions of uncertainty: non-cognitive predictors of achievement. In PAGE, C.F., and GIBSON, J. (eds.) *Motivation: Non-Cognitive Aspects of Student Performance.* London: SRHE.

KELSALL, R. (1963) University student selection in relation to subsequent academic performance: a critical appraisal of the British evidence. *Sociol. Rev. Monogr.*, **7**, 99-115.

KELVIN, R.P., LUCAS, C.J., and OJHA, A.B. (1965) The relation between personality mental health and academic performance in university students. *Br. J. soc. clin. Psychol.*, **4**, 244-53.

KENDALL, M. (1964) Those who failed—I: the further education of former students. *Univ. Quart.*, **8,** 398-406.

KIRK, G., and CROCKETT, R.H. (1971) A validation study of the Aberdeen University bursary examination. *Scot. educ. Stud.*, **3**, 39-43.

KLINE, P., and GALE, A. (1971) Extraversion, neuroticism and performance in a psychology examination. *Br. J. educ. Psychol.*, **41**, 90-3.

KLINGENDER, F.D. (1955) Student recruitment in England. *Univ. Quart.*, **9,** 168-76.

LAVIN, D.E. (1965) *The Prediction of Academic Performance.* New York: Wiley Science Editions.

LEWIS, D.G. (1958) The effect of national service on academic performance. *Br. J. educ. Psychol.*, **28**, 135-40.

LYNN, R., and GORDON, I. E. (1961) The relation of neuroticism and extraversion to educational attainment. *Br. J. educ. Psychol.*, **31**, 194-203.

MCCLELLAND, D.C., and co-authors (1953) *The Achievement Motive.* New York: Appleton-Century-Crofts.

MCCLELLAND, D.C., and co-authors (1958) *Talent and Society.* Princeton: Van Nostrand.

MCCRACKEN, D. (1969) University Student Performance. (The changing pattern of medical and social factors over three years and their correlations with examination results.) Report of the Student Health Department, University of Leeds.

MCDONALD, R. (1974) Guidance system is on course for disaster. *Education in the North*, **11**, 51-5.

MCDOWELL, J.V. (1967) Student role orientation in the freshman year: its stability, change and correlates at thirteen small colleges. In FELDMAN, K.A., and NEWCOMB, T.M. (1969). *The Impact of College on Students* (2 vols). New York: Jossey-Bass.

174   *Degrees of Excellence*

MACKENZIE, N., ERAUT, M., and JONES, H.C. (1970) *Teaching and Learning: an Introduction to New Methods and Resources in Higher Education.* Paris: UNESCO.
MACNAUGHTON-SMITH, P. (1965) *Some Statistical and other Numerical Techniques for Classifying Individuals.* London: HMSO.
MCPHERSON, A.F. (1970) Selections and survivals—a sociology of the ancient Scottish universities. In BROWN, R. (ed.) (1973). *Knowledge, Education and Cultural Change.* London: Tavistock.
MCPHERSON, A.F., and NEAVE, G. (1974) *An Improper Sixth Year.* Mimeograph. Centre for Educational Sociology, University of Edinburgh.
MALLESON, N.B. (1959) University student, 1953. I—Profile. *Univ. Quart.,* **13**, 287-98.
MALLESON, N.B. (1963) The influence of emotional factors in university education. *Sociol. Rev. Monogr.,* **7**, 141-59.
MALLESON, N.B. (1967) Redeployment to avoid student wastage. *Education,* March 3rd, 449-51.
MARRIS, P. (1964) *The Experience of Higher Education.* London: Routledge and Kegan Paul.
MEHRABIAN, A. (1968) Male and female scales of the tendency to achieve. *Educ. psychol. Measur.,* **28**, 493-502.
MILLER, C.M.L., and PARLETT, M.R. (1974) *Up to the Mark: a Study of the Examination Game.* London: SRHE.
MITCHELL, J.V. (1961) An analysis of the factorial dimensions of the achievement motivational construct. *J. educ. Psychol.,* **52**, 179-87.
NEWMAN, S.E. (1957) Student vs. instructor design of study method. *J. educ. Psychol.,* **48**, 328-33.
NISBET, J.D., and ENTWISTLE, N.J. (1969) *The Transition from Primary to Secondary Education.* London: University of London Press.
NISBET, J.D., and WELSH, J. (1966) Predicting student performance. *Univ. Quart.,* **20**, 468-81.
NISBET, S.D., and NAPIER, B.L. (1969) *Promise and Progress.* University of Glasgow Student Survey 1962-68. First Report. Department of Education, University of Glasgow.
ORR, L. (1974) *A Year Between School and University.* Slough: NFER.
PACE, C.R. (1967) *College and University Environment Scales.* Princeton, New Jersey: Educational Testing Service.
PARKYN, G.W. (1959) *Success and Failure in University—I. Academic Performance and the Entrance Standard.* Wellington: New Zealand Council for Educational Research.
PARKYN, G.W. (1967) *Success and Failure in University—II. The Problem of Failure.* Wellington: New Zealand Council for Educational Research.
PARLETT, M.R. (1970) The syllabus-bound student. In HUDSON, L., *The Ecology of Human Intelligence.* Harmondsworth: Penguin.
PARLETT, M.R., and HAMILTON, D. (1972) *Evaluation as Illumination: a New Approach to the Study of Innovatory Programs.* Occasional Paper—9 University of Edinburgh: Centre for Research in Educational Sciences.
PERVIN, L.A. (1967) A twenty-college study of student by college interaction using TAPE (Transactional Analysis of Personality and Environment). *J. educ. Psychol.,* **58**, 290-302.
PETCH, J.A. (1961) *GCE and Degree—I.* Manchester: NUJMB.
PETCH, J.A. (1963) *GCE and Degree—II.* Manchester: NUJMB.
PETERS, R.S. (1958) *The Concept of Motivation.* London: Routledge.
PETERSON, R.E. (1965a) *Technical Manual: College Student Questionnaires.* Princeton: Educational Testing Service.

PETERSON, R.E. (1965b) On a typology of college students. Research Bulletin, R.B. 65-9. Princeton: Educational Testing Service.

PIERON, H. (1963) *Examens et Docimologie.* Paris: Presses Universitaires de France.

PILKINGTON, G.W., and HARRISON, G.J. (1967) The relative value of two high-level intelligence tests, advanced level and first-year university marks for predicting degree classification. *Br. J. educ. Psychol.,* **37**, 382-9.

PILLINER, A.E.G. (1960) Prediction of success in the arts faculty of the University of Edinburgh by marks obtained at the Scottish Leaving Certificate Examination. Unpublished report. University of Edinburgh: Department of Education.

POND, L. (1964) A study of high achieving and low achieving freshmen. *Aust. J. Higher Educ.,* **2**, 73-8.

POWELL, J.L. (1973) *Selection for University in Scotland.* Edinburgh: Scottish Council for Research in Education.

RICHARDS, J.P.G., and WILSON, A.J.C. (1961) A level and pass degree in physics. *Univ. Quart.,* **15**, 389-91.

RICHARDSON, S. (1965) *Manual for Study of Values* (British Version). Slough: NFER.

Robbins Report (1963) *Higher Education* (Cmnd 2154). London: HMSO.

ROOK, A. (1959) Student suicides. *Br. Med. J.,* **2**, 551-5.

RORER, L.G., HOFFMAN, F.J., LA FORGE, C.E., and NEISH, K. (1966) Optimum cutting scores to discriminate groups of unequal size and variance. *J. appl. Psychol.,* **50**, 153-64.

RYLE, A. (1969) *Student Casualties.* Harmondsworth: Penguin.

SAINSBURY, A.B. (1970) Supplementary predictive information for university admission. In, *Research into Higher Education, 1969.* London: SRHE.

SANDERS, C. (1961) *Psychological and Educational Bases of Academic Performance.* Brisbane: Australian Council for Educational Research.

SANFORD, N. (1959) Motivation of high achievers. In DAVID, O.D. (ed.). *The Education of Women.* Washington, D.C.: American Council on Education.

SAVAGE, R.D. (1962) Personality factors and academic performance. *Br. J. educ. Psychol.,* **32**, 251-3.

SCANNELL, D.P. (1960) Prediction of college success from elementary and secondary school performance. *J. educ. Psychol.,* **51**, 130-4.

SCEEB (1974) *An Investigation into the Comparability of School Estimates and Examination Performance.* Edinburgh: Scottish Certificate of Education Examination Board.

SCHONELL, F.J., ROE, E., and MEDDLETON, I.G. (1962) *Promise and Performance: a Study of Student Progress at University Level.* Brisbane: University of Queensland Press.

Schools Council (1973) *Preparation for Degree Courses.* London: Evans/Methuen.

SCRE (1936) *The Prognostic Value of University Entrance Examinations in Scotland.* London: University of London Press.

SIMON, F.H. (1971) *Prediction Methods in Criminology.* Home Office Research Studies. London: HMSO.

SMALL, J.J. (1966) *Achievement and Adjustment in the First Year at University.* Wellington: New Zealand Council for Educational Research.

SMITHERS, A.G., and BATCOCK, A. (1970) Success and failure among social scientists and health scientists at a technological university. *Br. J. educ. Psychol.,* **40**, 144-53.

SNOW, C.P. (1964) *The Two Cultures and a Second Look.* London: Cambridge University Press.

SPIELBERGER, C.D. (1962) The effects of manifest anxiety on the academic achievement of college students. *Ment. Hyg.,* **46**, 420-6.

SPRANGER, E. (1928) *Types of Men: the Psychology and Ethics of Personality.* Reprinted by Johnson Reprint Co., New York (1966).

STERN, G.G. (1963) Characteristics of the intellectual climate of college environments. *Harv. Educ. Rev.,* **33**, 5-41.

STERN, G.G., and PACE, C.R. (1958) *College Characteristics Index.* Syracuse University, NY: Psychological Research Centre.

STILL, R.J. (1954) The prevention of psychological illness among students. *Univ. Quart.,* **9**, 32-45.

STOTT, M.B. (1950) What is occupational success? *Occupational psychol.,* **24**, 105-12.

THODAY, D. (1957) How undergraduates work. *Univ. Quart.,* **11**, 172-81.

THOMPSON, J.B. (1976) An interview study of the motivations and personality characteristics of 124 students in higher education. Ph.D. study, University of Lancaster (in progress).

TORGERSON, W.S. (1965) Multidimensional representations of similarity structures. In KATZ, M.M., COLE, J.O., and BARTON, W.E. *The Role and Methodology of Classification in Psychiatry and Psychopathology.* Washington: US Department of Health, Education and Welfare.

UCCA (1967) *Statistical Supplement to the Fourth Report.* London: UCCA.

UCCA (1969) *Statistical Supplement to the Sixth Report.* London: UCCA.

University Grants Committee (1968) *Enquiry into Student Progress.* London: HMSO.

VERNON, P.E. (1959) Trends in selection, I and II. *Times Educ. Supp.,* March 13th and 20th, 1959.

WALTON, H.J., DREWERY, J., and PHILIP, A.E. (1964) Typical medical students. *Br. Med. J.,* **2**, 744-8.

WANKOWSKI, J.A. (1969) Some aspects of motivation in success and failure at university. In *Report of the Fourth Annual Conference of SRHE.* London: SRHE.

WANKOWSKI, J.A. (1970) *Random Sample Analysis: Motives and Goals in University Studies.* Birmingham: University of Birmingham Educational Survey.

WANKOWSKI, J.A. (1973) *Temperament, Motivation and Academic Achievement* (2 vols). University of Birmingham: Educational Survey.

WARWICK, D.W. (1973) (ed.) *Counselling in Colleges of Education.* Lancaster: University of Lancaster, School of Education.

WATTS, A.G. (1972) *Diversity and Choice in Higher Education.* London: Routledge and Kegan Paul.

WHITELEY, J.M., and RESNIKOFF, A. (1972) *Perspectives on Vocational Development.* Washington, D.C.: American Personnel and Guidance Association.

WILLIAMS, E.M. (1950) An investigation of the value of higher school certificate results in predicting performance in first year university examinations. *Br. J. educ. Psychol.,* **20**, 83-98.

WILLIAMS, G.L. (1974) The events of 1973-74 in a long term planning perspective. *Higher Educ. Bull.,* **3**, 17-44.

WILSON, J. (1972) *Philosophy and Educational Research.* Slough: NFER.

WILSON, J.D. (1968) Predicting student performance in first year arts and science. *Scot. educ. Stud.,* **1**, 68-74.

WILSON, J.D. (1969) Predicting levels of first year student performance. Unpublished Ph.D. thesis, University of Aberdeen.

WILSON, J.D. (1973) Predicting levels of student performance. Final Report submitted to SSRC, September 1973.

WILSON, J.D. (1974) Head-teachers' estimates and student performance. *Scot. educ. Stud.*, **6**, 67-76.

WILSON, J.D. (1977) The Academic Achievement Game: experience with entering students. *Higher Education* (in press).

WISEMAN, S. (1961) *Examinations and English Education.* Manchester: University Press.

WISHART, D. (1969) *Clustan IA: Users' Manual.* University of St Andrews: Computing Laboratory.

Appendices

Appendix A1 Student Attitudes Questionnaire (Rowntree version)

The following statements cover a wide range of students' comments on their life at university or college and on certain more general social problems. The questions deliberately follow no logical order; we are interested in your *immediate* response to each separate item. Please work *quickly* through these statements indicating your agreement or disagreement by circling either '1' or '0'.* It is most important that you do make a definite response to every statement, even though your feelings may be rather indefinite.

	RESPONSE	SCALE
Background music helps me to study more effectively	(D)	SM
War is inherent in human nature	(D)	R
It is most unusual for me to be late handing-in work		M
I find I cover the assigned syllabus equally well whether it interests me or not		SB
I am often involved in following up my own ideas when I am supposed to be doing set work		SF
Persons with serious hereditary diseases should be compulsorily sterilized	(D)	T
My habit of putting off work leaves me with far too much to do at the end of term	(D)	SM
In the interests of peace, we must give up part of our national sovereignty		R
I enjoy the challenge of a difficult new topic in lectures		M
In the past few years I have read a lot of books covering widely different topics		SF
I like to be told precisely what to do in essays or in other assignments		SB
Our present difficulties are due rather to moral than to economic causes		T
It's rather difficult for me to organise my study time: at school this was done for me	(D)	SM
'My country, right or wrong' is a saying which expresses a fundamentally desirable kind of attitude	(D)	R
I usually tackle the easy things first and leave the more difficult ones until the end	(D)	M
Without the stimulus of exams, I doubt whether I would do much effective studying		SB
I often find myself questioning things that I hear from lecturers in lectures or tutorials		SF
Only by going back to religion can civilization hope to survive		T

---

* On the questionnaire used with the students the code '(1)' indicated an 'Agree' response and '(0)' indicated a 'Disagree' response.

Appendix A1 cont.

	RESPONSE	SCALE
I seem to have plenty of free time during the week	(D)	SM
Our treatment of criminals is too harsh; we should try to cure them, not to punish them		R
Examination marks provide a useful and necessary indication of one's progress		SB
I get very concerned about work which is overdue		SB
I enjoy collecting things such as stamps, minerals plants etc.		M
I spend too long on certain topics because I get very interested and involved in them		SF
People suffering from incurable diseases should have the choice of being put painlessly to death	(D)	T
I don't find much time to study during the holidays	(D)	SM
Ultimately, private ownership of the means of production and distribution should be abolished and complete socialism introduced		R
I play any game to win, not just for the fun of it		M
I consider the best possible way of learning is by completing the set work and doing the required reading		SB
The laws against abortion should be strengthened not weakened		T
My lecture notes are often difficult to decipher afterwards	(D)	SM
Workers in industry should have a voice in the running of their factory		R
I sometimes wish I had gone straight into work after school	(D)	M
Worrying about an exam or about work that's overdue often prevents me from sleeping		SB
Sunday observance is old-fashioned and should cease to govern our behaviour	(D)	T
I usually plan my week's work in advance, either on paper or in my head		SM
No unjust or aggressive war has ever been waged by England	(D)	R
I get disheartened and give up easily if something is too difficult for me	(D)	M
I like to play around with certain ideas of my own even if they do not come to very much		SF
It is right that the divorce laws should be altered to make divorce easier	(D)	T
I find it difficult to pick out the relevant points in a lecture unless they are written on the board or in a hand-out	(D)	SM
The threat of unemployment is the only incentive which will cause people to work hard at unpleasant jobs	(D)	R
I can't see any relevance in most of the work we do here	(D)	M
I feel nervous before an exam, but it seems to make me work better once I start		M

continues overleaf

Appendix A1 cont.

	RESPONSE	SCALE
Immigrants should be encouraged to return to their country of origin	(D)	T
I need to be in the right mood before I can study effectively	(D)	SM
Crimes of violence should be punished by flogging	(D)	R
I'm a pretty average student: I'll never be particularly good, so there's no point in striving to be something I'm not	(D)	M
I tend to learn more effectively by studying along my own lines than through doing the set work		SF
There is no survival of any kind after death	(D)	T
I find it difficult to keep awake during some lectures	(D)	SM
Under no circumstances can war ever be justified		R
It's important for me to do really well in the courses here		M
I usually study only what I am required to study		SB
It is right and proper that religious education in schools should be compulsory		T
There seems to be little point in following up the references we are given in lectures	(D)	SM
Nationalisation of the great industries leads to inefficiency, bureaucracy and stagnation	(D)	R
It's not often that I can stick at work for more than an hour at a time	(D)	M
I should prefer the set work to be less structured and organised		SF
The Jews have too much power and influence in this country	(D)	T
There are very few of the recommended text-books which are really worth buying	(D)	SM
Often I try to think of a better way of doing something or explaining something than is described in a lecture or book		SF
The death-penalty is an effective deterrent and should be reintroduced	(D)	R
I hate admitting defeat, even in trivial matters		M
The nation exists for the benefit of the individuals composing it, not the individuals for the benefit of the nation		T
I don't often join in tutorial discussions: I prefer to listen	(D)	SM
Unofficial strikes should be declared illegal	(D)	R
There's no point in trying to do things in a hurry: I prefer to take my time	(D)	M
I'm rather slow at starting work in the evenings	(D)	SM
Immigrants are as valuable, honest, and public-spirited citizens as any other group		T

Appendix A1 cont.

	RESPONSE	SCALE
My friends always seem to be able to do things better than me	(D)	M
Our national life suffers from a lack of discipline		T
I don't believe in challenging what lecturers say: they are better informed than I am		SB
The present over-emphasis on social services makes people less self-reliant, and is therefore not in the best interest of the country	(D)	R

BEFORE CONTINUING PLEASE LOOK BACK OVER THESE ATTITUDE STATEMENTS TO CHECK THAT YOU HAVE ANSWERED <u>ALL</u> OF THEM BY CIRCLING EITHER '1' OR '0'.

Key to scoring

The 'Agree' response is scored as '1' unless there is a (D) sign before the scale name; then the 'Disagree' response counts as '1'. The scales are: M – Motivation; SM – Study methods; SB – Syllabus-bound; SF – Syllabus-free; R – Radicalism; T – Tendermindedness.

Appendix A2 Headteacher's rating scale

Confidential Report on Students

Put a cross in the appropriate column below to indicate whether any of these handicaps to good performance at university apply in the case of

....

who was a pupil at your school last session.

Handicap	Applies		
	Not at all	To some extent	To a great extent
1. Lack of good health			
2. Lack of adequate intelligence			
3. Lack of a stable temperament			
4. Lack of a mature outlook			
5. Lack of a stable home background			
6. Lack of perseverance			
7. Lack of capacity to work independently			
8. Lack of interest in academic work			
9. Lack of articulate expression			
10. Other: (*a*)			
(*b*)			
(*c*)			

11. Is he/she a hardworking student?   ....

....

Appendix A3 Follow-up questionnaire to all third-year students

Name .... Home Address ....

....

1. Please list below the subjects which you studied last session, in
    2nd year, and which you are studying this session. Indicate
    whether ordinary, Advanced, Junior Honours etc.,

    Mark X in the appropriate column to indicate your degree examina-
    tion results last session.

Year of Study	Subject	Degree Examination Results Pass-June	Fail-June	Pass-Sept	Fail-Sept
2nd Year	1.	...	...	...	...
	2.	...	...	...	...
	3.	...	...	...	...
	4.	...	...	...	...
3rd Year	1.				
	2.				
	3.				
	4.				

2.(a) What degree do you expect to graduate with (e.g. Ordinary B.Sc.,
      Honours English)?

  (b) If you are studying for Honours, what class of degree do you
      expect to get?

      A first   ....   A lower second ....   Mark X
      An upper second ....   A third   ....   if applies

3. If you expect to study for a post-graduate qualification (e.g.
    Teacher Training, Social Work, Secretarial Course, M-Litt,Ph.D.
    etc.) please specify.

    (a) Course ....
    (b) Institution ....

4. What career do you intend to take up? ....

5. List below any *university* sports team you have played for, or any
    university society or organisation of which you have been a leading
    member at any time during the past three years (Include S.R.C.,
    Charities, Rectorial etc.). State any post of responsibility
    (e.g. captain, secretary) you have held.

        (a) Sporting activities   (b) Other activities
    Team member Post of responsibility Organisation   Post of
                                                         responsibility

1.   1.
2.   2.
3.   3.
4.   4.
5.   5.
6.   6.

continues overleaf

Appendix A3 cont.

6. Looking back to before you came up to university, can you remember who was chiefly responsible for taking the decision that
   you would apply for and attend university?

   (1) Yourself   ...   (5) A teacher   ...
   (2) Your father   ...   (6) Some other person   ...   Mark
   (3) Your mother   ...   (specify)   X
   (4) Some other relative ...   (7) Impossible to answer ...

7. How did you feel when you were told that you had been accepted
   for university?

   (1) Very excited   ...   (4) Indifferent   ...   Mark
   (2) Quite pleased   ...   (5) Can't remember   ...   X
   (3) Uncertain as to how
       I felt   ...

8. Did you encounter any special problems in making the transition
   from school to university?

   (1) No special problems   ...
   (2) A few minor problems   ...   Mark X
   (3) Some special problems ...

   (If 2 or 3, please specify as precisely as possible).

9. Over the past three years, have you ever felt seriously that you
   made the wrong decision in coming to university?
   (1) No - never   ...
   (2) Yes - very occasionally ...   Mark X
   (3) Yes - quite often   ...

10. If you could choose your course again, would you make any changes
    in what you would study?
                    Yes ......   No ......   Mark X
    If 'yes' what changes would you make? (Some possible changes are
    listed, but there are probably others you would wish to suggest).
    (a) Level of degree (e.g. take Honours rather
                              than Ordinary)   ......
   *(b) Faculty of study (e.g. take science
                              rather than arts)   ......
    (c) Subject of study within your present
        faculty (e.g. take Honours History   Mark X
        rather than Honours English)   ......
    (d) Optional subjects (e.g. take different
                'outside' subjects)   ......
    (e)   .   ...
    (f)   ......
    Please specify the exact change you would make and briefly
    explain the reasons.

11. During your period at Aberdeen, have you found any serious de-
    ficiencies in any of the following respects?
                (a) Quality of teaching   Yes/No
                (b) Extent of informal staff-student contact Yes/No
                (c) Student facilities (e.g. libraries,
                                        equipment)   Yes/No
                (d) Adequate personal and curricular guidance Yes/No
                (e) Other   Yes/No

                    Underline, if applies.

12. What do you think you have gained most from coming to university?

---

* If you have already transferred, write T and the year in which you
   transferred (e.g. T.2.)

Appendix A3 cont.

11

STUDENT ATTITUDES TO LIFE AT UNIVERSITY

The following statements cover a wide range of students' comments on their life at University and their feelings about it. Read each statement, and decide whether you AGREE or DISAGREE with it, as it stands, from your own experience. Then put a clearly visible cross through THE ANSWER YOU WISH TO GIVE, A or D. It is very important that you make a definite response to EACH statement as it stands, even if your own feelings are rather indefinite. Don't spend too much time over any question: only your immediate reaction is wanted. There are no right or wrong answers. Be sure not to omit any questions.

	AGREE	DISAGREE
1. I like to do things on the spur of the moment.	A	D
2. I find that I can learn more from a book than from most lectures.	A	D
3. There is at least one member of staff I feel I could ask if I needed help or advice.	A	D
4. I generally read through a lecture afterwards, underlining or noting the important points.	A	D
5. I tend to do much less work now than in first year.	A	D
6. I sometimes get the feeling that everyone is against me.	A	D
7. I hope to do research at University after the degree course.	A	D
8. I easily become depressed if I do badly in an exam, even though it isn't an important one.	A	D
9. Background music helps me to study more effectively.	A	D
10. I spend ages revising the work I have to submit because I never feel that it's good enough.	A	D
11. I certainly want a degree, but it doesn't matter much if it's not a particularly good one.	A	D
12. I've often had to refuse to go out with friends because I've needed the time for studying.	A	D
13. I try to keep a note of all the money I spend.	A	D
14. I generally do quite a bit of work during the holidays, reorganising lecture notes or doing background reading.	A	D
15. I get depressed easily – too easily.	A	D
16. I think I'm rather an anxious person: I seem to worry more than most people.	A	D
17. I don't mind competition, in fact I thrive on it.	A	D
18. Sport or social activities take up quite a lot of my time.	A	D
19. I rarely get interested in the work we are given here.	A	D
20. If I get into an argument with someone, I usually blame myself afterwards.	A	D
21. I find it difficult to organize my study time satisfactorily.	A	D
22. It annoys me intensely if I do badly at anything.	A	D
23. I feel rather self-conscious when I meet people for the first time.	A	D
24. I often find that my mind goes blank when I'm faced with a particularly difficult problem.	A	D
25. Naturally I want to do well at University, but not if it means working flat out most of the time.	A	D

continues overleaf

Appendix A3 cont.

	AGREE	DISAGREE
26. I find that I can get through the work best by working steadily for most of the evening.	A	D
27. Good lecture notes are all you need to pass exams.	A	D
28. I like to be in the swim of things; if there is anything going on, I like to be there.	A	D
29. I'm sure I'll never be better than an average student.	A	D
30. What you do later in life is much more important than the marks you obtain here.	A	D
31. I'm rather slow at starting work in the evenings.	A	D
32. Life is much more fun if you're with a crowd.	A	D
33. My life at University has been intellectually unstimulating.	A	D
34. I dislike competition: I always expect to lose.	A	D
35. I like to be the centre of attraction when I'm with friends.	A	D
36. I'd never ask a question in a lecture: it would be too much of an ordeal for me.	A	D
37. When I'm with a group of friends, I prefer to keep in the background and let others take the lead.	A	D
38. I seem to have plenty of free time during the week.	A	D
39. I usually plan out my week's work in advance, either on paper or in my head.	A	D
40. If I had to state my order of priorities, exam success would be at the top.	A	D
41. To pass exams I rely mostly on a concentrated last week of revision.	A	D
42. I'm not keen on parties: I prefer to be alone or with one or two friends.	A	D
43. I often find myself worrying about whether other people really like me.	A	D

PLEASE MAKE SURE THAT YOU HAVE GIVEN ONE RESPONSE TO EVERY ITEM IN THIS SECTION.

Appendix A3 cont.

111 Students express many different opinions about their purpose in being at university. Below are listed four points of view, which, it is believed, are widely held among Aberdeen university students. Read through each statement in turn and try to decide which best expresses YOUR OWN opinion, which expresses it next best, and so on. At the end, list the statements in the order in which you agree with them.

A. This is the view held by students who see themselves at university primarily to get a degree qualification which will be useful in a career. Their emphasis is on getting a marketable qualification, and they subordinate other aspects of university life to this purpose. They cover the necessary course-work in their subjects adequately, but are rarely interested in getting to grips with the fundamental intellectual issues in the discipline. They participate in extra-curricular and social activities, but make sure that these do not interfere with their academic progress.

B. This is the view held by students who are searching for a personal philosophy of life, and who question or reject the common values underlying our society. Such students emphasise their individual points of view: they are interested in ideas, and in making explicit their personal reactions to them. They are particularly concerned with philosophical and social problems. They are likely to show little interest in getting a 'good' degree or in using it in subsequent careers in business or the professions: they may even despise such activities. They attach little importance to participation in formal extra-curricular activities.

C. This is the view held by students who get deeply involved in theoretical issues at the heart of their subjects. Their wish to deepen and broaden their understanding makes them work well beyond the prescribed minimum. They identify with their subjects and teachers, and may even see themselves as future scholars. The vocational usefulness of the qualification they are studying for is probably regarded as of minor importance. Participation in social life and in extra-curricular activities not related to the area of study is likely to be limited.

D. This is the view held by students who believe that a great deal of value in a university education is gained by meeting fellow-students outside the formal class sessions, and participating in extra-curricular activities, in clubs and societies, in parties and in casual chat over coffee. Such students may have a moderate interest in the courses they are following, and certainly wish to get a degree, but they also believe strongly that an essential part of a university education is gained from the friendships which are formed, and the different points of view which are encountered, in contacts with fellow-students outside the classroom or laboratory.

After you have read all four statements, list them in the order in which they express your point of view, as follows:-
(1) Best description of my point of view   ......   Mark A, B, C or
(2) Second best description   ......   D as appropriate
(3) Third best description   ......
(4) Least accurate description   ......

PLEASE CHECK TO SEE THAT YOU HAVE ANSWERED ALL THE QUESTIONS.
THANK YOU.

Appendix A4 First questionnaire to unsatisfactory students

NAME ....

Home Address ....

1. Did you re-sit in September all the subjects you had not passed by June?

2. Did you prepare thoroughly, quite thoroughly or only moderately for the September re-sits?

3. How have you been employed since the September re-sits?

4. What are your plans for the immediate future? Will you

   (*a*) Try for re-admission to Aberdeen or some other university next session?
   (Specify course and university, e.g. M.A. (Ord.) Aberdeen)

OR (*b*) Continue your education at a technical college, college of education, etc?
   (Specify course and college)

OR (*c*) Take permanent employment?   (Specify occupation)

OR (*d*) Other?   (Specify)

If (*a*) or (*b*) -

   i Are there any changes in your approach to study that you would make in the light of your experience over the past session?

   ii Are you confident of ultimately qualifying in your course?

If (*c*) or (*d*) -

   i Is this to be your career?

   ii What further educational qualifications will you require for your career?

   iii Are you confident of obtaining further qualifications?

5. If you answered (*b*), (*c*) or (*d*) -

   Do you now feel that you should not have come to university?

6. Dropping out of university affects people differently. Some feel relieved to escape from a stressful situation, others feel depressed and anxious.   How has it affected you?

7. What do you think was the main reason for your difficulties at university?

Appendix A5 Second questionnaire to unsatisfactory students

<u>If you did not re-sit any subject in the June and September resit examinations answer the questions below:</u>

1. By what date did you decide not to re-sit?

2. Why did you decide not to re-sit?

3. Was your decision not to re-sit a free decision, or were you under any pressure to re-sit?

   If there was pressure, who exerted it?

4. Have you applied for admission to a course in another institution?

   If 'yes' - please give name of institution, course and award sought.

   (*a*) Have you been accepted?
   (*b*) How confident are you of completing your new course satisfactorily?
   (*c*) How relevant will your previous university course be to your new course?
   (*d*) On the whole, do you regard your new course as more or less suitable than your university course?

   If 'no' -

   (*e*) What are your future educational plans?

5. How are you presently employed?

   Is this to be your career?

6. Please indicate the level of your current earnings by ringing the appropriate number below.
Under £ 10 per week	1
Between £ 10 and £ 20 per week	2
Between £ 21 and £ 30 per week	3
Above £ 31 per week	4
Not earning	5

7. How do you now feel about your year at university?

8. Has your performance at university adversely affected your relationship with
   (*a*) your father?
   (*b*) your mother?

<u>If you re-sat examinations in June and/or September but failed to secure readmission, answer the questions below.</u>

1. (*a*) Did you re-sit all the subjects you had failed?

   (*b*) Did you pass all the subjects you re-sat?

2. Did you encounter any special problems in preparing to re-sit?

3. Was your decision to re-sit a free decision, or were you under any pressure to re-sit?

   If there was pressure, who exerted it?

Appendix A5 cont.

4. In your year away from university, and in your preparations for re-sitting, did you keep in touch with any member of the university staff?

   If 'yes' was this a member of staff who had taught you, or a member of staff in some other capacity (eg. Advisor, Regent etc).

5. Have you applied for admission to a course in another institution?

   If 'yes' - please give name of institution, course and award sought.

   (*a*) Have you been accepted?
   (*b*) How confident are you of completing your new course satisfactorily?
   (*c*) How relevant will your previous university course be to your new course?
   (*d*) On the whole do you regard your new course as more or less suitable than your university course?

   If 'no'

   (*a*) What are your future educational plans?

6. How are you presently employed?

   Is this to be your career?

7. Please indicate the level of your current earnings by ringing the appropriate number below.

Under £ 10 per week	1
Between £ 10 and £ 20 per week	2
Between £ 21 and £ 30 per week	3
Above £ 31 per week	4
Not earning	5

8. How do you now feel about your year at university?

9. Has your performance at university adversely affected your relationship with
   (*a*) your father?
   (*b*) your mother?

If you re-sat examinations in June and/or September and secured readmission to Aberdeen University, answer the questions below:

1. (*a*) Did you re-sit all the subjects you had failed?

   (*b*) Did you pass all the subjects you re-sat?

2. Did you encounter any special problems in preparing to re-sit?

3. Was your decision to re-sit a free decision, or were you under any pressure to re-sit?

   If there was pressure, who exerted it?

4. In your year away from university, and in your preparations for re-sitting, did you keep in touch with any member of the university staff?

   If 'yes' was this a member of staff who had taught you, or a member of staff in some other capacity (eg. Advisor, Regent etc)?

5. How confident are you of passing the degree examinations at the end of the session (June, September, 1970)?

6. How confident are you of graduating in your course?

7. Have you experienced any major problem in readjusting to university.
   If 'yes', please specify.

Appendix B1 End of course result and first-year performance category, by sex and faculty

End of course classification	ARTS									
	First-year academic category									
	Men (N = 295)					Women (N = 344)				
	Good	Weak	Fail	Other	Total	Good	Weak	Fail	Other	Total
Good Hons/Ord.	152	18	3	0	173	157	7	0	0	164
Weak Hons/Ord.	31	18	6	0	55	77	49	8	0	134
Fail	14	18	27	0	59	10	7	26	0	43
Other	5	3	0	0	8	2	1	0	0	3
All	202	57	36	0	295	246	64	34	0	344

End of course classification	SCIENCE									
	First-year academic category									
	Men (N = 264)					Women (N = 112)				
	Good	Weak	Fail	Other	Total	Good	Weak	Fail	Other	Total
Good Hons/Ord.	103	19	3	0	125	44	4	2	0	50
Weak Hons/Ord.	39	32	2	0	73	19	17	1	0	37
Fail	12	10	35	0	57	7	4	11	0	22
Other	6	3	0	0	9	2	1	0	0	3
All	160	64	40	0	264	72	26	14	0	112

Notes: Students listed as 'other' in final year include known voluntary withdrawals, and transfers to other faculties and universities. One student died.

Appendix B2 Head's ratings on hard work, letter of recommendation and failure, by sex, faculty and area of home residence

	Head's rating — Not hard-working						Head's letter — Reservations				
	Men	Women	All	Arts	Science		Men	Women	All	Arts	Science
1. *N* of students	87	39	126	64	62		71	41	112	64	48
2. *N* in (1) U/S*	35	11	46	20	26		20	12	32	19	13
3. % U/S ; (2) as % of (1)	40	28	37	31	42		28	29	29	30	27
4. % U/S : univ. region	38	26	34	35	32		34	25	30	33	24
5. % U/S rest of UK	43	40	42	23	49		21	38	26	20	29

* U/S = Unsatisfactory (as defined in Table 6.7)

Appendix B3 Number and percentage of students rated on check-list items, by sex, faculty and first-year performance

Check-list items	Arts				Science					
	Men (N=274)		Women (N=330)		Men (N=247)		Women (N=107)		All (N=958)	
Lack of	N	(%)	N	(%)	N	(%)	N	(%)	N	(%)
1. Good health	25	(9)	36	(11)	12	(5)	12	(11)	85	(9)
2. Adequate intelligence	88	(32)	79	(24)***	77	(31)	32	(30)	276	(29)
3. A stable temperament	71	(26)	59	(18)	46	(19)***	14	(13)**	190	(20)
4. A mature outlook	117	(43)***	106	(32)	75	(31)*	29	(27)	327	(34)
5. A stable home background	38	(14)	40	(12)	25	(10)	9	(8)	112	(12)
6. Perseverance	99	(37)***	50	(15)	69	(28)***	20	(19)*	238	(25)
7. Capacity to work independently	105	(39)***	73	(22)	66	(27)*	25	(23)	269	(28)
8. Interest in academic work	81	(30)***	46	(14)	46	(19)	16	(15)***	189	(20)
9. Articulate expression	95	(35)**	96	(29)	82	(33)	35	(33)*	308	(32)
10. Other	22	(8)	33	(10)	17	(7)	21	(20)	93	(10)
11. One or more of above.	219	(80)	218	(66)	173	(70)	69	(64)	679	(71)

First-year performance criteria:

Good = Pass all three (arts) or four (science) subjects by September 1968 (i.e. end of first year)

Weak = Fail one subject by September 1968

Fail = Fail two or more subjects by September 1968.

Difference between good and weak plus fail students in first year
$p < 0.01$ ***, $p < 0.02$ **, $p < 0.05$*.

Appendix B4 Means and standard deviations of check-list scores, by sex, faculty and first-year performance

First-year performance	Arts						Science					
	Men			Women			Men			Women		
	N	Mean	S.D.	*N*	Mean	S.D.	*N*	Mean	S.D.	*N*	Mean	S.D.
Good	184	2.4	2.8	235	1.8	2.4	150	1.8	2.0	70	1.6	1.8
Weak	55	3.6**	2.7	63	2.5*	2.4	60	2.8**	2.2	25	3.2*	3.2
Fail	35	4.0**	2.4	32	2.3*	2.3	37	2.9**	2.3	12	2.6*	2.6

Difference from 'good' mean significant at 0.01 level ** and at 0.05 level *

Appendix B5 Head's ratings on check-list items and failure to graduate

	Check-list items: students rated as lacking									
	(1) Good health	(2) Adequate intelligence	(3) Stable temperament	(4) Mature outlook	(5) Stable home background	(6) Perseverance	(7) Capacity for indep. work	(8) Interest in acad. work	(9) Articulate expression	(10) Other
1. N of students (N = 801)	66	228	163	281	92	197	228	157	257	77
2. N in (1) U/S*	13	57	44	72	24	65	64	41	55	13
3. % U/S: (2) as % of (1)	20	25	27	26	26	33	28	26	21	17
4. % U/S: univ.region	21	27	30	29	24	30	30	30	23	20
5. % U/S: rest of UK	17	21	23	20	29	38	28	19	19	15

* U/S = Unsatisfactory (as defined in Table 6.7)

Appendix B6 Dichotomised check-list scores, by sex, faculty and failure to graduate

	Check-list score									
	Low (good rating)					High (poor rating)				
	Men	Women	All	Arts	Science	Men	Women	All	Arts	Science
1. *N* of Students	209	210	419	271	148	202	180	382	247	135
2. *N* in (1) U/S*	29	24	53	35	18	65	35	100	57	43
3. % U/S: (2) as % of (1)	14	11	13	13	12	32	19	26	23	32
4. % U/S: univ. region	14	12	13	13	12	38	19	28	27	35
5. % U/S: rest of UK	15	10	12	12	13	26	20	23	14	31

* U/S = Unsatisfactory (as defined in Table 6.7)

Appendix B7 Summary of results of relationships between personality, motivation, study methods and academic performance, by sex

Relationship between high scores and performance	Men (*N*=265)	Women (*N*=270)
Motivation	0.02	NS
Study methods	0.01	0.01
Motivation and study methods	0.01	0.01
Relationship between personality scores and performance		
Extraversion	NS	NS
Emotional instability	NS	NS
Combined scores (personality group*)	NS	NS
Relationship between personality group* and scores on motivation and study methods		
Motivation	NS	NS
Study methods	0.01	0.01
Motivation and study methods	0.01	0.05

* Personality groups were stable introvert, stable extravert, unstable introvert, unstable extravert.

Appendix B8 Fail students—responses to second questionnaire

ITEM	MEN (N=51)	WOMEN (N=34)	ALL (N=85)	ARTS (N55)	SCIENCE (N=30)
FAIL STUDENTS					
Classification of students:					
Non-sitters	26	21	47	30	17
Non-passers	13	5	18	10	8
Re-entrants	12	8	20	15	5
Pressure to re-sit (all students):	(51)	(34)	(85)	(55)	(30)
Free decision	42	28	70	47	23
Some pressure	9	6	15	8	7
Further education (non-sitters and non-passers only):	(39)	(26)	(65)	(40)	(25)
Enrolled in new course	16	17	33	19	14
Applied but not yet enrolled	7	1	8	4	4
Not applied	16	8	24	17	7
New course and university course (students entering F.E. only):	(23)	(18)	(41)	(23)	(18)
(a) Confident of success in new course	19	17	36	22	14
Not confident of success	3	0	3	0	3
(b) University course helpful	9	13	22	12	10
University course not relevant	9	4	13	7	6
(c) New course more congenial	8	15	23	16	7
New course less congenial	4	0	4	0	4
My year at university was (non-sitters and non-passers only):	(39)	(26)	(65)	(40)	(25)
Useful/beneficial/enjoyable	19	13	32	20	12
A missed opportunity	8	3	11	6	5
A waste of time	4	6	10	7	3
Other/no opinion	8	4	12	7	5
Failure and relationship with parents (non-sitters and non-passers only):					
No adverse effect	17	19	36	30	6*
Some adverse effect	9	3	12	4	8

* $x_c^2 = 8.61$ $p < 0.01$.

Appendix B8 cont.

ITEM	FAIL STUDENTS				
	MEN (N=51)	WOMEN (N=34)	ALL (N=85)	ARTS (N=55)	SCIENCE (N=30)
Preparing for re-sits (non-passers and re-entrants only):	(25)	(13)	(38)	(25)	(13)
(a) Special problems	11	9	20	12	8
No special problems	14	4	18	13	5
(b) Kept in touch with staff	12	3	15	10	5
Did not keep in touch	13	10	23	15	8
Performance at end of second year (Sept. 1970) (re-entrants only):	(12)	(8)	(20)	(15)	(5)
(a) Passed all subjects by June 1970	6	5	11	8	3
(b) Passed all subjects by Sept. 1970	1	0	1	0	1
(c) Failed one subject by Sept. 1970	4	2	6	6	0
(d) Failed two or more subjects by Sept. 1970	1	1	2	1	1
Performance at end of study (October 1972) (re-entrants only):	(12)	(8)	(20)	(15)	(5)
(a) Honours degree	4	1	5	2	3
(b) Ordinary degree	6	7	13	12	1
(c) Did not graduate	2	0	2	1	1

Appendix C1 Mean scores of students in six areas of study, by sex

	YEAR (N)**	LANGUAGES			HUMANITIES			SOCIAL SCIENCES		
		Men	Women	Stand'd mean	Men	Women	Stand'd mean	Men	Women	Standard mean
Degree result	3	9.3	10.1	0.07	10.1	9.8	0.14	9.3	9.8	0.03
'A' level grades	0	13.3	13.9	0.26	12.8	13.0	- 0.02	12.4	12.8	- 0.13
No. of 'O' levels	0	7.9	8.4	0.05	7.4	8.2	- 0.27	7.7	8.4	- 0.05
Verbal aptitude	1	36.2	36.6	0.44	33.6	32.7	0.03	32.2	34.0	0.03
Mathematical aptitude	1	16.6	14.2	- 0.65	16.6	14.4	- 0.64	19.4	17.2	- 0.21
Motivation	3	7.2	7.8	- 0.08	8.0	6.8	- 0.09	7.8	7.2	- 0.08
	1	8.3	8.5	0.05	8.8	8.3	0.14	8.0	7.9	- 0.16
Study methods	3	7.4	8.2	0.08	8.0	7.8	0.11	7.5	7.4	- 0.09
	1	7.4	7.7	0.16	7.8	7.5	0.16	6.9	7.0	- 0.14
Hours studied	3	26.7	32.5	0.16	35.2	35.5	0.71	28.8	31.8	0.25
	1	24.0	27.5	0.28	27.7	27.0	0.44	22.4	25.3	0.07
Syllabus-bound	3	3.5	4.1	- 0.16	3.6	3.8	- 0.21	3.7	3.8	- 0.17
Syllabus-free	3	6.3	5.7	0.17	5.9	5.2	- 0.06	6.1	5.6	0.09
Extraversion	3	13.3	13.4	- 0.05	12.4	13.3	- 0.18	13.7	14.3	0.12
	1	13.2	13.2	- 0.07	12.2	13.3	- 0.17	13.5	14.5	0.15
Neuroticism	3	12.9	14.4	0.15	12.0	14.7	0.11	12.7	13.4	0.05
	1	14.5	15.0	0.35	12.2	14.4	- 0.01	13.0	14.4	- 0.08
Radicalism	3	9.1	9.5	0.10	9.5	9.3	0.12	10.6	10.2	0.44
	1	8.4	8.9	0.20	7.8	8.2	- 0.03	8.8	8.9	0.26
Tendermindedness	3	7.0	7.8	0.11	7.7	7.3	0.16	6.4	7.1	- 0.16
	1	7.5	8.1	0.18	8.0	7.5	0.15	6.6	7.4	- 0.15
Social values	3	41.6	42.8	0.04	41.0	43.0	0.01	41.4	44.7	0.19
	1	40.6	40.8	0.14	38.0	39.8	- 0.15	38.8	43.4	0.22
Political values	3	23.9	21.7	- 0.35	27.8	24.9	0.16	29.7	25.6	0.35
	1	23.7	23.1	- 0.32	28.2	25.1	- 0.16	29.7	25.4	0.30
Economic values	3	26.9	25.4	- 0.35	26.9	27.2	- 0.21	30.6	26.5	0.00
	1	27.6	26.0	- 0.43	28.2	27.7	- 0.25	32.2	28.0	0.07
Theoretical values	3	31.1	30.6	- 0.39	30.4	30.9	- 0.43	32.3	31.8	- 0.21
	1	29.9	29.5	- 0.17	28.4	30.2	- 0.52	31.8	30.7	- 0.23
Aesthetic values	3	34.4	33.0	0.57	29.4	37.4	0.23	28.2	30.4	- 0.02
	1	34.0	32.4	0.70	28.3	31.5	0.28	26.3	28.8	- 0.05
Religious values	3	22.1	26.4	0.19	24.5	21.8	0.12	17.9	21.3	- 0.18
	1	23.2	27.3	0.14	28.2	24.8	0.25	20.2	22.8	- 0.16

** Numbers of students in each sub-group will be found in Table 9.1.

Appendix C1 cont.

	YEAR (N)**	PURE SCIENCES			APP.SCIENCES		MATHEMATICS			FULL SAMPLE	
		Men	Women	Stand'd mean	Men	Stand'd mean*	Men	Women	Stand'd mean	Men	Women
Degree result	3	9.7	9.1	−0.06	8.8	0.00	8.7	8.1	−0.39	9.4	9.6
'A' level grades	0	12.6	12.4	−0.16	12.3	−0.18	13.6	13.3	0.20	12.7	13.1
No. of 'O' levels	0	8.1	8.5	0.15	7.9	0.08	7.4	8.4	−0.14	7.8	8.4
Verbal aptitude	1	31.0	31.2	−0.23	30.8	−0.43	30.7	29.6	−0.34	32.2	33.6
Mathematical aptitude	1	23.1	21.2	0.39	25.4	0.97	28.7	27.2	1.28	21.7	17.7
Motivation	3	8.2	7.9	0.21	7.1	−0.11	7.4	7.3	−0.12	7.8	7.5
	1	8.4	8.6	0.12	7.6	−0.35	8.1	8.2	−0.06	8.2	8.3
Study methods	3	7.9	8.1	0.13	6.2	−0.10	6.5	7.2	−0.31	7.4	7.9
	1	7.5	7.6	0.11	6.1	−0.20	6.3	7.4	−0.17	7.1	7.5
Hours studied	3	22.1	25.2	−0.41	20.0	−0.59	21.8	27.8	−0.31	25.2	30.6
	1	20.1	20.1	−0.33	16.7	−0.50	18.1	24.2	−0.20	21.4	24.9
Syllabus-bound	3	4.1	4.6	0.12	4.7	0.44	4.8	5.4	−0.49	4.0	4.2
Syllabus-free	3	5.8	5.4	−0.05	5.9	−0.18	5.4	4.5	−0.37	5.9	5.4
Extraversion	3	13.6	13.9	0.05	14.2	0.33	13.4	12.0	−0.21	13.5	13.6
	1	13.5	13.9	0.06	13.6	−0.01	13.6	12.2	−0.15	13.3	13.6
Neuroticism	3	11.5	12.6	−0.20	12.3	−0.28	11.8	12.8	−0.13	12.1	13.7
	1	11.5	13.2	−0.26	13.0	0.57	12.1	13.7	−0.12	12.5	14.2
Radicalism	3	8.1	8.2	−0.31	7.5	−0.40	8.5	8.2	−0.24	8.9	9.2
	1	7.4	7.6	−0.22	6.4	−0.31	7.6	7.6	−0.20	7.8	8.4
Tendermindedness	3	6.6	7.9	0.04	6.4	0.11	6.2	8.2	0.01	6.7	7.7
	1	6.8	7.8	−0.03	6.6	−0.09	6.7	8.4	0.06	6.9	7.9
Social values	3	40.0	42.3	−0.15	40.2	−0.07	40.6	43.6	0.03	40.7	43.2
	1	37.7	40.9	−0.09	37.8	−0.46	38.3	40.3	−0.08	38.4	41.2
Political values	3	26.8	22.7	−0.07	26.6	−0.16	27.6	21.6	−0.09	27.3	23.2
	1	27.3	22.8	−0.08	26.7	−0.18	28.1	21.9	0.09	27.5	23.7
Economic values	3	31.0	28.6	0.19	31.9	0.35	32.3	28.4	0.27	30.2	26.9
	1	32.4	29.7	0.22	34.0	0.52	32.3	29.6	0.21	31.4	27.8
Theoretical values	3	36.7	35.2	0.44	38.9	0.13	37.0	34.9	0.44	34.3	32.3
	1	36.4	34.6	0.44	35.4	0.73	37.8	35.9	0.66	33.8	31.6
Aesthetic values	3	26.4	26.5	−0.33	26.6	−0.43	25.1	25.4	−0.48	28.0	30.2
	1	24.8	25.0	−0.44	25.3	−0.31	23.9	24.6	−0.48	26.6	29.1
Religious values	3	18.9	24.8	−0.01	19.6	0.14	17.3	26.1	−0.03	19.5	24.3
	1	20.7	26.2	−0.01	20.0	−0.11	18.0	26.6	−0.10	21.3	25.7

* Standard mean of all students, including a small sample of women whose mean scores are not reported here.

** Number of students in each sub-group will be found in Table 9.1.

Appendix C2 Standard deviations of students in six areas of study, by sex

	YEAR	LANGUAGES		HUMANITIES		SOCIAL SCIENCES	
		Men	Women	Men	Women	Men	Women
Degree result	3	2.9	2.2	2.8	2.1	2.9	2.2
'A' level grades	0	2.6	2.6	2.2	2.2	2.6	3.0
No. of 'O' levels	0	1.2	0.9	1.3	1.2	1.3	0.9
Verbal aptitude	1	6.5	7.0	6.8	7.1	7.8	7.5
Mathematical aptitude	1	5.3	4.2	6.2	4.6	6.5	5.5
Motivation	3	2.2	2.2	2.2	2.2	2.1	2.5
	1	2.2	2.0	1.9	2.0	2.0	2.1
Study methods	3	2.4	2.2	2.8	2.5	2.6	2.4
	1	2.6	2.3	2.7	2.5	2.3	2.6
Hours studied	3	10.0	11.4	9.3	9.5	9.9	8.8
	1	9.2	9.3	10.2	8.4	9.1	8.5
Syllabus-bound	3	1.9	1.8	2.1	2.1	2.0	1.9
Syllabus-free	3	1.9	2.0	2.1	1.9	1.9	2.0
Extraversion	3	4.0	4.3	3.9	3.7	4.3	3.7
	1	4.0	4.0	4.5	4.1	4.3	3.7
Neuroticism	3	3.9	4.3	4.8	4.4	4.2	4.1
	1	4.0	3.8	4.7	3.5	4.1	3.7
Radicalism	3	2.9	2.6	3.2	3.2	2.5	2.6
	1	3.0	2.4	3.5	3.1	3.2	2.8
Tendermindedness	3	2.2	2.6	2.6	3.4	2.1	2.4
	1	2.5	2.8	2.9	2.3	2.4	2.3
Social values	3	5.7	5.2	6.5	6.1	6.1	6.1
	1	5.9	6.0	6.9	6.1	6.1	5.4
Political values	3	6.9	6.5	7.0	6.5	6.6	7.4
	1	6.8	6.3	7.8	6.7	6.7	6.0
Economic values	3	6.6	5.8	6.8	7.0	7.2	6.0
	1	6.4	6.1	8.0	5.8	6.9	5.6
Theoretical values	3	4.8	5.6	5.8	4.8	5.6	5.6
	1	5.3	5.0	6.1	5.7	5.8	5.4
Aesthetic values	3	7.4	7.2	7.5	8.2	7.5	7.4
	1	7.0	7.1	7.7	7.2	7.8	6.0
Religious values	3	11.1	13.6	15.0	12.0	11.4	11.8
	1	11.6	13.0	16.0	12.7	11.1	11.7

Appendix C2 cont.

	YEAR	PURE SCIENCES		APPLIED SCIENCES	MATHEMATICS		FULL SAMPLE	
		Men	Women	Men	Men	Women	Men	Women
Degree result	3	3.6	3.3	4.0	4.7	3.6	3.5	2.7
'A' level grades	0	3.0	2.4	2.9	3.1	2.7	2.8	2.8
No. of 'O' levels	0	1.1	0.8	1.5	1.7	0.9	1.3	0.9
Verbal aptitude	1	8.5	8.6	8.9	9.2	6.8	8.3	7.9
Mathematical aptitude	1	5.5	5.3	4.9	4.0	4.2	6.7	6.3
Motivation	3	2.1	2.1	2.2	2.3	2.2	2.2	2.3
	1	2.2	2.2	2.2	2.3	2.0.	2.2	2.1
Study methods	3	2.6	2.5	2.8	2.7	2.2	2.7	2.4
	1	2.5	2.7	2.6	2.4	2.8	2.5	2.5
Hours studied	3	8.7	9.2	10.2	10.0	8.0	10.5	10.4
	1	9.6	8.1	8.3	9.1	8.1	9.8	9.1
Syllabus-bound	3	2.1	1.9	1.9	2.2	1.9	2.1	2.0
Syllabus-free	3	1.9	1.9	1.9	2.0	1.6	2.0	1.9
Extraversion	3	3.9	3.6	3.8	4.1	3.5	4.0	3.9
	1	4.0	3.7	3.9	4.0	3.5	4.1	3.9
Neuroticism	3	4.4	4.4	4.1	4.3	4.4	4.3	4.4
	1	4.2	3.9	3.7	4.2	4.7	4.3	4.0
Radicalism	3	3.3	2.6	2.9	2.2	2.6	3.1	2.8
	1	3.0	2.6	2.8	2.7	2.4	3.1	2.7
Tendermindedness	3	2.4	2.9	2.6	2.2	3.0	2.4	2.7
	1	2.5	2.9	2.5	2.3	2.9	2.5	2.7
Social values	3	6.3	5.9	5.8	4.9	5.3	6.0	5.7
	1	6.3	5.8	5.5	5.7	6.9	6.3	6.0
Political values	3	6.7	7.7	6.0	6.1	6.5	6.8	7.2
	1	6.5	7.1	6.3	6.8	6.1	6.9	6.6
Economic values	3	7.3	6.6	6.1	6.6	6.0	7.2	6.4
	1	6.5	6.1	6.2	5.2	6.0	6.9	6.2
Theoretical values	3	6.2	5.7	6.5	6.3	5.1	6.4	5.8
	1	6.4	5.4	5.4	6.0	6.2	6.8	5.6
Aesthetic values	3	7.8	7.4	7.5	8.3	7.4	8.2	8.0
	1	6.6	6.7	5.6	6.8	6.4	6.6	7.4
Religious values	3	11.3	14.7	12.5	11.4	12.8	12.0	13.4
	1	11.1	13.4	12.9	11.4	12.2	12.3	12.9

Appendix C3 Standard mean scores of students in ten honours subjects

	YEAR	ENGLISH	FRENCH	HISTORY	ECONOMICS	SOCIOLOGY
'A' level grades	0	0.35	0.13	0.11	−0.19	−0.02
Verbal aptitude	1	0.65	0.33	−0.01	−0.07	0.25
Mathematical aptitude	1	−0.63	−0.73	−0.68	−0.22	−0.37
Motivation	3	−0.02	0.09	−0.03	0.19	−0.09
	1	0.06	0.04	0.25	0.09	0.00
Study method	3	0.15	−0.03	0.27	0.29	−0.08
	1	0.11	0.15	0.27	−0.07	0.01
Hours studied	3	0.46	−0.31	0.92	0.40	0.29
	1	0.37	0.14	0.67	0.20	0.23
Syllabus-bound	3	−0.46	0.28	−0.15	−0.20	−0.38
Syllabus-free	3	0.30	−0.13	−0.24	−0.03	0.21
Extraversion	3	−0.11	0.07	−0.25	0.12	0.13
	1	−0.05	0.11	−0.19	0.10	0.16
Neuroticism	3	0.16	−0.03	−0.01	0.23	0.12
	1	0.36	0.25	−0.16	0.05	0.03
Radicalism	3	0.24	−0.05	−0.04	0.16	0.67
	1	0.36	0.12	−0.21	−0.20	0.49
Tendermindedness	3	0.10	0.18	0.16	−0.31	−0.12
	1	0.21	0.27	0.10	−0.01	−0.06
Social values	3	−0.05	0.35	−0.04	0.38	0.36
	1	0.10	0.49	−0.14	0.18	0.43
Political values	3	−0.49	−0.69	0.18	0.09	0.39
	1	−0.43	−0.55	0.25	0.22	0.25
Economic values	3	−0.59	−0.15	−0.15	0.33	−0.31
	1	−0.50	−0.39	−0.14	0.22	−0.13
Theoretical values	3	−0.43	−0.55	−0.40	−0.41	−0.19
	1	−0.53	−0.64	−0.48	−0.31	−0.20
Aesthetic values	3	0.85	0.46	0.07	−0.20	0.09
	1	0.94	0.65	0.12	−0.19	−0.06
Religious values	3	0.25	0.25	0.19	−0.02	−0.19
	1	0.14	0.23	0.23	−0.08	−0.13

Appendix C3 cont.

	YEAR	BIOLOGY	CHEMISTRY	PHYSICS	ENGINEERING	MATHEMATICS
'A' level grades	0	-0.31	0.06	0.24	0.05	0.49
Verbal aptitude	1	-0.26	-0.25	-0.11	-0.21	-0.20
Mathematical aptitude	1	0.01	0.59	0.91	0.59	1.39
Motivation	3	0.29	0.13	0.30	-0.20	-0.01
	1	-0.03	0.14	0.26	-0.22	0.14
Study method	3	0.25	0.13	0.23	-0.48	-0.31
	1	0.12	0.11	0.18	-0.30	-0.08
Hours studied	3	-0.19	-0.60	-0.56	-0.42	-0.25
	1	-0.47	-0.37	-0.27	-0.38	0.01
Syllabus-bound	3	0.08	0.34	0.01	0.39	0.47
Syllabus-free	3	0.08	-0.26	-0.10	0.09	-0.47
Extraversion	3	0.04	0.00	0.14	0.05	-0.23
	1	0.08	-0.11	0.04	0.07	-0.21
Neuroticism	3	-0.02	-0.19	-0.30	0.08	-0.25
	1	-0.12	-0.29	-0.33	0.11	-0.21
Radicalism	3	-0.05	-0.50	-0.28	-0.47	-0.18
	1	0.09	-0.36	-0.23	-0.35	-0.18
Tendermindedness	3	-0.10	-0.01	0.12	-0.14	0.07
	1	-0.21	-0.05	0.05	-0.12	0.14
Social values	3	-0.11	-0.03	-0.70	-0.07	0.04
	1	0.08	-0.17	-0.35	-0.14	-0.07
Political values	3	-0.16	-0.05	0.14	-0.10	-0.01
	1	-0.23	-0.11	0.05	-0.05	0.01
Economic values	3	0.16	0.22	0.14	0.30	0.22
	1	0.09	0.35	0.21	0.47	0.19
Theoretical values	3	0.44	0.62	0.52	0.11	0.38
	1	0.48	0.61	0.70	0.27	0.65
Aesthetic values	3	-0.16	-0.48	-0.36	-0.20	-0.52
	1	0.21	-0.42	-0.48	-0.31	-0.56
Religious values	3	-0.05	-0.08	0.00	-0.01	0.02
	1	-0.05	-0.08	-0.03	-0.11	-0.10

Appendix C4 Correlations of predictive variables with degree results, by honours disciplines

	ENGLISH		FRENCH		HISTORY		ECONOMICS		SOCIOLOGY	
	YEAR		*YEAR*		*YEAR*		*YEAR*		*YEAR*	
	1	*3*	*1*	*3*	*1*	*3*	*1*	*3*	*1*	*3*
First-year marks	40		29		54		31		39	
No. of 'O' levels	17		-03		-15		15		32	
'A' level grades	24		11		17		10		16	
Verbal aptitude	27		-03		26		08		24	
Mathematical aptitude	22		11		23		01		09	
Motivation	10	25	11	-06	09	-02	10	13	-03	29
Study methods	05	16	20	19	21	23	-04	08	12	-09
Hours studied	16	13	08	01	22	27	-17	18	15	01
Syllabus-bound		21		20		-24		17		01
Syllabus-free		-13		-13		-05		-17		-09
Self-ratings of:										
Good at maths	13		-04		12		00		-15	
Hard-working	23		22		17		-18		07	
Ambitious	-08		-11		-03		09		-14	
Sociable	-29		-30		-27		01		-09	
Seriousminded	12		-06		15		04		02	
Extraversion	-29	-11	-12	-19	-34	-25	07	00	-20	-15
Neuroticism	09	-01	-03	-14	-09	-09	-02	-01	19	04
Radicalism	-01	-12	12	08	02	14	-10	-02	-03	06
Tendermindedness	12	25	06	16	05	-12	33	19	-25	-04
Social values	06	06	-06	00	-02	08	06	-03	-06	-21
Political values	-03	-10	-10	-19	09	00	09	-15	11	16
Economic values	-10	-13	-03	-12	-05	-19	-30	-11	-06	02
Theoretical values	-21	-19	-07	-04	-04	12	-33	01	01	09
Aesthetic values	-21	-19	-17	-19	-05	04	21	-03	06	13
Religious values	24	28	18	24	02	-03	13	20	-04	-08

$p < 0.05$ if $r \geqslant$ 19   27   21   33   23

Appendix C4 cont.

	BIOLOGY		CHEMISTRY		PHYSICS		ENGINEERING		MATHEMATICS	
	YEAR		*YEAR*		*YEAR*		*YEAR*		*YEAR*	
	1	*3*	*1*	*3*	*1*	*3*	*1*	*3*	*1*	*3*
First-year marks	43		63		61		78		73	
No. of 'O' levels	03		00		05		11		07	
'A' level grades	21		37		12		46		56	
Verbal aptitude	-02		-05		-13		-01		22	
Mathematical aptitude	02		09		16		11		38	
Motivation	16	23	19	34	06	18	25	30	21	18
Study methods	20	39	17	21	16	31	39	33	11	25
Hours studied	06	19	06	08	35	15	34	09	-02	08
Syllabus-bound		-17		-03		23		-18		-10
Syllabus-free		03		-06		18		-10		-03
Self-ratings of:										
Good at maths	-15		-02		04		20		37	
Hard-working	01		13		12		41		35	
Ambitious	00		03		17		14		-05	
Sociable	-13		-09		-31		01		-02	
Seriousminded	17		07		02		26		-15	
Extraversion	-16	-23	00	-08	-25	-10	-28	-20	-05	04
Neuroticism	-02	-07	-07	00	-15	-06	-09	-12	-17	-01
Radicalism	24	25	-18	-19	05	02	-05	-05	08	20
Tendermindedness	-02	10	-04	-05	-13	03	20	14	-05	-06
Social values	-07	01	08	01	-02	01	19	25	-13	-10
Political values	15	01	-10	03	-08	-28	-16	-15	09	11
Economic values	-16	-12	11	14	14	-06	-05	03	04	13
Theoretical values	26	23	04	14	02	02	-05	02	16	26
Aesthetic values	07	-09	-29	-28	03	05	-10	-18	-03	-16
Religious values	-11	-01	06	01	-05	13	11	08	-11	-10

$p < 0.05$ if $r \geqslant$ 22   20   25   29   24

Appendix C5 Mean degree results, first-year marks and aptitude scores for different 'A' level grades

'A' level grades	LANGUAGES	HUMANITIES	SOCIAL SCIENCES	PURE SCIENCES	APPLIED SCIENCES	MATHEMATICS
ABB or higher	10.3 13.1 / 37.2 15.4 (N =76)	10.9 15.8 / 35.6 15.7 (21)	10.4 13.4 / 35.3 17.4 (40)	10.7 14.7 / 31.3 23.5 (50)	12.0 17.0 / 29.4 26.6 (10)	11.3 15.9 / 33.7 29.4 (27)
BBB / BBC	9.7 12.6 / 35.6 14.5 (99)	10.7 13.3 / 33.6 15.4 (39)	9.2 12.6 / 32.6 17.6 (47)	9.7 12.7 / 32.7 22.8 (67)	8.9 12.3 / 32.8 24.0 (9)	8.4 12.9 / 30.7 28.3 (18)
BCC / CCC	9.4 12.2 / 35.4 14.8 (75)	9.3 12.1 / 30.7 14.0 (46)	9.2 11.9 / 32.4 17.7 (93)	8.8 12.0 / 30.3 22.0 (85)	7.9 11.6 / 28.1 24.0 (14)	7.7 12.4 / 28.5 28.0 (26)
CCD / CDD	8.4 10.9 / 34.8 15.3 (37)	8.9 11.3 / 33.3 16.0 (26)	8.2 11.5 / 32.8 19.7 (41)	8.1 11.7 / 29.6 22.0 (72)	7.8 11.7 / 32.0 24.5 (12)	5.5 10.6 / 26.9 25.1 (17)
DDD or lower	6.2 8.7 / 29.0 15.8 (6)	8.8 11.0 / 37.8 18.0 (4)	9.8 12.3 / 31.4 16.5 (26)	7.3 10.8 / 28.6 21.6 (49)	6.0 8.8 / 28.3 23.4 (12)	5.1 9.6 / 27.1 26.3 (16)

Key:

Academic Performance

Degree	First Year
Verbal	Mathematics

Academic Aptitude

Appendix C6 Inter-correlations between variables for men and women

	DR	COS	ASL	SWC	FYM	OL	AL	VA	MA	GM
Degree results		37	−16	27	55	13	26	09	00	01
Concentrating on studying	26		−27	25	23	05	09	−09	−13	−04
Active social life	−07	−15		−08	−15	−01	00	−01	00	00
Satisfied with courses	10	18	05		18	01	00	01	−01	03
First-year marks	47	18	−05	10		07	30	07	15	13
No. of 'O' levels	08	02	00	−04	07		08	16	07	05
'A' level grades	29	07	01	02	30	16		10	11	04
Verbal aptitude	18	−12	13	08	07	07	20		−06	−04
Mathematical aptitude	−01	−02	05	07	07	10	−01	09		63
Good at maths	−11	05	00	10	03	17	−06	−16	66	
Motivation	15	22	05	11	13	−02	05	10	03	12
Study methods	18	24	−07	07	17	05	11	−03	−09	00
Hours studied	18	17	−12	03	15	−07	13	−03	−22	−17
Syllabus-boundness	−01	05	−04	05	04	12	−04	−14	10	18
Syllabus-freedom	−05	02	16	−04	−04	−05	02	20	−10	−15
Hard-working	20	37	−07	16	25	08	−07	−06	−18	07
Ambitious	01	13	08	08	06	−07	−04	−15	−08	03
Serious-minded	08	23	−10	13	11	06	06	−02	−09	06
Sociable	05	02	23	−07	00	−03	−02	−14	−04	−04
Extraversion	−11	−10	27	−05	−09	−06	−11	−07	−09	−07
Neuroticism	−06	−09	02	−17	−09	−06	−01	00	−13	−19
Radicalism	08	−03	01	−08	−03	05	03	17	−13	−18
Tendermindedness	00	05	−04	05	05	13	04	04	02	09

continues overleaf

Appendix C6 cont.

	MTV	SM	HS	SB	SF	HW	AM	SM	SS	EXT	NEU	RAD	TEN
Degree results	23	22	22	-06	-09	25	01	06	-13	-11	-04	04	01
Concentrating on studying	30	32	30	-01	-07	36	15	11	-07	-11	-07	-08	08
Active social life	01	-07	-15	-13	12	-17	03	-11	38	37	-11	04	-10
Satisfied with courses	13	20	14	04	-08	07	03	03	-05	00	-11	03	12
First-year marks	23	23	16	-01	-07	26	01	08	-18	-14	-06	02	00
No. of '0' levels	11	05	-03	04	-05	06	07	03	00	00	01	-01	-06
'A' level grades	16	12	12	-04	-04	13	03	-03	-05	-12	-10	02	08
Verbal aptitude	09	04	-01	-20	10	-09	-18	08	-10	-13	-06	20	07
Mathematical aptitude	05	-10	-25	09	-07	-06	-02	-07	-05	-05	-14	-09	-06
Good at maths	05	-05	-16	10	-05	07	09	02	-10	-04	-10	-06	-02
Motivation		44	24	-16	07	33	28	11	04	07	-26	-07	08
Study methods	39		38	-13	-11	41	11	09	-07	-05	-32	02	11
Hours studied	18	37		-06	-05	51	07	17	-10	-13	-10	03	16
Syllabus-boundness	-13	-10	-09		-43	-01	03	03	-04	-09	21	-24	-02
Syllabus-freedom	15	02	05	44		-11	-03	08	07	04	09	17	04
Hard-working	34	45	44	07	-04		24	27	-12	-17	-13	-11	14
Ambitious	34	14	05	06	09	20		15	17	10	-06	-20	03
Serious-minded	12	17	21	02	04	36	22		-13	-29	04	-02	19
Sociable	05	-01	-15	-08	13	01	12	-16		57	-10	01	-07
Extraversion	07	-05	-19	-16	18	-13	12	-29	52		-19	03	-11
Neuroticism	-24	-27	-04	09	08	-18	04	-01	-02	-06		05	03
Radicalism	-01	02	05	-28	13	-09	-15	-01	08	05	-01		00
Tendermindedness	06	05	08	05	-13	13	-14	15	-15	-12	-07	-02	

Appendix C7 Test- retest correlations of variables measured in first and third years

VARIABLE	CORRELATION	
	MEN	WOMEN
Motivation	0.47	0.42
Study methods	0.55	0.51
Hours studied	0.50	0.46
Extraversion	0.67	0.62
Neuroticism	0.66	0.63
Radicalism	0.69	0.66
Tendermindedness	0.58	0.67
Social values	0.62	0.56
Political values	0.59	0.63
Economic values	0.60	0.55
Theoretical values	0.64	0.60
Aesthetic values	0.68	0.66
Religious values	0.70	0.76

Appendix C8 Factor loadings on six factors for men and women

Factors	MEN (N = 594)						WOMEN (N = 493)					
	I	II	III	IV	V	VI	I	II	III	IV	V	VI
Degree	76	26					75					
Concentration on study	34	42						52		27		
Active social life					63						37	26
Satisfied with courses	70	41					71		31	-32		
First-year marks												
No. of 'O' levels	48						26					
'A' level grades	51						66					
Verbal aptitude			88				38		82			
Mathematical aptitude			78						81			
Good at maths						57						59
Motivation	28	49		42				61				28
Study methods		74						72				
Hours studied		55	-34					55				
Syllabus-bound				26		-74			-35		-26	-75
Syllabus-free				51		65				28		67
Hard-working		49						74				
Ambitious				68	26			34		68		
Serious-minded				62	-30					40	-40	
Sociable					78						79	
Extraversion		-65			80					41	81	
Neuroticism			-32		-27			-43	-34	-37		
Radicalism				-28		53				-35		44
Tendermindedness					-28							
Percentage variance	8.5	10.5	8.1	7.3	9.8	8.0	8.1	11.9	8.5	6.1	8.5	8.1

Notes 1. Decimal points and factor loadings below /0.25/ have been omitted.
   2. The six-factor solution was chosen from inspection of a 'scree plot', although nine factors had eigen values in excess of unity and explained 66 per cent of the variance.
   3. Rotation was by Kaiser's Varimax criterion, retaining orthogonal factors.

Appendix C9 Standard mean scores of cluster centroids for 443 split-half sample

Variable	Year	1 (N=47)	3 (37)	5 (52)	6 (22)	9 (30)	10 (47)	11 (44)	12 (40)	14 (28)	15 (53)
Degree result	3	10	1	4	5	3	- 4	1	- 9*	-10*	2
First-year marks	1	10	0	3	6	7	- 4	- 2*	- 8	- 4	0*
Satisfied with courses	3						4*			- 7	- 4
Active social life	3			9*	-11*	- 6			4	- 4	
Using sports facilities	3			- 4*	- 7			7*	4*		- 5
Aesthetic interests	3	- 4	6*	7	- 5*					7	- 4*
'A' level grades	0	9			5				- 7		
Verbal aptitude	1		4		- 9*				- 5*	6	
Maths aptitude	1	8		- 5	6*	- 5			5	8	- 6
Motivation	1	8		6	- 6					- 8	- 5
Motivation	3	7		5*						- 9*	- 6*
Study methods	1	6		5	- 5*	7		6		- 8*	- 5
Study methods	3							4		- 7	- 4
Hours studied	3			9*		9		5	- 6	-10	
Syllabus-bound	3		-10	- 8	10		5	4			
Syllabus-free	3		7	6	- 6		- 6	- 6			
Extraversion	1		10		- 4	- 9	- 5*				
Neuroticism	1	- 6	- 7*		9						6*
Sociable	1		10			- 5*					
Likeable	1		7							- 6*	
Self-confident	1		9*		- 5	- 5				- 5	
Social values	1										6
Political values	1		8			- 7	-11				
Economic values	1			- 7*	12	- 9		6	8		
Theoretical values	1	7*			8*	-10	- 8		8	5	
Aesthetic values	1	- 5		7*	- 5		-10		- 4	8	6
Religious values	1		- 5		- 6	14	17		- 6		
Radicalism	1	- 5*	4	6	- 4		.		-10*		6
Tendermindedness	1				- 6	11	12		- 9		

* Indicates *F* ratio ⩾ 0.7.

Note: In Appendices C9 – C13 cluster numbers refer to the summary table (10.2). Scores are shown to one decimal place (multiply 10). Scores below 4 have been omitted.

Appendix C10 Standard mean scores of cluster centroids for language students

Variable	Year	4 (N= 8)	7 (12)	9 (26)	12 (28)	15 (24)
Degree result	3	1	3	5	1	-3
First-year marks	1	5	0*	4*	4	-6
Satisfied with courses	3					
Active social life	3					
Using sports facilities	3					
Aesthetic interests	3					
'A' level grades	0	10				-7*
Verbal aptitude	1	11				
Maths aptitude	1					
Motivation	1	6		5	(3)	-5*
Motivation	3	-10		4	-5	
Study methods	1	(3)		6*		
Study methods	3	-8		6*		
Hours studied	3	-9		5*		-4
Syllabus-bound	3		11			-6
Syllabus-free	3	9	-10			4
Extraversion	1		-11			
Neuroticism	1		4			
Sociable	1	-8	- 5			
Likeable	1					
Self-confident	1					
Social values	1		- 7		5	
Political values	1	5		-6		
Economic values	1		6	-9*	5	
Theoretical values	1			-7*		
Aesthetic values	1	7				5
Religious values	1	-6		11	-5	
Radicalism	1		- 9			5*
Tendermindedness	1			9	-5	-4

* Indicates F ratio > 0.7.

Appendix C11 Standard mean scores of cluster centroids for humanities students

Variable	Year	2 (N=24)	9 (23)	11 (17)	13 (35)
Degree result	3	6	1	1	-2
First-year marks	1	5*	1	1	-5*
Satisfied with courses	3				
Active social life	3				
Using sports facilities	3				
Aesthetic interests	3				
'A' level grades	0	6			
Verbal aptitude	1	4*			
Maths aptitude	1	5*			
Motivation	1			6	
Motivation	3				
Study methods	1	6*			
Study methods	3				
Hours studied	3	4			
Syllabus-bound	3			-9	
Syllabus-free	3	-5*		7*	
Extraversion	1	-8		9	
Neuroticism	1			-7	7
Sociable	1	-6		6	
Likeable	1			7	
Self-confident	1	-6		7	
Social values	1				6*
Political values	1		-5*		
Economic values	1	6*		-8*	
Theoretical values	1		-14	6*	
Aesthetic values	1		-9	7*	
Religious values	1		16		-6*
Radicalism	1			4*	
Tendermindedness	1		12		-5

* Indicates *F* ratio $\geq$ 0.7.

Appendix C12 Standard mean scores of cluster centroids for social science students

Variable	Year	3 (N= 38)	7 (31)	8 (28)	10 (29)	11 (18)	15 (45)
Degree result	3	3	0	3	-1*	-1	-2*
First-year marks	1	3	3	4	-2	-5	-3
Satisfied with courses	3						
Active social life	3						
Using sports facilities	3					7*	
Aesthetic interests	3	5	-5				
'A' level grades	0					-5*	
Verbal aptitude	1			-6		-4*	6
Maths aptitude	1						
Motivation	1		-8	5		5	-6*
Motivation	3		-6*	8		6	-6
Study methods	1		-5	10		(-1)	-6
Study methods	3		(-2)	8*		8	-9
Hours studied	3			6*			
Syllabus-bound	3	-7	7		8		
Syllabus-free	3	5	-9			-8	
Extraversion	1	6				8	
Neuroticism	1	-4*				-9*	
Sociable	1	6				8	
Likeable	1	7					
Self-confident	1	6				5	
Social values	1						
Political values	1				-12		
Economic values	1	-5	7		-4	8	
Theoretical values	1				-10		
Aesthetic values	1	6*		-6	-8		
Religious values	1				18	-7	
Radicalism	1	6		-5*			6
Tendermindedness	1				13	-9	

* Indicates F ratio $\geqslant$ 0.7.

Appendix C13 Standard mean scores of cluster centroids for pure science students

Variable	Year	2 (N= 33)	5 (20)	7 (28)	8 (24)	10 (20)	11 (41)	15 (26)
Degree result	3	8	-2	2	6	-1	-5	-6
First-year marks	1	7	-2	-1	8	-1	-4	-6
Satisfied with courses	3				5			-7
Active social life	3						5	
Using sports facilities	3							
Aesthetic interests	3							
'A' level grades	0	6		-5	8			
Verbal aptitude	1	4	9	-5	-6			
Maths aptitude	1	6		-5				
Motivation	1				7			-10
Motivation	3				9			-9
Study methods	1			4	7			-7
Study methods	3			6	8	-5		-5
Hours studied	3			7				-6
Syllabus-bound	3		-9					
Syllabus-free	3	-5	9					
Extraversion	1	-4*		4			4	
Neuroticism	1			5	-5			
Sociable	1						6	
Likeable	1						5	
Self-confident	1	-5						
Social values	1			4				6
Political values	1					-9		
Economic values	1			4	7	-6	8	
Theoretical values	1				7	-8		-4
Aesthetic values	1		9			-6		7
Religious values	1		-7	-4	-4	15	-5	
Radicalism	1		5			-9		
Tendermindedness	1	5			-6	11		

* Indicates F ratio $\geqslant$ 0.7.

Appendix D Rules for The Academic Achievement Game

1. <u>GENERAL</u>

TAAG is a game which attempts to create the experience of university for you. It is based on the findings of research on students. We hope it will help you to become aware of the kinds of things that may affect your performance at university.

Students differ enormously in ability, temperament and motivation. They follow different courses in different faculties, and although all are taught by means of lectures, tutorials and practical classes, and are assessed in examinations and on written work, they react to these experiences in unique ways. It is impossible to capture all of this complexity for each individual, but TAAG does attempt to show how student types with different personality and intellectual character- istics react to these standard features of student life. We hope that by getting you to define your personal characteristics, and by showing how these interact with the circumstances of life as a stu- dent, we will help you to know yourself better and thus to cope more effectively with the opportunities that university life offers.

2.   <u>STARTING CONDITIONS</u>

It is essential, if you wish to learn as much as possible about how you are likely to cope at university, that you make the most realistic self-assessments from the choices given below.

(*a*) In which faculty do you intend to study? You may choose from Science, Social Science or Arts. (If your course is in Medicine, choose Science; if in Law, choose Social Science; if in Divinity, choose Arts).

(*b*) How clever are you? University students are, of course, a very able group compared to the population as a whole. But even so, some students have outstanding ability, while others have high or moderate ability in relation to the majority of entrants. Ability is not always related to the level of degree taken, but one would expect students of outstanding ability to be potential first-class honours graduates, while students of moderate ability would not expect to graduate with more than an ordinary degree. Decide how you compare and select the appropriate die: if your ability is well above that of the average entrant take a die with values 3-8; if it is a little above that of the average entrant take a die with values 2-7; if you have moderate ability take a die from 1-6.

(*c*) What kind of entrance qualifications do you have (if you have come from school within the past two years)? If you got a 'good' group, e.g. four SCE Highers at 'B' grade or two 'A' levels at 'B' grade, or better, at the first attempt, the following con- ditions apply:
    i   Science   -   two free throws to start
    ii Arts   -   one free throw to start

A 'good' entrance group (as defined above) does not entitle you to a free throw in Social Sciences.

(*d*) How well has school or further education trained you to work by yourself? Take <u>one</u> free throw if you have had such training in a subject you intend to study at university.

(*e*) What kind of temperament, personality and motivation to study do you have? Below are brief descriptions of four ideal 'student types'. All students, in fact, have something of each in their make-up, but we want you to select the coloured counter of the type which you believe is the most accurate description of you.

Appendix D cont.

   i. Are you the emotionally stable, hard-working and persevering type of person who is not easily upset, and is highly ambitious and eager to succeed? *(Orange)*

  ii. Are you the rather anxious, somewhat withdrawn type of person who is not sure about how he will do at university, or what standard of performance will be expected of him, but who is nevertheless hardworking and keen to do well? *(Black)*

 iii. Are you the self-confident and assured, sociable type of person, who is outward going and likes to be 'in the swim', and who is keen to develop and propagate his own ideas, even to the point of deviating from the prescribed course of study? *(Green)*

  iv. Are you the relaxed kind of person who certainly wants to get a degree, but who finds it hard to get down to work, and who is also keen to sample fully the social life of university, believing that a great deal and even most of value in university education is gained outside the formal class sessions? *(Brown)*

(*f*) How many people can play? Universities are crowded places with large lecture classes and generally overcrowded facilities. This situation could be simulated in the game. In theory thirty-six people could play on one board (3 ability levels multiply 4 student types multiply 3 faculties), but this would slow the game down too much. Between nine and twelve people are recommended (at least three per faculty).

3. THE TRACK, CHANCE, HAZARD AND BONUS ELEMENTS

(*a*) The track is divided into three faculties. It is numbered from 1 to 168, and some squares contain a star (Chance) or the letter H (Hazard) or B (Bonus). If you land on one of these squares you must draw a card from the appropriate pile and follow the instructions it sets out. Chance happenings include such events as breaking a leg, hazards include being assigned to an incompetent tutor, and bonuses include getting a good mark for an essay. Students react to such factors in different ways according to temperament and motivation and the cards are loaded accordingly.

(*b*) Return the card to the bottom of the appropriate pile (face down) when you have followed the instructions.

(*c*) The end of the board is separated off into sections corresponding to the results of honours degree examinations.

4. THE GAME

The object of the game is to get a good degree. The player(s) with most free throws start first, and the other players then throw their die in turn. <u>Each faculty finishes separately</u>. When the first student in a faculty gets to 'Graduation' the results for the other students in that faculty are then read off from their position on the board. The winner must get a score which takes him the exact number of moves into 'Graduation', and he cannot move closer than the lowest number on his die (e.g. a student of 'outstanding ability' must remain three or more squares away from 'Graduation' until he gets the requisite score). However, after waiting three throws, a player may proceed to 'Graduation' on the fourth throw, irrespective of whether he has got the exact number of moves or not.

The course can be negotiated up to three times if you wish.

Index

Mehrabian, A., 31
MHAI, *see* Moray House Adult Intelligence Test
Miller, C. M. L., 161, 166
'missing middle', 8
Mitchell, J. V., 31
Moray House Adult Intelligence Test (MHAI), 51, 52, 59, 142
motivation, 29-31, 63, 64, 65, 99, 145
  goal oriented, 30
  tests of, 40
multiple regression analysis, 14, 116-18

'n-ach', *see* need for achievement
Napier, R. L., 19, 21, 24, 62
National Foundation for Educational Research (NFER), 103-4, *see also* Choppin, B. H. L.
Neave, G., 160
need for achievemnt ('n-ach'), 30-1
Neish, K., 58
neuroticism, 25-7, 32, 118, 144
  characteristics of, 26
  tests of, 39
  see also extraversion, introversion, personality
Newcomb, T. M., 34, 36
Newman, S. E., 32
NFER, *see* National Foundation for Educational Research
Nisbet, J. B., 42, 91, *see also* Thompson, J. B.
Nisbet, J. D., viii, 6, 13, 19, 22, 47, 97, 159
Nisbet, S. D., 19, 21, 24, 62
Nufferno tests, 20
Nuffield Group, *see* Becher, R. A.

Ojha, A. B., 20, 28, 29
Orr, L., 23

PAA, *see* predictive attribute analysis
Pace, C. R., 34, 38
Parkyn, G. W., 6, 20, 21, 48
Parlett, M. R., 9, 33, 43, 157, 161, 166
Pavlov, I. P., 28
Percy, K. A., viii, 42, 91, 161
Personal Values Inventory, *see* Finger, J. A.
personality, 55-6, 75-7, 99-100, 122-7
  variations between disciplines, 105-9
  tests of, 111, App. C7
  see also extraversion, introversion, neuroticism
Pervin, L. A., 34
Petch, J. A., 18
Peters, F. R., 22
Peters, R. S., 29
Peterson, R. E., 36, 52
Pieron, H., 11
Philip, A. E., 14, 147

Pilkington, G. W., 18, 20
Pilliner, A. E. G., 19, 20
Pond, L., 32-3
Powell, J. L., 20, 21, 159
predictive attribute analysis (PAA), 14-15
psychological disorders, 25, *see also* neuroticism

questionnaires, 39-41, 59-60, 77-9, 83-4, 96, App. A3-A5, *see also* Student Attitude Questionnaire

radicalism, 127
  tests of, 37
Reid, I., 31
religious sentiments among students, tests of, 40
research strategies, 7-16
Resnikoff, A., 164
Richards, J. P. G., 18
Richardson, S., 96
Robbins Committee, 24, 78, 91
Roe, E., 20
Rook, A., 25
Rorer, L. G., 58
Rowntree Project, 4, 33, 38, 43, 50, 70, 91-138, 157, 161, App. C1-C12
  and Aberdeen study, 141-5
Ryle, A., 25, 32

Sainsbury, A. B., 20, 95, 96
sampling, 9-10
Sanders, C., 21, 23
Sanford, N., 29
SAQ, *see* Student Attitude Questionnaire
Sarnoff, I., 24, 29, 30
Savage, R. D., 26, 28
Scannell, D. P., 21, 23
Schlesser, G. E., 31, 32, 38
Scholastic Aptitude Test, 21
Schonell, F. J., 20, 21
science students, 36, 94, 116, 118, 129, 131, 132, 133, 134, 135, 137, 138, 142-3, App. B2
  in Aberdeen study, 51
Scottish Council for Research in Education (SCRE), 20, 21, 23
sex differences in academic performance, 23, 62, 67, 70, 73, 104, 119, 144, App. B2, C6, C8
  predictions of, 49
Simon, F. H., 15
Small, J. J., 15, 21, 23, 28, 32, 47, 48, 57, 147
Smithers, A. G., 24
Snow, C. P. (Lord Snow), 104-5
social background and academic performance, 24-5, 60, 63, 64, 65, 129, 143
Social Science Research Council, ix
social science students, 113, 116-18, 133
Spielberger, C. D., 27